Eric Johnson

Legislative Hand Book and Manual of the State of Nebraska, 1897

Eric Johnson

Legislative Hand Book and Manual of the State of Nebraska, 1897

ISBN/EAN: 9783744728874

Printed in Europe, USA, Canada, Australia, Japan

Cover: Foto ©Suzi / pixelio.de

More available books at **www.hansebooks.com**

LEGISLATIVE HAND BOOK

——◆AND◆——

MANUAL

OF THE   STATE OF

NEBRASKA.

1897.

Published by Authority of the Senate and House
of Representatives.

Compiled and Edited by

ERIC JOHNSON,

Formerly Chief Clerk of the House of Representatives.

LINCOLN:
JACOB NORTH & CO., PRINTERS,
1897.

PREFACE.

The very favorable reception and commendation accorded the first edition of the Legislative Hand Book and Manual of 1893, and the specific endorsement by the Legislature of 1897, which by resolution ordered a new edition of my compilation, is the reason for the publication of this second edition.

Election returns and other valuable information have been compiled and revised up to date. Pains have been taken to make the Legislative Hand Book as near accurate as is possible.   ERIC JOHNSON.

WAHOO, NEB., 1897.

TABLE OF CONTENTS.

THE DECLARATION OF INDEPENDENCE
IN CONGRESS, JULY 4TH, 1776.

—The Unanimous Declaration of the Thirteen United States of America:

When, in the course of human events, it becomes necessary for one people to dissolve the political bands which have connected them with another, and to assume among the powers of the earth the separate an l equal station to which the laws of nature and of nature's God entitle them, a decent respect to the opinions of mankind requires that they should declare the causes which impel them to the separation.

We hold these truths to be self-evident, that all men are created equal; that they are endowed by their Creator with certain unalienable rights; that among these are life, liberty, and the pursuit of happiness. That, to secure these rights, governments are instituted among men, deriving their just powers from the consent of the governed; that, whenever any form of government becomes destructive of these ends, it is the right of the people to alter or abolish it, and to institute a new government, laying its foundation on such principles, and organizing its powers in such form as to them shall seem most likely to effect their safety and happiness. Prudence, indeed, will dictate that governments long established should not be changed for light and transient causes; and, accordingly, all experience hath shown that mankind are more disposed to suffer, while evils are sufferable, than to right themselves by abolishing the forms to which they are accustomed. But when a long train of abuses and unsurpations, pursuing invariably the same object, evinces a design to reduce them under absolute despotism, it is their right, it is their duty, to throw off such government and to provide new guards for their future security.

Such has been the patient sufferance of these colonies, and such is now the necessity which constrains them to alter their former systems of government. The history of the present king of Great Britain is a history of repeated injuries and usurpations, all having in direct object the establishment of an absolute tyranny over these states. To prove this, let facts be submitted to a candid world:

He has refused his assent to laws the most wholesome and necessary for the public good.

He has forbidden his governors to pass laws of immediate and pressing importance, unless suspended in their operations till his assent should be obtained, and, when so suspended, he has utterly neglected to attend to them.

He has refused to pass other laws for the accommodation of large districts of people, unless those people would relinquish the right of representation in the legislature, a right inestimable to them, and formidable to tyrants only.

He has called together legislative bodies at places unusual, uncomfortable, and distant from the depository of their public records, for the sole purpose of fatiguing them into compliance with his measures.

He has dissolved representative houses repeatedly, for opposing with manly firmness his invasions on the rights of the people.

He has refused, for a long time after such dissolutions, to cause others to be elected, whereby the legislative powers, incapable of annihilation, have returned to the people at large for their exercise, the state remaining in the meantime exposed to all the dangers of invasion from without and convulsions within.

He has endeavored to prevent the population of these states, for that purpose obstructing the laws for the naturalization of foreigners, refusing to pass others to encourage their migration hither, and raising the conditions of new appropriations of lands.

He has obstructed the administration of justice by refusing his assent to laws for establishing judiciary powers.

He has made judges dependent on his will alone for the tenure of their offices, and the amount and payment of their salaries.

He has erected a multitude of new offices and sent hither swarms of officers to harass our people and eat out their substance.

He has kept among us, in times of peace, standing armies, without the consent of our legislature.

He has effected to render the military independent of and superior to the civil power.

He has combined with others to subject us to a jurisdiction foreign to our constitution and unacknowledged by our laws, giving his assent to their acts of pretended legislation.

For quartering large bodies of armed troops among us.

For protecting them, by a mock trial, from punishment for any murders which they should commit on the inhabitants of these states.

For cutting off our trade with all parts of the world.

For imposing taxes on us without our consent.

For depriving us, in many cases, of the benefit of trial by jury.

For transporting us beyond seas to be tried for pretended offences.

For abolishing the free system of English laws in a neighboring province, establishing therein an arbitrary government, and enlarging its boundaries so as to render it at once an example and fit instrument for introducing the same absolute rule into these colonies.

For taking away our charters, abolishing our most valuable laws, and altering, fundamentally, the powers of our governments.

For suspending our own legislatures, and declaring themselves invested with power to legislate for us in all cases whatsoever.

He has abdicated government here by declaring us out of his protection, and waging war against us.

He has plundered our seas, ravaged our coasts, burnt our towns, and destroyed the lives of our people.

He is, at this time, transporting large armies of foreign mercenaries to complete the works of death, desolation, and tyranny already begun, with circumstances of cruelty and perfidy scarcely paralled in the most barbarous ages, and totally unworthy the head of a civilized nation.

He has constrained our fellow citizens, taken captive on the high seas, to bear arms against their country, to become the executioners of their friends and brethern, or to fall themselves by their hands.

He has excited domestic insurrections amongst us, and has endeavored to bring on the inhabitants of our frontier the merciless Indian savages, whose known rule of warfare is an undistinguished destruction of all ages, sexes, and conditions.

In every stage of these oppressions we have petitioned for redress in the most humble terms. Our repeated petitions have been answered only by repeated injury. A prince whose character is thus marked by every act which may define a tyrant, is unfit to be the ruler of a free people.

Nor have we been wanting in attentions to our British brethren. We have warned them from time to time of attempts made by their legislature to extend an unwarrantable jurisdiction over us. We have reminded them of the circumstances of our emigration and settlement here. We have appealed to their native justice and magnanimity, and we have conjured them by the ties of our common kindred, to disavow these usurpations, which would inevitably interrupt our connections and correspondence. They, too, have been deaf to the voice of justice and consanguinity. We must, therefore, acquiesce in the necessity which denounces our seperation, and hold them, as we hold the rest of mankind, enemies in war; in peace, friends.

We, therefore, the representatives of the UNITED STATES OF AMERICA IN GENERAL CONGRESS assembled, appealing to the Supreme Judge of the world for the rectitude of our intentions, do, in the name and by the authority of the good people of these colonies, solemnly publish and declare, That these United Colonies are, and of right ought to be, FREE AND INDEPENDENT STATES; that they are absolved from all allegiance to the British crown, and that all political connection between them and the state of Great Britain is, and ought to be, totally dissolved; and that as FREE AND INDEPENDENT STATES, they have full power to levy war, conclude peace, contract alliances, establish commerce, and do all other acts and things which INDEPENDENT STATES may of right do. And for the support of this declaration, with firm reliance on the protection of DEVINE PROVIDENCE, we mutually pledge to each other our lives, our fortunes, and our sacred honor.

The foregoing declaration was, by order of congress, engrossed and signed by the following members. JOHN HANCOCK.

New Hampshire.
JOSIAH BARTLETT,
WILLIAM WHIPPLE,
MATTHEW THORNTON.

Rhode Island.
STEPHEN HOPKINS,
WILLIAM ELLERY.

Connecticut.
ROGER SHERMAN,
SAMUEL HUNTINGTON,
WILLIAM WILLIAMS,
OLIVER WOLCOT.

New York.
WILLIAM FLOYD,
PHILIP LIVINGSTON,
FRANCIS LEWIS,
LEWIS MORRIS.

New Jersey.
RICHARD STOCKTON,
JOHN WITHERSPOON,
FRANCIS HOPKINSON,
JOHN HART,
ABRAHAM CLARK.

Pennsylvania.
ROBERT MORRIS,
BENJAMIN RUSH,
BENJAMIN FRANKLIN,
JOHN MORTON,
GEORGE CLYMER,
JAMES SMITH,
GEORGE TAYLOR,
JAMES WILSON,
GEORGE ROSS.

Massachusetts.
SAMUEL ADAMS,
JOHN ADAMS,
ROBERT TREAT PAYNE,
ELDRIDGE GERRY.

Delaware
CÆSAR RODNEY,
GEORGE READ,
THOMAS M'KEAN.

Maryland.
SAMUEL CHASE,
WILLIAM PACA,
THOMAS STONE,
CHAS. CARROLL, of Carrollton.

Virginia.
GEORGE WYTHE,
RICHARD HENRY LEE,
THOMAS JEFFERSON,
BENJAMIN HARRISON,
THOMAS NELSON, Jr.
FRANCIS LIGHTFOOT LEE,
CARTER BRAXTON.

North Carolina.
WILLIAM HOOPER,
JOSEPH HEWS,
JOHN PENN.

South Carolina.
EDWARD RUTLEDGE,
THOMAS HEYWARD, Jr.,
THOMAS LYNCH, Jr.,
ARTHUR MIDDLETON.

Georgia.
BUTTON GWINNETT,
LYMAN HALL,
GEORGE WALTON.

SIGNERS OF THE DECLARATION OF INDEPENDENCE.

NAME.	FROM COLONY.	OCCUPATION.	Born.	Died.
Josiah Bartlett	New Hampshire	Physician	1729	1795
William Whipple	New Hampshire	Sailor	1730	1785
Matthew Thornton	New Hampshire	Physician	1714	1803
John Hancock	Massachusetts Bay	Merchant	1737	1793
John Adams	Massachusetts Bay	Lawyer	1735	1826
Samuel Adams	Massachusetts Bay	Merchant	1722	1803
Robert T. Payne	Massachusetts Bay	Lawyer	1731	1814
Eldridge Gerry	Massachusetts Bay	Merchant	—	1814
Stephen Hopkins	Rhode Island	Farmer	1744	1785
William Ellery	Rhode Island	Lawyer	1707	1820
Roger Sherman	Connecticut	Shoemaker	1727	1793
Samuel Huntington	Connecticut	Lawyer	1721	1796
William Williams	Connecticut	Statesman	1731	1811
Oliver Wolcott	Connecticut	Soldier	1726	1797
William Floyd	New York	Farmer	1734	1821
Philip Livingston	New York	Merchant	1716	1778
Francis Lewis	New York	Merchant	1713	1803
Lewis Morris	New York	Farmer	1726	1798
Richard Stockton	New Jersey	Lawyer	1730	1781
John Witherspoon	New Jersey	Educator	1722	1794
Francis Hopkinson	New Jersey	Lawyer	1731	1796
John Hart	New Jersey	Farmer	1708	1780
Abraham Clark	New Jersey	Lawyer	1726	1794
Robert Morris	Pennsylvania	Merchant	1733	1806
Benjamin Rush	Pennsylvania	Physician	1746	1813
Benjamin Franklin	Pennsylvania	Printer	1706	1790
John Morton	Pennsylvania	Surveyor	1724	1777
George Clymer	Pennsylvania	Merchant	1739	1813
James Smith	Pennsylvania	Lawyer	1719	1806
George Taylor	Pennsylvania	Foundryman	1716	1781
James Wilson	Pennsylvania	Lawyer	1742	1798
George Ross	Pennsylvania	Lawyer	1730	1779
Cæsar Rodney	Delaware	General	1730	1783
George Reed	Delaware	Lawyer	1733	1798
Thomas McKean	Delaware	Lawyer	1734	1817
Samuel Chase	Maryland	Lawyer	1741	1811
Thomas Stone	Maryland	Lawyer	1743	1787
William Paca	Maryland	Lawyer	1740	1799
Charles Carroll	Maryland	Lawyer	1737	1832
George Wythe	Virginia	Lawyer	1726	1806
Richard Henry Lee	Virginia	Statesman	1732	1794
Thomas Jefferson	Virginia	Lawyer	1743	1826
Benjamin Harrison	Virginia	Farmer	1740	1791
Thomas Nelson Jr.	Virginia	Statesman	1738	1789
Francis L. Lee	Virginia	Farmer	1734	1797
Carter Braxton	Virginia	Planter	1736	1777
William Hooper	North Carolina	Lawyer	1742	1790
Joseph Hewes	North Carolina	Merchant	1730	1779
John Penn	North Carolina	Lawyer	1741	1788
Edward Rutledge	South Carolina	Lawyer	1749	1800
Thomas Heyward Jr.	South Carolina	Lawyer	1746	1809
Thomas Lynch Jr.	South Carolina	Lawyer	1749	1779
Arthur Middleton	South Carolina	Planter	1743	1787
Button Gwinnett	Georgia	Merchant	1732	1777
Lyman Hall	Georgia	Physician	1725	1790
George Walton	Georgia	Lawyer	1740	1804

CONSTITUTION OF THE UNITED STATES OF AMERICA.
PREAMBLE.

We, the people of the United States, in order to form a more perfect union, establish justice, insure domestic tranquility, provide for the common defense, promote the general welfare, and secure the blessings of liberty to ourselves and our posterity, do ordain and establish this Constitution for the United States of America.

ARTICLE I.
Of the Legislative Power.

SECTION I. All legislative power herein granted shall be vested in a Congress of the United States, which shall consist of a Senate and House of Representatives.

Of the House of Representatives.

SEC. II. 1. The House of Representatives shall be composed of members chosen every second year by the people of the several states; and the electors in each state shall have the qualifications requisite for electors of the most numerous branch of the state legislature.

Qualifications of Members.

2. No person shall be a represenative who shall not have attained the age of twenty-five years and been seven years a citizen of the United States, and who shall not, when elected, be an inhabitant of that state in which he shall be chosen.

Apportionment of Representatives and Direct Taxes—Census.

3. Representatives and direct taxes shall be apportioned among the several states which may be included within this Union according to their respective numbers, which shall be determined by adding to the whole number of free persons, including those bound to service for a term of years and excluding Indians not taxed, three-fifths of all other persons. The actual enumeration shall be made within three years after the first meeting of the Congress of the United States, and within every subsequent term of ten years, in such manner as they shall by law direct. The number of representatives shall not exceed one for every thirty thousand, but each state shall have at least one representative; and until such enumeration shall be made, the state of New Hampshire shall be entitled to choose three; Massachusetts, eight; Rhode Island and Providence Plantations, one; Connecticut, five; New York, six; New Jersey, four; Pennylvania, eight; Delaware, one; Maryland, six; Virginia, ten; North Carolina, five; South Carolina, five; and Georgia, three.

Vacancies.

4. When vacancies happen in the representation from any state, the executive authority thereof shall issue writs of election to fill such vacancies.

Of Their Officers—Impeachment.

5. The house of representatives shall choose their speaker and other officers, and shall have the sole power of impeachment.

Of the Senate.

SEC.III. 1. The senate of the United States shall be composed of two senators from each state, chosen by the legislature thereof, for six years and each senator shall have one vote.

Their Classes—Vacancies.

2. Immediately after they shall be assembled, in consequence of the first election, they shall be divided as equally as may be into three classes

The seats of the senators of the first class shall be vacated **at the expiration of the second year, of** the second class at the expiration **of the fourth year,** and of the third class at the expiration of the **sixth year, so that** one-third may be **chosen** every second **year; and** if vacancies happen, by resignation or otherwise, during the recess of the legislature of any state, **the** executive thereof may make temporary appointments until the next **meeting** of the legislature, **which** shall then fill such vacancies.

Qualification of Senators.

3. **No person shall** be a senator who shall **not** have attained to the age **of** thirty years and been nine **years a citizen of the** United States, and who shall not, **when elected, be an inhabitant of that state** for which he shall **be chosen.**

Of the Vice President.

4. **The** vice-president **of the United States shall be president of** the senate, **but shall** have no vote **unless they be equally divided.**

Of the Officers of the Senate.

5. **The senate** shall choose **their other officers, and also** a president *pro tempore* **in the** absence **of the vice-president, or when** he shall exercise the office of president of the **United States.**

Of Impeachment.

6. **The** senate shall have **the** sole power to try all impeachments. **When** sitting for that purpose they **shall** be **on oath** or affirmation. When the president **of the** United States **is** tried the chief **justice** shall preside, and no person shall be convicted without the concurrence **of** two-thirds **of the** members present.

Judgment in Cases of.

7. Judgment in cases of impeachment shall not extend further than to **removal** from office and disqualification to hold and enjoy any office of **honor, trust, or** profit under the United States; but the party convicted **shall, nevertheless, be liable** and **subject to** indictment, trial, judgment **and punishment, according to law.**

Manner of Electing Members of Congress.

SEC. IV. 1. **The times, places, and manner of holding** elections for **senators and representatives shall be** prescribed **in each state by** the **legislature thereof, but the congress may at any time, by law, make or** alter such regulations, except as **to** the **places of choosing senators.**

Of the Meeting of Congress.

2. The congress shall assemble **at least once in every year, and such** meeting shall be **on the first Monday in December, unless** they shall by **law** appoint **a different day.**

Powers of Each House.

SEC. 5. 1. **Each house shall be** the **judge** of elections, returns, and qualifications **of its own** members, and **a** majority of each shall constitute a quorum **to do** business; but a smaller number may adjourn **from** day to **day, and may be** authorized to **compel the** attendance of absent members, **in such manner and under such penalties as** each house may provide.

Expulsion.

2. Each house **may determine the rules of** its proceedings, punish its **members for disorderly behavior, and, with** the concurrence of two-thirds **expel a member.**

Journals and Yeas and Nays.

3. Each house **shall keep** a journal of **its** proceedings, and from **time to** time publish the **same,** excepting **such parts as** may, in their

judgment, require secrecy; **and the yeas and nays of** the members of **either house, on any question, shall, at the desire of one-fifth of those** present, be entered **on the journal.**

Of Adjournment.

4. Neither house, **during the session of congress, shall, without the con-** sent of the **other,** adjourn for more **than three days, nor to any other place than in which** the two houses **shall** be sitting.

Compensation, Privileges and Incapacities **of Members.**

SEC. VI. 1. The senators and representatives shall **receive a compen- sation for** their services, to be ascertained by law, and paid **out of the treasury** of the United States. They shall, in all cases, except **treason,** felony, and breach of the peace, be privileged from arrest, **during their** attendance at the session of their **respective** houses, and in **going** to or returning from the same; and for any speech or debate in **either** house they shall not be questioned in any other place.

Exclusion from Office.

2. No senator **or representative shall, during the** time for which **he was** elected, be **appointed to any civil office, under** the authority of **the United** States, which **shall have been created, or the** emoluments where- **of shall have been increased, during such time, and no person holding any office under the United States shall be a member** of either **house during his** continuance **in office.**

Revenue Bills.

SEC. VII. 1. **All bills for** raising revenue shall **originate in the house of** representatives, but the senate may propose **or concur with amend- ments as on other bills.**

Manner of Passing Bills, etc.

2. **Every bill which shall have passed the house of** representatives and **the senate shall, before it** becomes a law, be presented to the president of **the United** States; if he approves, he shall sign it; but if not, he shall re- turn it, with his objections, to that house in which it shall have origin- ated, who shall enter the objections at large on **their** journal, and pro- ceed to reconsider it. If, after such reconsideration, two-thirds **of** that house shall agree to pass the bill, it **shall be sent,** together **with the** objec- tions, to the other house, by which **it shall likewise** be reconsidered, and **if** approved **by** two-thirds **of** that **house, it shall** become a law. But, in **all such** cases, the votes of **both houses shall be determined** by yeas and nays; and the **names of the persons voting for and** against the bill, shall be entered on the **journal of each house respectively. If any** bill shall **not be** returned by the **president within ten days, (Sunday** excepted), **after** it shall have **been presented to him, the same shall** be a law, in like manner as if he **had signed it, unless the congress,** by their adjournment, prevents its return; **in which case it shall** not be a law.

Orders, Resolutions and Votes.

3. Every order, **resolution, or vote,** to which the concurrence of the **senate** and **house of representatives may be** necessary (except on a ques- **tion of adjournment), shall be presented to the** president of the United **States; and before the same shall take effect** shall be approved by him, or **being disapproved by** him, **shall be repassed by** two-thirds of the senate **and house of** representatives, according to the rules and limitations pre- **scribed in the case of** a bill.

General Power of Congress—Taxes, Duties Imports, Uniformity.

SEC. VIII.   The congress shall have power—

1.   **To lay** and collect taxes, duties, imposts, and excises; **to pay** the **debts, and to** provide for the common defense and general welfare of the **United States; but** all duties, imposts, and excises shall be uniform throughout the United States.

Borrow Money.

2.   **To borrow money on the credit of the United States.**

Commerce.

3.   **To regulate commerce with foreign nations, and** among the several states, and with the Indian tribes.

Naturalization—Bankruptcy.

4.   **To** establish **an uniform rule of naturalization, and uniform** laws on the subject of bankruptcies thoughout the United States.

Money, Weights and Measures.

5.   **To coin** money, regulate **the value thereof, and of foreign** coin, and **fix the standard** of weights and measures.

Counterfeiting.

6.   **To provide for the punishment of counterfeiting** the securities and current coin of the United States.

Post Offices.

7.   **To** establish post-offices and **post roads.**

Authors—Inventors.

8.   To promote the progress of science and useful **arts by** securing, for limited times to authors and **inventors, the exclusive** right to their respective writings and discoveries.

Inferior Tribunals.

9.   **To** constitute tribunals inferior to the supreme court.

Piracies—Offences.

10.   **To define and punish piracies and** felonies committed on the high **seas, and** offenses against the law of nations.

War—Marque and Reprisals.

11.   **To** declare war, **grant letters of marque and** reprisal, **and make** rules concerning captures on land and water.

Armies.

12.   **To raise and support armies; but no appropriation of money to** that use shall be for a longer term than two years.

Navy.

13.   **To provide and maintain a navy.**

Rules for Land and Naval Forces.

14.   **To make rules for the government** and regulation of **the land and** naval forces.

Calling out Militia.

15.   **To provide for calling forth the** militia **to execute the laws** of the **Union, su**ppress insurrections, and repel invasions.

Organizing, Arming and Disciplining Militia.

16.   **To** provide for **organizing, arming, and** disciplining **the militia, and** for governing **such part of them as** may be employed **in the** service **of the** United States, **reserving to the** states respectively the appointment **of the** officers, and **the authority of** training the militia according to the discipline prescribed **by congress.**

Exclusive Legislation over Seat of Government—Forts, etc.

17.   To exercise exclusive **legislation in** all cases whatsoever **over** such

district (not exceeding ten miles square) as may, by session of particular states, and the **acceptance of congress,** become the seat of government of the United States, **and to exercise like authority over all** places purchased by the consent of **the legislature of the state in which the same** shall be, for the **erections of forts, magazines, arsenals,** dock-yards, and other needful **buildings.**

Power Given to Enforce Constitution.

18. **To make all** laws which shall be necessary and proper **for carrying into execution the** foregoing powers, and all other powers **vested by this constitution** in the government of the United States, **or in any department or officer thereof.**

Limitation of Power—Migration of Slaves.

SEC. IX. 1. The migration or importation of such persons as **any of** the states now existing shall think **proper to admit** shall not be prohibited by the congress prior to the year one **thousand** eight hundred **and** eight, but a tax **on duty** may be imposed on such importation, **not exceed-**ing ten dollars for such person.

Habeas Corpus.

2. The privilege of **the** writ of **ha**beas corpus **shall** not be suspended, unless when, in cases **of rebellion or** invasion, **the public** safety may require **it.**

Attainder—Ex-Post Facto.

3. **No** bill of attainder or *ex-post facto* law shall **be passed.**

Capitation—Taxes.

4. No capitation **or** other direct tax shall **be laid unless in proportion** to the census or **enumeration herein**before **directed to be** taken.

Exports.

5. No tax **or duty shall be laid on articles exported from** any state. No **preference shall be given by any regulation of commerce** or revenue to the **ports of one state over those of another; nor shall** vessels bound to or **from one state be obliged to enter clear, or** pay duties in another.

Money, how Drawn From the Treasury.

6. No money shall be drawn from the treasury but in consequence of appropriations made by law; and a regular statement and account of the receipts and expenditures of all public **money** shall be published from time to time.

Nobility—Presents—Offices.

7. No title of nobility shall **be granted by** the United States, and no person holding any office of profit or trust under them shall, without the consent of the congress, accept **any present,** emolument, office, or title of any kind whatever, from any king, prince, **or** foreign state.

Limitations of the Powers of Individual States.

SEC. X. 1. No state **shall enter into any treaty, alliance** or confederation; grant letters of marque and **reprisal, coin money;** emit bills of credit; make anything but gold and **silver coin a tender in** payment of debts; pass any **bills of** attainder, *ex-post facto* la**w, or law** impairing the obligation of contracts, or grant any **title of** nobility.

Powers of States, Consent of Congress, when Necessary,

2. **No state shall, without the** consent of congress, lay any imposts or duties **on imports or exports,** except what may **be** absolutely necessary for executing **its inspection laws;** and the net **produce** of all duties and imposts laid by any state **on** imports **or exports** shall be for the use of the treasury **of the** United States, **and all such laws shall** be subject to the

revision and control of congress. No state shall, without the consent of congress, lay any duty of tonnage, keep troops or ships of war in time of peace, enter into any agreement or compact with another state, or with a foreign power, or engage in war, unless actually invaded, or in such imminent danger as will not admit of delay.

ARTICLE II.

Of the President—The Executive Power.

SEC. 1. 1. **The executive** power shall be vested in a president of the United States of America. He shall hold his office during the term of four years, and together with the vice-president, chosen for the same term, be elected as follows:

Manner of Electing.

2. **Each state** shall appoint in such manner as the legislature thereof may direct, a number of electors, equal to the whole number of senators and representatives to which the state may be entitled in the congress, but no senator or representative, or person holding an office of trust or profit under the United States, shall be appointed an elector.

Time of Meeting of Electors, and Manner of Voting.

3. (12th Amendment). The electors shall meet in their respective states and vote by ballot, for president and vice president, one of whom, at least shall not be an inhabitant of the same state with themselves; They shall name in their ballot the person voted for as president, and in distinct ballots, the person voted for as vice-president, and they shall make distinct lists of all persons voted for as president, and of all persons voted for as vice-president, and of the number of votes for each, which lists they shall sign and certify, and transmit sealed to the seat of government of the United States directed to the president of the senate; the president of the senate shall, in the presence of the senate and house of representatives, open all the certificates, and the votes shall then be counted; the person having the greatest number of votes for president shall be the president, if such number be a majority of the whole number of electors appointed; and if no person have such a majority, then from the persons having the highest number not exceeding three, on the list of those voted for as president, the house of representatives shall choose immediately, by ballot, the president. But, in choosing the president, the votes shall be taken by states, the representatives from each state having one vote; a quorum for this purpose shall consist of a member or members from two-thirds of the states, and a majority of all the states shall be necessary to a choice. And if the house of representatives shall not choose a president, whenever the right of choice shall devolve upon them, before the fourth day of March, next following, then the vice-president shall act as president, as in the case of the death or other constitutional disability of the president.

The person having the greatest number of votes as vice-president shall be the vice-president, if such number be a majority of the whole number of electors appointed; and if no person have a majority, then from the two highest numbers on the list the senate shall choose the vice-president; a quorum for that purpose shall consist of two-thirds of the whole number of senators, and a majority of the whole number shall be necessary to a choice.

But no person constitutionally ineligible to the office of president shall be eligible to that of vice-president of the United States.

Time of Choosing Electors.

4. The congress may determine the time of choosing the electors, and the day on which they shall give their votes, which day shall be the same throughout the United States.

Who May be Elected President.

5. No person except a natural born citizen, or a citizen of the United States at the time of the adoption of this constitution, shall be eligible to the office of president, neither shall any person be eligible to that office who shall not have attained to the age of thirty-five years, and been fourteen years a resident within the United States.

In Case of Removal etc., of the President, his Powers to Devolve Upon the Vice-President, etc.

1. In case of the removal of the president from office, or of his death, resignation or inability to discharge the powers and duties of the said office, the same shall devolve on the vice-president, and the congress may, by law, provide for the case of removal, death, resignation or inability, both of the president and vice-president, declaring what officer shall then act as president, and such officer shall act accordingly, until the disability be removed or a president shall be elected.

President's Compensation.

7. The president shall, at stated times, receive for his services a compensation which shall neither be increased nor diminished during the period for which he shall have been elected, and he shall not receive during that period any other emolument from the United States or any of them.

His Oath.

8. Before he enters on the execution of his office he shall take the following oath or affirmation:

"I do solemnly swear (or affirm) that I will faithfully execute the office of president of the United States, and will, to the best of my ability, preserve, protect, and defend the constitution of the United States."

Power and Duties.

SEC. II. 1. The president shall be commander-in-chief of the army and navy of the United States, and of the militia of the several states when called into the actual service of the United States. He may require the opinion in writing of the principal officer in each of the executive departments, upon any subject relating to the duties of their respective offices; and he shall have power to grant reprieves and pardons for offenses against the United States, except in cases of impeachment.

Of Making Treaties—Appointments.

2. He shall have power, by and with the advice and consent of the senate, to make treaties, provided two-thirds of the senators present concur; and he shall nominate, and by and with the consent of the senate, shall appoint ambassadors, other public ministers and consuls, judges of the supreme court, and all other officers of the United States whose appointments are not herein otherwise provided for, and which shall be established by law. But the congress may, by law, vest the appointment of such inferior officers as they think proper in the president alone, in the courts of law, or in the heads of departments.

Power of Appointment.

3. The president shall have power to fill up all vacancies that may happen during the recess of the senate, by granting commissions, which shall expire at the end of their next session.

Further Powers and Duties.

SEC. III. 1. He shall from time to time give to the congress information of the state of the Union, and recommend to their consideration such measures as he shall judge necessary and expedient. He may, on extraordinary occasions, convene both houses or either of them, and in case of disagreement between them, with respect to the time of adjournment he may adjourn them to such time as he may think proper. He shall receive ambassadors and other public ministers. He shall take care that the laws be faithfully executed; and shall commission all the officers of the United States.

Of Impeachments.

SEC. IV. 1 The president, vice-president and all civil officers of the United States, shall be removed from office on impeachment for, and conviction of, treason, bribery, or other high crimes and misdemeanors.

ARTICLE III.

OF THE JUDICIARY.

Of the Judicial Power—Concerning the Judges

SEC. 1. 1. The judicial power of the United States shall be vested in one supreme court, and in such inferior courts as the congress may from time to time ordain and establish.

The judges, both of the supreme and inferior courts, shall hold their offices during good behavior, and shall, at stated times, receive for their services a compensation, which shall not be diminished during their continuance in office.

Extent of the Judicial Power—This Clause Alters Portea—See Amendment Art. XI. That Follows:

SEC. II. 1. The judicial power shall extend to all cases in law and equity arising under this constitution, the laws of the United States, and treaties made, or which shall be made, under their authority; to all cases affecting ambassadors, or other public ministers and consuls; to all cases of admiralty and maritime jurisdiction; to controversies to which the United States shall be a party; to controversies between two or more states, between a state and citizens of another state; between citizens of different states; between citizens of the same state, claiming land under grants of different states, and between a state or the citizens thereof and foreign states, citizens, or subjects.

Of Original and Appellate Jurisdiction of the Supreme Court.

2. In all cases affecting ambassadors, or other public ministers or consuls, and those in which a state shall be a party, the supreme court shall have original jurisdiction. In all the other cases before mentioned, the supreme court shall have appellate jurisdiction, both as to law and fact, with such exceptions and under such regulations as the congress shall make.

Of Trials for Crimes.

3. The trial of all crimes, except in cases of impeachment, shall be by a jury; and such trial shall be held in the state where the said crimes shall

have been committed; but when not committed within any state, the trial shall be at such place or places as the congress may by law have directed.

Of the Judicial Power.

(Amendment Art. XI). The judicial power of the United States shall not be construed to extend to any suit in law or in equity, commenced or prosecuted against one of the United States by citizens of another state, or by citizens or subjects of any foreign state.

Of Treason.

SEC. III. 1. Treason against the United States shall consist only in levying war against them, or in adhering to their enemies; giving them aid and comfort. No person shall be convicted of treason, unless on the testimony of two witnesses to the same overt act, or on confession in open court.

Punishment of Treason.

2. The congress shall have power to declare the punishment of treason; but no attainder of treason shall work corruption of blood or forfeiture, except during the life of the person attained.

ARTICLE IV.

Of State Records.

SEC. I. 1. Full faith and credit shall be given in each state to the public acts, records, and judicial proceedings of every other state. And the congress may, by general law, prescribe the manner in which such acts, records, and proceedings shall be proved, and effect thereof.

Of Citizenship.

SEC. II. 1. The citizens of each state shall be entitled to all privileges and immunities of citizens in the several states.

Fugitives from Justice.

2. A person charged in any state with treason, felony, or other crime, who shall flee from justice, and be found in another state, shall, on demand of the executive authority of the state from which he fled, be delivered up, to be removed to the state having jurisdiction of the crime.

Of Persons held to Service.

3. No person held to service or labor in one state, under the laws thereof, escaping into another, shall, in consequence of any law or regulation therein, be discharged from such service or labor; but shall be delivered up on claim of the party to whom such service or labor may be due.

Admission of New States.

SEC. III. 1. New states may be admitted by the congress into this Union, but no new state shall be formed or erected within the jurisdiction of any other state, nor any state be formed by the junction of two or more states, or parts of states, without the consent of the legislatures of the states concerned, as well as of the congress.

Property—Claims.

2. The congress shall have power to dispose of, and make all needful rules and regulations respecting the territory of other property belonging

to the United States; and nothing in this constitution shall be so construed as to prejudice any claims of the United States, or of any particular state.

Republican Form of Government Guaranteed.

S c. IV. 1. The United States shall guarantee to every state in this Union a republican form of government, and shall protect each of them against invasion; and on application of the legislature, or of the executive (when the legislature can not be convened), against domestic violence.

ARTICLE V.

Of Amendments to the Constitution.

1. The congress, whenever two-thirds of both houses shall deem it necessary, shall propose amendments to this constitution; or on the application of the legislatures of two-thirds of the several states, shall call a convention for proposing amendments, which, in either case, shall be valid, to all intents and purposes, as part of this constitution, when ratified by the legislatures of three-fourths of the several states, or by conventions in three-fourths thereof, as the one or the other mode of ratification may be proposed by the congress; *Provided*, That no amendment which be made prior to the year one thousand eight hundred and eight, shall in any manner affect the first and fourth clauses in the ninth section of the first article; and that no state, without its consent, shall be deprived of its equal suffrage in the senate.

ARTICLE VI.

Of Public Debt.

SEC. I. All debts contracted, and engagements entered into, before the adoption of this constitution, shall be as valid against the United States, under this constitution, as under the confederation.

The Supreme Law of the Land.

SEC. II. This constitution, and the laws of the United States which shall be made in pursuance thereof, and all treaties made, or which shall be made under the authority of the United States, shall be the supreme law of the land, and the judges in every state shall be bound thereby; anything in the constitution or laws of any state to the contrary notwithstanding.

Constitutional Oath—No Religious Test.

SEC. III. The senators and representatives, before mentioned, and the members of the several state legislatures, and all executive and judicial officers, both of the United States and of the several states, shall be bound by oath or affirmation to support this constitution; but no religious test shall ever be required as a qualification to any office or public trust under the United States.

ARTICLE VII.

The ratification of the conventions of nine states shall be sufficient for the establishment of this constitution between the states so ratifying the same.

Done in convention, by the unanimous consent of the states present, the seventeenth day of September, in the year of our Lord one thousand seven hundred and eighty-seven, and of the independence of the United States of America, the twelfth.

In witness whereof, we have hereunto subscribed our names:

GEORGE WASHINGTON,
President and Deputy from Virginia.

New Hampshire.
JOHN LANGDON,
NICHOLAS GILMAN.
Connecticut.
WILLIAM SAMUEL JOHNSON,
ROGER SHERMAN.
New York.
ALEXANDER HAMILTON.
New Jersey.
WILLIAM LIVINGSTON,
DAVID BREARLEY,
WILLIAM PATTERSON,
JONATHAN DAYTON.
Pennsylvania.
BENJAMIN FRANKLIN,
THOMAS MIFFLIN,
ROBERT MORRIS,
GEORGE CLYMER,
THOMAS FITZIMMONS,
JARED INGERSOLL,
JAMES WILSON,
GOVERNEUR MORRIS.
Delaware.
GEORGE REED,
GUNNING BEDFORD, JR.

Massachusetts.
NATHANIEL GORMAN,
RUFUS KING,
JOHN DICKINSON,
RICHARD BASSETT,
JACOB BROOM.
Maryland.
JAMES M'HENRY,
DANIEL OF ST. THO. JENIFER,
DANIEL CARROLL.
Virginia.
JOHN BLAIR,
JAMES MADISON, JR.
North Carolina.
WILLIAM BLOUNT,
RICHARDS DOBBS SPAIGHT,
HUGH WILLIAMSON.
South Carolina.
JOHN RUTLEDGE,
CHAS. COTESWORTH PINCKNEY,
CHAS. PINCKNEY,
PIERCE BUTLER.
Georgia.
WILLIAM FEW,
ABRAHAM BALDWIN.

ATTEST: WILLIAM JACKSON, *Secretary.*

NOTE. This constitution was ratified by the several states in the order and dates here given, viz: Delaware, December 7, 1787; Pennsylvania, December 12, 1787; New Jersey, December 18, 1787; Georgia, January 2, 1788; Connecticut, January 9, 1788; Massachusetts, February 6, 1788; Maryland, April 28, 1788; South Carolina, May 23, 1788; New Hampshire, June 21, 1788; Virginia, June 26, 1788; New York, July 26, 1788; North Carolina, November 21, 1789; Rhode Island, May 29, 1790.

Amendments to the Constitution.

(The first ten amendments to the constitution of the United States were proposed to the legislatures of the several states by the First congress on the 25th of September, 1789. They were ratified by the following states and the notifications of the ratification by the governors thereof were successively communicated by the president to congress: New Jersey, November 20, 1789, Maryland, December 19, 1789; North Carolina, December 22, 1789; South Carolina, January 19, 1790; New Hampshire, January 25, 1790; Delaware, January 28, 1790; Pennsylvania, March 10, 1790; New York March 27, 1790; Rhode Island, June 15, 1790; Vermont, November 3, 1791, and Virginia, December 15, 1791.)

ARTICLE I.

Of the Right of Conscience—Freedom of the Press.

Congress shall make no law respecting the establishment of religion, or preventing the free exercise thereof; or abridging the freedom of speech, or of the press; or the right of the people peaceably to assemble, and to petition the government for a redress of grievances.

ARTICLE II.

Of the Right to Bear Arms.

A well regulated militia being necessary to the security of a free state, the right of the people to keep and bear arms shall not be infringed.

ARTICLE III.

Of Quartering Troops.

No soldier shall, in time of peace, be quartered in any house without the

consent of the owner, nor in time of war, but in a manner to be pre
scribed law.

ARTICLE IV.
Of the Right to be Secure from Search.

The right of the people to be secure in their persons, houses, papers, and
effects, against unreasonable searches and seizures, shall not be violated;
and no warrants shall be issued but upon probable cause, supported by
oath or affirmation, and particularly describing the place to be searched,
and the persons or things to be seized.

ARTICLE V.
Of Indictment, Punishment, etc.

No person shall be held to answer for a capital, or otherwise infamous
crime, unless on a presentment or indictment of a grand jury, except in a
case arising in the land or naval forces, or in the militia, when in actual
service, in time of war or public danger; nor shall any person be subject,
for the same offense, to be twice put in jeopardy of life or limb, nor shall
be compelled, in any criminal case, to be a witness against himself, or be
deprived of life, liberty or property, without due process of law; nor shall
private property be taken for public use without just compensation.

ARTICLE VI.
Of Trial in Criminal Cases, and the Rights of Defendant.

In all criminal prosecutions the accused shall enjoy the right to a
speedy and public trial, by an impartial jury of the state and district
wherein the crime shall have been committed, which district shall have
been previously ascertained by law, and to be informed of the nature and
cause of the accusation; to be confronted with the witness against him; to
have compulsory process for obtaining witnesses in his favor, and to have
the assistance of counsel for his defense.

ARTICLE VII.
Of Trial in Civil Cases.

In suits at common law, where the value in controversy shall exceed
twenty dollars, the right of trial by jury shall be preserved, and no fact,
tried by a jury, shall be otherwise re-examined in any court of the United
States than according to the rules of the common law.

ARTICLE VIII.
Of Bail and Fines.

Excessive bail shall not be required, nor excessive fines imposed, nor
cruel or unusual punishments inflicted.

ARTICLE IX.
Of Rights Reserved.

The enumeration, in the constitution, of certain rights, shall not be construed to deny or disparage others retained by the people.

ARTICLE X.
Of Powers Reserved to the States.

The powers not delegated to the United States, by the constitution, nor
prohibited by it to the states, are reserved to the states, respectively, or to
the people.

ARTICLE XI.
Of the Judicial Power.   See Article 3, Section 2.

(The eleventh amendment was proposed to the legislatures of the several
states by the Third Congress, on the 5th of September, 1794, and was declared in a message from the President to Congress dated the 8th of January, 1798, to have been ratified by the legislatures of three-fourths of the
states)

ARTICLE XII.

Manner of Electing the President and Vice-President. See Article 2, Section 3.

(The twelfth amendment was proposed to the legislatures of the several states by the eighth congress, on the 12th day of December, 1803, and was declared in a proclamation of the Secretary of State, dated the 25th of September, 1804, to have been ratified by the legislatures of three-fourths of the states.)

ARTICLE XIII.

Slavery Prohibited.

SEC. I   Neither slavery nor involuntary servitude, except as a punishment for crime, whereof the party shall have been duly convicted, shall exist within the United States, or any place subject to their jurisdiction.

Congress Given the Power to Enforce.

SEC. II.   Congress shall have power to enforce this article by appropriate legislation.

(The thirteenth amendment was proposed to the legislatures of the several states by the thirty-eighth congress, on the first of February, 1865, and was declared in a Proclamation of the Secretary of State, dated the 18th of of December, 1865 to have been ratified by the legislatures of twenty-seven of the thirty-six states, viz: Illinois, Rhode Island, Michigan, Maryland, New York, West Virginia, Maine, Kansas, Massachusetts,, Pennsylvania, Virginia, Ohio, Missouri, Nevada, Indiana, Louisiana, Minnesota, Wisconsin, Vermont, Tennessee, Arkansas, Connecticut, New Hampshire, South Carolina, Alabama, North Carolina and Georgia.)

ARTICLE XIV.

Citizenship Defined.

SEC. I.   All persons born or naturalized in the United States, and subject to the jurisdiction thereof, are citizens of the United States and of the state wherein they reside.   No state shall make or enforce any law which shall abridge the privileges or immunities of citizens of the United States, nor shall any state deprive any person of life, liberty, or property, without due process of law; nor deny to any person within its jurisdiction the equal protection of the laws.

Apportionment of Representatives.

SEC. II.   Representatives shall be apportioned among the several states according to their respective numbers, counting the whole number of persons in each state, excluding Indians not taxed.   But when the right to vote at any election for the choice of electors for president and vice-president of the United States, representatives in congress, the executive and judicial officers of a state, or the members of the legislatures thereof, is denied to any of the male inhabitants of such state, being twenty-one years of age, and citizens of the United States, or in way abridged, except for participation in rebellion, or other crime, the basis of representation therein shall be reduced in the proportion which the number of such male citizens shall bear to the whole number of male citizens twenty one years of age in such state.

Of Persons Disqualified From Holding Office and Removal of Disabilities.

SEC. III.   No person shall be a senator or representative in congress, or elector of president and vice-president, or hold any office, civil or military, under the United States, or under any state, who, having previously taken an oath, as a member of congress or as an officer of the United States, or as a member of any state legislature, or as an executive or judicial officer of

any state, **to** support the constitution **of** the United States, shall have **en-**
gaged in insurrection or rebellion against the same, or given aid or comfort
to the enemies thereof. But congress may, **by** a vote of **two-thirds of each**
house; remove such disability.

**Of Debts of the United States, and Debts incurred in aid of Rebell-
ions Prohibited.**

SEC. IV. **The validity of** the public debt of the United States, authorized
by law, including debts incurred for payment of pensions and bounties
for services in suppressing insurrection or rebellion, shall not be questioned. But neither **the United** States nor **any state shall assume** or pay
any debt or obligation **incurred** in aid of **insurrection or rebellion** against
the United States, **or any claim for** the **loss** or **emancipation of any** slave:
but all such debts, **obligations and** claims shall **be held illegal and** void.

Congress Given Power to Enforce.

SEC. V. Congress shall **have power** to enforce, by appropriate **legislation,**
the provisions of this article.

(The fourteenth amendment **was** proposed to the legislatures of **the sev-**
eral states by the thirtyninth congress, on the 16th day of June, **1866.** On
the 21st of July 1868, congress adopted and transmitted to the department
of state a concurrent resolution, declaring that "the legislatures of the
states of Connecticut, Tennessee, New Jersey, Oregon, Vermont, New York,
Ohio, Illinois, West Virginia, Kansas, Maine, Nevada, Missouri, Indiana,
Minnesota, New Hampshire, Massachutes, Nebraska, Iowa, Arkansas,
Florida, North Carolina, Alabama, South Carolina and Louisiana being
three-fourths and more **of** the several states **of the** union, having ratified
the fourteenth article **of** amendment of **the** constitution of the United
States, duly proposed **by** two-thirds of each **house of the** thirty-ninth congress; therefore,
Resolved, That said fourteenth article is hereby declared **to be a** part of
the constitution of the United States, and it shall be duly promulgated as
such by the secretary of state." The secretary of state accordingly issued
a proclamation, dated the 28th **of** July, 1868, declaring that the proposed
fourteenth amendment had been ratified by the legislatures, of thirty of
the thirty-sixstates, Pennsylvania ratified it February 13, 1867).

ARTICLE XV.

The Right to Vote.

SEC. 1. The right of citizens of **the United States to vote shall not be**
denied or abridged by the United **States or by any state on account of**
race, color **or** previous condition **of servitude.**

SEC. **2.** The congress shall have **power to enforce this article by ap-**
propriate legislation.

(The fifteenth amendment to the Constitution of the United States was
proposed to the legislatures of the several states by the fortieth congress,
on the 27th day of February 1869, and was declared in a proclamation of
the secretary of state, dated March 30, 1870 to have been ratified by the
legislatures of twenty-nine of the thirty-seven states. Pennsylvania
ratified it **March** 26, 1869).

ORGANIC ACT.

AN ACT to Organize the Territory of Nebraska.

Be it enacted by the Senate and House of Representatives of the United States of America in Congress Assembled. That all that part of the territory of the United States included within the following limits, except such portions thereof as are hereinafter expressly exempted from the operations of this act, to-wit: beginning at a point on the Missouri river, where the fortieth parallel of north latitude crosses the same; thence west on said parellel to the east boundry of the territory of Utah, on the summit of the rocky mountains; thence on said summit northward to the forty-ninth parallel of north latitude; thence east on said parallel to the western boundary of the territory of Minnesota; thence southward on said boundary to the Missouri river; thence down the main chaunel of said river to the place of beginning, be and the same is hereby created into a temporary government, by the name of the Territory of Nebraska; and when admitted as a state or states, the said territory, or any portion of the same, shall be received into the Union with or without slavery, as their constitution may prescribe at the time of their admission: *Provided,* That nothing in this act contained shall be construed to inhibit the government of the United States from dividing said territory into two or more territories, in such manner and at such times as congress shall deem convenient and proper, or from attaching any portion of said territory to any other state or territory of the United States: *Provided further,* That nothing in this act contained shall be construed to impair the rights of person or property now pertaining to the Indians in said territory, so long as such rights shall remain unextinguished by treaty between the United States and such Indians, or to include any territory, which, by treaty with any Indian tribe, is not, without the consent of said tribe, to be included within the territorial limits or jurisdiction of any state or territory; but all such territory shall be excepted out of the boundaries, and constitute no part of the territory of Nebraska, until said tribe shall signify their assent to the president of the United States to be included within the said territory of Nebraska, or to affect the authority of the government of the United States to make any regulations respecting such Indians, their lands, property or other rights, by treaty, law, or otherwise, which it would have been competent to the government to make if this act had never passed.

SEC. 2. *And be it further enacted,* That the executive power and authority, in and over said territory of Nebraska, shall be vested in a governor, who shall hold his office for four years, and until his successor shall be appointed and qualified, unless sooner removed by the president of the United States. The governor shall reside within said territory, and shall be commander-in-chief of the militia thereof. He may grant pardons and respite for offenses against the laws of said territory, and reprieves for offenses against the laws of the United States, until the decision of the president can be made known thereon; he shall commission all officers who shall be appointed to office under the laws of the said territory, and shall take care that the laws be faithfully executed.

SEC. 3. *And be it further enacted,* That there shall be a secretary of the said territory, who shall reside therein, and hold his office for five years, unless sooner removed by the president of the United States: he shall record and preserve all the laws and proceedings of the legislative assembly hereinafter constituted, and all the acts, and proceedings of the governor in his executive department; he shall transmit one copy of the laws and journals of the legislative assembly within thirty days after the end of each session, and one copy of the executive proceedings and official correspondence, semi-annually, on the first days of January and July in each year, to the president of the United States, and two copies of the laws to the president of the senate, and to the speaker of the house of representatives, to be deposited in the libraries of congress: and in case of the death, removal, resignation, or absence of the governor from the territory, the secretary shall be, and he is hereby authorized and required to execute and perform all the powers and duties of the governor ,during such vacancy or absence, or until another governor shall be duly appointed and qualified to fill such vacancy.

SEC. 4. *And be it further enacted,* That the legislative power and authority of said territory shall be vested in the governor and a legislative assembly. The legislative assembly shall consist of a council and house of representatives. The council shall consist of thirteen members, having the qualification of voters, as hereinafter prescribed, whose term of service shall continue two years. The house of representatives shall, at its first session, consist of twenty-six members, possessing the same qualifications as prescribed for members of the council, and whose term of service shall continue one year. The number of representatives may be increased by the legislative assembly, from time to time, in proportion to the increase of qualified voters; *Provided*, That the whole number shall never exceed thirty-nine. An apportionment shall be made, as nearly equal as practicable, among the several counties or districts, for the election of the council and representatives, giving to each section of the territory representation in the ratio of its qualified voters as nearly as may be. And the members of the council and of the house of representatives shall reside in, and be inhabitants of, the district or county or counties for which they may be elected respectively. Previous to the first election the governor shall cause a census or enumeration of the inhabitants and qualified voters of the several counties and districts of the territory, to be taken by such persons and in such mode as the governor shall designate and appoint; and the person so appointed shall receive a reasonable compensation therefor. And the first election shall be held at such time and places, and be conducted in such a manner, both as to the persons who shall superintend such election and the returns thereof, as the governor shall appoint and direct; and he shall at the same time declare the number of members of the council and house of representatives to which each of the counties or districts shall be entitled under this act. The persons having the highest number of legal votes in each of said council districts for members of the council shall be declared by the governor to be duly elected to the council; and the persons having the highest number of legal votes for the house of representatives shall be declared by the governor to be duly elected members of said house; *Provided*, That in case two or more persons voted for shall have an equal number of votes, and in case a vacancy shall otherwise occur in either branch of the legislative assembly, the governor shall order a new election, and the persons thus elected to the legislative assembly shall meet at such place and on such day as the governor shall appoint; but thereafter, the time, place, and manner of holding and conducting all elections by the people, and the apportioning the representation in the several counties and districts to the council and house of representatives, according to the number of qualified voters, shall be prescribed by law, as well as the day of the commencement of the regular sessions of the legislative assembly; *Provided*, That no session in any one year shall exceed the term of forty days, except the first session, which may continue sixty days.

SEC. 5. *And be it further enacted*, That every free white male inhabitant above the age of twenty-one years, who shall be an actual resident of said territory, and shall possess the qualifications hereinafter prescribed, shall be entitled to vote at the first election, and shall be eligible to any office within the said territory; but the qualifications of voters, and of holding office, at all subsequent elections, shall be such as shall be prescribed by the legislative assembly; *Provided*, That the right of suffrage and of holding office shall be exercised only by citizens of the United States, and those who shall have declared on oath their intention to become such, and shall have taken an oath to support the constitution of the United States, and the provisions of this act. *And provided further*, That no officer, soldier, seaman, or marine, or other person in the army or navy of the United States, or attached to troops in the service of the United States, shall be allowed to vote or hold office in said territory, by reason of being in service therein.

SEC. 6. *And be it further enacted*, That the legislative power of the territory shall extend to all rightful subjects of legislation consistent with the constitution of the United States and the provisions of this act, but no law shall be passed interfering with the primary disposal of the soil; no tax shall be imposed upon the property of the United States; nor shall the lands or other property of non-residents be taxed higher than the lands or other property of residents. Every bill which shall have passed the council and house of representatives of the said territory, shall, before it becomes a law, be presented to the governor of the territory, if he approves, he shall sign it; but if not, he shall return it, with his objections, to the house in which it originated, who shall enter the objections at large on their journal, and proceed to reconsider it. If, after such reconsideration, two-thirds of that house shall agree to pass the bill, it shall be sent, together with the objections, to the other house, by which it shall likewise be reconsidered, and if approved by two-thirds of that house it shall become a law. But in all such cases the votes of both houses shall be determined by yeas and nays, to be entered on the journal of each house respectively. If any bill shall not be returned by the governor within three days (Sundays excepted) after it shall have been presented to him, the same shall be a law in like manner as if he had signed it, unless the assembly, by adjournment, prevent its return, in which case it shall not be a law.

SEC. 7. *And be it further enacted,* That all township, district, and county officers, not herein otherwise provided for, shall be appointed or elected, as the case may be, in such manner as shall be provided by the governor and legislative assembly of the territory of Nebraska. The governor shall nominate, and, by and with the advice and consent of the legislative council, appoint all officers not herein otherwise provided for; and in the first instance the governor alone may appoint all said officers, who shall hold their offices until the end of the first session of the legislative assembly; and shall lay off the necessary districts for members of the council and house of representatives, and all other officers.

SEC. 8. *And be it further enacted,* That no member of the legislative assembly shall hold, or be appointed to, any office which shall have been created, or the salary or emoluments of which shall have been increased, while he was a member, during the term for which he was elected, and for one year after the expiration of such term; but this restriction shall not be applicable to members of the first legislative assembly; and no person holding a commission or appointment under the United States, except postmasters, shall be a member of the legislative assembly, or hold any office under the government of said territory.

SEC. 9. *And be it further enacted,* That the judicial power of said territory shall be invested in a supreme court, district courts, probate courts, and in justices of the peace. The supreme court shall consist of a chief justice, and two associate justices, any two of whom shall constitute a quorum, and who shall hold a term at the seat of government of said territory annually, and they shall hold their offices during the period of four years, and until their successors shall be appointed and quallified. The said territory shall be divided into three judicial districts, and a district court shall be held in each of said districts by one of the justices of the supreme court, at such times and places as may be prescribed by law; and the said judges shall, after their appointments, respectively reside in the districts which shall be assigned them. The jurisdiction of the several courts herein provided for, both appellate and original, and that of the probate courts and of justices of the peace, shall be as limited by law; *Provided,* That justices of the peace shall not have jurisdiction of any matter in controversy when the title or boundaries of land may be in dispute, or where the debt or sum claimed shall exceed one hundred dollars; and the said supreme and district courts respectively shall possess chancery as well as common law jurisdiction. Each district court, or the judge thereof, shall appoint its clerk, who shall also be the register in chancery, and shall keep his office at the place where the court may be held. Writs of error, bills of exception, and appeals, shall be allowed in all cases from the final decisions of said district courts, to the supreme court, under such regulations as may be prescribed by law; but in no case removed to the supreme court, shall trial by jury be allowed in said court. The supreme court or the justices thereof, shall appoint its own clerk, and every clerk shall hold his office at the pleasure of the court for which he shall have been appointed. Writs of error and appeals from the final decisions of said supreme court, shall be allowed, and may be taken to the supreme court of the United States in the same manner and under the same regulations as from the circuit courts of the United States, where the the value of the property, or the amount in controversy, to be ascertained by the oath or affirmation of either party, or other competent witness, shall exceed one thousand dollars, except only that in all cases involving title to slaves, the said writs of errors or appeals, shall be allowed and decided by the supreme court, without regard to the value of the matter, property, or title in controversy; and except also that a writ of error or appeal shall also be allowed to the supreme court of the United States, from the decision of the said supreme court created by this act, or of any judge thereof, or of the district courts created by this act or of any judge thereof, upon any writ of *habeas corpus,* involving the question of personal freedom; *Provided,* That nothing herein contained shall be construed to

apply to or affect the provisions of the "act respecting fugitives from jus
tice, and persons escaping from the service of their masters," approved
February twelfth, seventeen hundred and ninety-three, and the "act to
amend and supplementary to the aforesaid act," approved September
eighteenth, eighteen hundred and fifty; and each of the said district courts
shall have and exercise the same jurisdiction in all cases arising under the
constitution and laws of the United States as is vested in the circuit and
district courts of the United States, and the said supreme and district
court of the said territory, and the respective judges thereof shall
and may grant writs of *habeas corpus* in all cases in which the same are
granted by the judges of the United States in the District of Columbia;
and the first six days of every term of said courts, or so much thereof as
shall be necessary, shall be appropriated to the trial of causes arising under the said constitution and laws, and writs of error and appeal in all
such cases shall be made to the supreme court of said territory, the same
as in other cases. The said clerk shall receive in all such cases the same
fees which the clerks of the district courts of Utah territory now receive
for similar services.

SEC. 10.   *And be it further enacted,* That the provisions of an act entitled
"an act respecting fugitives from justice and persons escaping from the
service of their masters," approved February twelve, seventeen hundred
and ninety-three, and the provisions of the act entitled, "An act to amend
and supplementary to the aforesaid act," approved September eighteen,
eighteen hundred and fifty, be and the same are hereby declared to extend
to and be in full force within the limits of said territory of Nebraska.

SEC. 11.   *And be it further enacted,* That there shall be appointed an attorney for said territory, who shall continue in office for four years, and
until his successor shall be appointed and qualified, unless sooner removed by the president, and who shall receive the same fees and salary as
the attorney of the United States for the present territory of Utah. There
shall also be a marshal for the territory appointed, who shall hold his office for four years, and until his successor shall be appointed and qualified, unless sooner removed by the president, and who shall execute all
processes issuing from the said courts, when exercising their jurisdiction
as circuit and district courts of the United States; he shall perform the
duties, be subject to the same regulations and penalties, and be entitled to
the same fees as the marshal of the district court of the United States for
the present territory of Utah, and shall, in addition, be paid two hundred
dollars annually as a compensation for extra services.

SEC. 12.   *And be it further enacted,* That the governor, secretary, chief
justices and associate justices, attorney and marshal, shall be nominated,
and, by and with the advice and consent of the senate, appointed by the
president of the United States. The governor and secretary to be appointed as aforesaid, shall, before they act as such, respectively take an oath or
affirmation before the district judge or some justice of the peace in the
limits of said territory duly authorized to administer oaths and affirmations by the laws now in force therein, or before the chief justice, or
some associate justice of the supreme court of the United States, to support the constitution of the United States and faithfully to discharge the
of their respective offices, which said oaths when so taken, shall be certified by the person by whom the same shall have been taken; and such
certificates shall be received and recorded by the said secretary among the
executive proceedings; and the chief justice and associate justices, and all
other civil officers in said territory, before they act as such, shall take a
like oath or affirmation before the said governor or secretary, or some
judge or justice of the peace of the territory, who may be duly com-
missioned and qualified, which said oath or affirmation shall be certified
and transmitted by the person taking the same to the secretary, to be by
him, recorded as aforesaid; and afterwards the like oath or affirmation
shall be taken, certified, and recorded, in such manner and form as may
be prescribed by law. The governor shall receive an annual salary of two
thousand five hundred dollars. The chief justice and associate justices
shall each receive an annual salary of two thousand dollars. The secretary shall receive an annual salary of two thousand dollars. The said
salaries shall be paid quarter-yearly from the dates of the respective appointments, at the treasury of the United States; but no such payment
shall be made until said officers shall have entered upon the duties of
their respective appointments. The members of the legislative assembly
shall be entitled to three dollars each per day, during their attendance at
the sessions thereof, and three dollars each for every twenty miles' travel

in going to and returning from th said sessions, estimated according to the nearest usually traveled route, and an additional allowance of three dollars shall be paid to the presiding officer of each house for each day he shall so preside. And a chief clerk, and assistant clerk, a sergeant-at-arms, and door-keeper may be chosen for each house; and the chief clerk shall receive four dollars per day, and the said other officers three dollars per day during the s ssion of the legislative assembly; but no other officer shall be paid by the United States; *Provided*, that there shall be but one session of the legislature annually, unless, on an extraordinary occasion, the governor sh-ll think proper to call the legislature together There shall be appropriated annually the usual sum, to be expended by the governor, to defray the contingent expenses of the territory, including the salary of a clerk of the executive department; and there shall also be appropriated annually a sufficient sum, to be expended by the secretary of the territory, and upon an estimate to be made by the secretary of the treasury of the United States, to defray the expenses of the legislative assembly, the printing of laws, and other incidental expenses; and the governor and secretary of the territor., shall, in the disbursements of all moneys in-trusted to them, be governed solely by the instructions of the secretary of the treasury of the United States, and shall, semi-annually, account to the said secretary for the manner in which the aforesaid moneys shall have been expended; and no expenditures shall be made by said legislative assembly for objects not specially authorized by the acts of congress making the appropriations, nor beyond the sums thus appropriated fo; such objects.

SEC. 13. *And be it further enacted*, That the legislative assembly of the territory of Nebraska shall hold its first session at such time and place in said territory as the governor thereof shall appoint and direct; and at the said first session, or as soon thereafter as they shall deem expedient, the governor and legislative assembly shall proceed to locate and establish the seat of government for said territory at such place as they may dee eligible; which place, however, shall thereafter be subject to be change.l by the said governor and legislative assembly.

SEC. 14. *And be it further enacted*, That a delegate to the house of representatives of the United States, to serve for the term of two years, who shall be a citizen of the United States, may be elected by the voters qualified to elect members of the legislative assembly, who shall be entitled to the same rights and privileges as are exercised and enjoyed by the delegates of the several other territories of the United States to the said house of representatives; but the delegate first elected shall hold his seat only during the term of congress to which he shall be elected. The first election shall be held at such time and places, and be conducted in such manner, as the governor shall appoint and direct, and at all subsequent elections the times, places and manner of holding the elections shall be prescribed by law. The person having the great.st number of votes shall be declared by the governor to be duly elected, and a certificate thereof shall be given accordingly. That the constitution and laws of the United States, which are not locally inapplicable, shall have the same force and effect within the said territory of Nebraska as elsewhere within the United States, except the eighth section of the act preparatory to the admission of Missouri into the Union, approved March sixth, eighteen hundred and twenty, which, being inconsistent with the principle of non-intervention by congress with slavery in the states and territories, as recognized by the legislation of eighteen hundred and fifty, commonly called the compromise measures, is hereby declared inoperative and void, it being the true intent and meaning of this act not to legislate slavery into any territory or state nor to exclude it therefrom, but leave the people thereof perfectly free to form and regulate their domestic institutions in their own way, subject only to the constitution of the United States; *Provided*, That nothing herein contained shall be construed to revive or put in force any law or regulation which may have existed prior to the act of sixth March, eighteen hundred and twenty, either protecting, establishing, prohibiting, or abolishing slavery.

SEC. 15. *And be it further enacted*, That there shall hereafter be appropriated, as has been customary for the territorial governments, a sufficient amount, to be expended under the direction of the said governor of the territory of Nebraska, not exceeding the sums heretofore appropriated for similar objects, for the erection of suitable public buildings at the seat of government, and for the purchase of a library, to be kept at the seat of government for the use of the governor, legislative assembly, judges of the supreme court, secretary, marshall, and attorney of said territory, and such other persons and under such regulations as shall be prescribed by law.

SEC. 16. *And be it further enacted,* That when the lands in the said territory shall be surveyed under the direction of the government of the United States, prepaitory to bringing the same into market, sections number sixteen to thirty-six in each township in said territory shall be and the same are hereby reserved for the purpose of being applied to schools in said territory, and in the states and territories hereafter to be erected out of the same.

SEC. 17. *And be it further enacted,* That until otherwise provided by law, the governor of said territory may define the judicial districts of said territory and assign the judges who may be appointed for said territory to the several districts, and also appoint the times and places for holding courts in the several counties or subdivisions in each of said judicial districts by proclamation to be issued by him; but the legislative assembly, at their first or any subsequent session, may organize, alter, or modify such judicial districts, and assign the judges, and alter the times and places of holding the courts, as to them shall seem proper and convenient.

SEC. 18. *And be it further enacted,* That all officers to be appointed by the president, by and with the advice and consent of the senate, for the territory of Nebraska, who, by virtue of the provisions of any law now existing or which may be enacted during the present congress, are required to give security for moneys that may be intrusted with them for disbursement, shall give such security at such time and place, and in such manner, as the secretary of the territory may prescribe.

Approved May 30, 1854.

ENABLING ACT.

AN ACT to enable the people of Nebraska to form a constitution and state government, and for the admission of such stat e into the Union on an equal footing with the original states.

[*Passed April 19, 1864, 13th U. S. Statutes at large, Page 47.*]

Be it enacted by the Senate and House of Representatives of the United States of America in Congress Assembled: That the inhabitants of that portion of the territory of Nebraska included in the boundaries hereinafter designated be and they are hereby authorized to form for themselves a constitution and state government with the name aforesaid, which states, when so formed, shall be admitted into the Union as hereinafter provided.

SEC. 2. *And be it further enacted,* That the said state of Nebraska shall consist of all the territory included within the following boundaries, to-wit: Commencing at a point formed by the intersection of the western boundry of the state of Missouri with the fortieth degree of north latitude; extending thence due west along said fortieth degree of north latitude to a point formed by its intersection with the twenty-fifth degree of longitude west from Washington; thence north along said twenty-fifth degree of longitude to a point formed by its intersection with the forty-first degree of north latitude; thence west along said forty-first degree of north latitude to a point formed by its intersection with the twenty-seventh degree of longitude west from Washington; thence north along said twenty-seventh degree of west longitude to a point formed by its intersection with the forty-third degree of north latitude; thence east along said forty-third degree of no th latitude to the Keya Paha river; thence down the middle of the channel of said river, with its meanderings, to its junction with the Niobrara river; thence down the middle of the channel of said Niobrara river, and following the meanderings thereof, to its junction with the Missouri river; thence down the middle of the channel of said Missouri river, and following the meanderings thereof, to the place of beginning.

SEC. 3. *And be it further enacted,* That all persons qualified by law to vote for representatives to the general assembly of said territory shall be qualified to be elected; and they are hereby authorized to vote for and choose representatives to form a convention, under such rules and regulations as the governor of said territory may prescribe, and also to vote upon the acceptance or rejection of such constitution as may be formed by said convention, under such rules and regulations as said convention may prescribe; and if any of said citizens are enlisted in the army of the United States, and are still within said territory, they shall be permitted to vote at their place of rendezvous; and if any are absent from said territory by reason of their enlistment in the army of the United States, they shall be permitted to vote at their place of service, under the rules and regulations in each case to be prescribed as aforesaid; and the aforesaid representative to form the aforesaid convention shall be apportioned among the several counties in said territory in proportion to the population, as near as may be, and said apportionment shall be made for said territory by the governor, United States district attorney, and chief justice thereof, or any two of them. And the governor of said territory shall, by proclamation, on or before the first Monday of May next, order an election of the representatives aforesaid to be held on the first Monday in June thereafter throughout the territory; and such election shall be conducted in the same manner as is prescribed by the laws of said territory regulating elections therein for members of the house of representatives; and the number of members to said convention shall be the same as now constitute both branches of the legislature of the aforesaid territory

SEC. 4. *And be it further enacted,* That the members of the convention thus elected shall meet at the capital of said territory on the first Monday in July next, and after organization shall declare, on behalf of the people of said territory, that they adopt the constitution of the United States; whereupon the said convention shall be and it is hereby authorized to form a constitution and state government: *Provided,* That the constitution when formed shall be republican, and not repugnant to the constitution of the United States and the principles of the Declaration of Independence; *And provided further,* That said constitution shall provide, by an article forever irrevocable, without the consent of the congress of the United States:

First, That slavery or involuntary servitude shall be forever prohibited in said state.

Second, That perfect toleration of religious sentiment shall be secured, and no inhabitant of said state shall ever be molested in person or property on account of his or her mode of religious worship.

Third, That the people inhabiting said territory do agree and declare that they forever disclaim all right and title to the unappropriated public lands lying within said territory, and that the same shall be and remain at the sole and entire disposition of the United States, and that the lands belonging to citizens of the United States residing without the said state shall never be taxed higher than the land belonging to residents thereof; and that no taxes shall be imposed by said state on lands or property therein belonging to or which may hereafter be purchased by the United States.

SEC. 5. *Ane be it further enacted*, That in case a constitution and state government shall be formed for the people of said territory of Nebraska in compliance with the provisions of this act, that said convention forming the same shall provide by ordinance for submitting said constitution to the people of said state for their ratification or rejection at an election to be held on the second Tuesday of October, one thousand, eight hundred and sixty-four, at such places and under such regulations as may be prescribed therein, at which election the qualified voters as heretofore provided, shall vote directly for or against the proposed constitution, and the returns of said election shall be made to the acting governor of the territory, who together with the United States district attorney, and chief justice of the said territory, or any two of them, shall canvass the same, and if a majority of the legal votes shall be cast for said constitution in in said proposed state, the said acting governor shall certify the same to the president of the United States, together with a copy of the said constitution and ordinances; whereupon it shall be the duty of the president of the United States to issue his proclamation declaring the state admitted into the Union on an equal footing with the original states, without any further action whatever on the part of congress.

SEC. 6. *And be it further enacted*, That until the next general census shall be taken said state of Nebraska shall be entitled to one representative in the house of representatives of the United States, which representative together with the governor and state and other officers provided for in said constitution, may be elected on the same day a vote is taken for or against the proposed constitution and state government.

SEC. 7. *And be it further enacted*, That sections number sixteen and thirty-six in every township, and when such sections have been sold or otherwise disposed of by any act of congress, other lands equivalent thereto, in legal subdivisions of not less than one quarter-section, and as contiguous as may be, shall be and are hereby granted to said state for the support of common schools.

SEC. 8. *And be it further enacted*, That provided the state of Nebraska shall be admitted into the Union in accordance with the foregoing provisions of this act, that twenty entire sections of the unappropriated public lands within said state, to be selected and located by direction of the legislature thereof, on or before the first day of January, Anno Domini eighteen hundred and sixty-eight, shall be and they are hereby granted, in legal subdivisions of not less than one hundred and sixty acres, to said state for the purpose of erecting public buildings at the capital of said state for legislative and judicial purposes, in such manner as the legislature shall prescribe.

SEC. 9. *And be it further enacted*, That fifty other entire sections of land, as aforesaid, to be selected and located as aforesaid, in legal subdivisions as aforesaid, shall be and they are hereby granted to said state for the purpose of erecting a suitable building for a penitentiary or state prison in the manner aforesaid.

SEC. 10. *And be it further enacted*, That seventy-two other sections of land shall be set apart and reserved for the use and support of a state university, to be selected in manner as aforesaid, and to be appropriated and applied as the legislature of said state may prescribe for the purpose named, and for no other purpose.

SEC. 11. *And be it further enacted*, That all salt springs within said state, not exceeding twelve in number, with six sections of land adjoining, or as contiguous as may be to each, shall be granted to said state for its use, the said land to be selected by the governor thereof within one year after the admission of the state, and when so selected to be used or disposed of on such terms, conditions, and regulations as the legislature shall direct; *Provided,* That no salt spring or lands, the right whereof is now vested in any individual or individuals, or which hereafter shall be confirmed or adjudged to any individual or individuals, shall, by this act, be granted to said state.

SEC. 12. *And be it further enacted,* That five per centum of the proceeds of the sales of all public lands lying within said state, which have been or shall be sold by the United States prior or subsequent to the admission of said state into the Union, after deducting all expenses incident to the same, shall be paid to the said state for the support of the common schools.

SEC. 13. *And be it further enacted,* That from and after the admission of said state of Nebraska into the Union in pursuance of this act, the laws of the United States, not locally inapplicable, shall have the same force and effect within the said state as elsewhere within the United States; and said state shall constitute one judicial district, and be called the district of Nebraska.

SEC. 14. *And be it further enacted,* That any unexpended balance of the appropriations for said territorial legislative expenses of Nebraska remaining for the fiscal years eighteen hundred and sixty-three and eighteen hundred and sixty-four, or so much thereof as may be necessary, shall be applied to and used for defraying the expenses of said convention and for the payment of the members thereof, under the same rules, regulations, and rates as are now provided by law for the payment of the territorial legislature.

CONSTITUTION OF THE STATE OF NEBRASKA.

IN FORCE NOVE ᴀ BER 1, 1875.

PREAMBLE.

We, the people, grateful to Almighty God for our freedom, do ordain and establish the following declaration of rights and frame of government, as the constitution of the state of Nebraska.

ARTICLE I.

Bill of Rights.

SEC. 1. All persons are by nature free and independent, and have certain inherent and inalienable rights; among these are life, liberty, and the pursuit of happiness. To secure these rights, and the protection of property, governments are instituted among people, deriving their just powers from the consent of the governed.

SEC. 2. There shall be neither slavery or unvoluntary servitude in this state, otherwise than for punishment of crime whereof the party shall have been duly convicted.

SEC. 3. No person shall be deprived of life, liberty, or property, without due process of law. *Turner v. Althaus*, 6 Neb., 54.

SEC. 4. All persons have a natural and indefeasible right to worship Almighty God according to the dictates of their own consciences. No person shall be compelled to attend, erect, or support any place of worship against his consent, and no preference shall be given by law to any religious society, nor shall any interference with the rights of conscience be permitted. No religious test shall be required as a qualification for office, nor shall any person be incompetent to be a witness on account of his religious belief; but nothing herein shall be construed to dispense with oaths and affirmations. Religion, morality, and knowledge, however, being essential to good government, it shall be the duty of the legislature to pass suitable laws to protect every religious denomination in the peaceable enjoyment of its own mode of public worship, and to encourage schools and the means of instruction.

Freedom of Speech and Press.

SEC. 5. Every person may freely speak, write and publish on all subjects, being responsible for the abuse of that liberty; and in all trials for libel, both civil and criminal, the truth, when published with good motives and for justifiable ends, shall be a sufficient defense.

Trial by Jury Inviolate.

SEC. 6. The right of trial by jury shall remain inviolate, but the legislature may authorize trial by jury of a less number than twelve men in courts inferior to the district court. *Lamaster v. Scofield*, 5 Neb., 148.

The People Secure in Their Persons, Houses and Effects, etc.

SEC. 7. The right of the people to be secure in their persons, houses, papers, and effects, against unreasonable searches and seizures, shall not be violated; and no warrant shall issue but upon probable cause, supported by oath of affirmation, and particularly describing the place to be searched and the person or thing to be seized.

Writ of Habeas Corpus Guaranteed.

SEC. 8. The privilege of the writ of habeas corpus shall not be suspended unless, in case of rebellion or invasion, the public safety requires it, and then only in such manner as shall be prescribed by law.

Bail; Excessive Fines. etc.

SEC. 9. All persons shall be bailable by sufficient sureties, except for treason and murder, where tne proof is evident or the presumption great. Excessive bail shall not be required, nor excessive fines imposed, nor cruel and unusual punishment inflicted.

Criminal Offenses—Indictment of a Grand Jury—Legislature may Abolish, etc.

SEC. 10. No person shall be held to answer for a criminal offense, except in cases in which the punishment is by fine or imprisonment, otherwise than in the penitentiary, in case of impeachment, and in cases arising in the army and navy or in the militia when in actual service in time of war or public danger, unless on a presentment or indictment of a grand jury; *Provided,* That the legislature may by law provide for holding persons to answer for criminal offences on information of a public prosecutor, and may by law abolish, limit, change, amend, or otherwise regulate the grand jury system.

Accused Guaranteed the Right to Appear and Defend.

SEC. 11. In all criminal prosecutions the accused shall have the right to appear and defend in person or by counsel, to demand the nature and cause of accusation, and to have a copy thereof; to meet the witnesses against him face to face; to have process to compel the attendance of witnesses in his behalf, and a speedy public trial by an impartial jury of the county or district in which the offense is alleged to have been committed.

Not to Give Evidence Against Himself.

SEC. 12 No person shall be compelled, in any criminal case, to give evidence against himself, or be twice put in jeopardy for the same offense.

Justice to be Administered Without Denial or Delay.

SEC. 13. All courts shall be open, and every person, for any injury done him in his lands, goods, person, or reputation, shall have a remedy by due course of law, and justice administered without denial or delay.

Treason Against the State.

SEC. 14. Treason against the state shall consist only in levying war against the state, or in adhering to its enemies, giving them aid and comfort. No person shall be convicted of treason unless on the testimony of two witnesses to the same overt act, or on confession in open court.

Penalties to be Proportionate to Offense.

SEC. 15. All penalties shall be proportioned to the nature of the offense, and no conviction shall work corruption of blood or forfeiture of estate; nor shall any person be transported out of the state for any offense committed within the state.

No Bill of Attainder.

SEC. 16. No bill of attainder, *ex post facto* law, or law impairing the obligation of contracts, or making any irrevocable grant of special privileges or immunities, shall be passed. *Jones v. Davis,* 6 Neb., 33.

Military.

SEC. 17. The military shall be in strict subordination to the civil power.

Quartering of Soldiers.

SEC. 18. No soldier shall, in time of peace, be quartered in any house without the consent of the owner; nor in time of war, except in the manner prescribed by law.

Peaceable Assembly and the Right of Petition Guaranteed.

SEC. 19. The right of the people peaceably to assemble to consult for the common good, and to petition the government, or any department thereof, shall never be abridged.

No Imprisonment for Debt.

SEC. 20. No person shall be imprisoned for debt in any civil action on mesne or final process, unless in cases of fraud.

Private Property for Public Use.

SEC. 21. The property of no person shall be taken or damaged for public use without just compensation therefor.

All Elections free and Without Hindrance.

SEC. 22. All elections shall be free; and there shall be no hindrance or impediment to the right of a qualified voter to exercise the elective franchise.

Of Writ of Error.

SEC. 23. The writ of error shall be a writ of right in all cases of felony, and in capital cases shall operate as a supersedeas to stay the execution of the the sentence of death until the further order of the supreme court in the premises.

The Right of Appeal.

SEC. 24. The right to be heard in all civil cases in the court of last resort, by appeal, error, or otherwise, shall not be denied.

No Distinction Between Resident Aliens and Citizens in Reference to Property.

SEC. 25. No distinction shall ever be made by law between resident aliens and citizens in reference to the possession, enjoyment or descent of property.

Reserved Rights.

SEC. 26. This enumeration of rights shall not be construed to impair or deny others retained by the people, and all powers not herein delegated remain with the people.

ARTICLE II.

Distribution of Powers.

SEC. 1. The powers of the goverment of this state are divided into three distinct departments—the legislative, executive, and judicial; and no person or collection of persons being one of these departments shall exercise any power properly belonging to either of the others, except as hereinafter expressly directed or permitted.

ARTICLE III.

The Legislative.

SEC. 1. The legislative authority is vested in a senate and house of representatives.

Enumeration and Apportionment.

SEC. 2. The legislature shall provide by law for an enumeration of the inhabitants of the state in the year eighteen hundred and eighty-five, and every ten years thereafter; and at its first regular session after each enumeration, and also after each enumeration made by the authority of the United States, but at no other time, the legislature shall apportion the senators and representatives according to the number of inhabitants, excluding Indians not taxed and soldiers and officers of the United States army and navy.

Number of Senators and Representatives.

SEC. 3. The house of representatives shall consist of eighty-four members, and the senate shall consist of thirty members, until the year eighteen hundred and eighty, after which time the number of members of each house shall be regulated by law; but the number of representatives shall never exceed one hundred, nor that of senators thirty-three.

Biennial Sessions.

The sessions of the legislature shall be biennial, except as otherwise provided in this constitution.

Term of Office and Pay of Members (as amended).

"SEC. 4. The term of office of members of the legislature shall be two years, and they shall each receive pay at the rate of five dollars per day, during their sitting, and ten cents for every mile they shall travel in going to and returning from the place of meeting of the legislature on the most usual route; Provided, however, That they shall not receive pay for more than sixty days at any one sitting, nor more than one hundred days during their term. That neither members of the legislature nor employes shall receive any pay or perquisites other than their salary and mileage. Each session, except special sessions, shall be not less than sixty days. After the expiration of forty days of the session, no bills or joint resolutions of the nature of bills shall be introduced, unless the governor shall, by special message call the attention of the legislature to the necessity of passing a law on the subject-matter embraced in the message, and the introduction of the bills shall be restricted thereto."

Eligibility.

SEC. 5. No person shall be eligible to the office of senator or member of the house of representatives who shall not be an elector and have resided within the district from which he is elected for the term of one year next before his election, unless he shall have been absent on the public business of the United States or of this state. And no person elected as aforesaid shall hold his office after he shall have removed from such district.

SEC. 6. No person holding office under the authority of the United States or any lucrative office under the authority of the state, shall be eligible to or have a seat in the legislature; but this provision shall not extend to precinct or township officers, justices of the peace, notaries public, or officers of the militia; nor shall any person interested in a contract with, or an unadjusted claim against the state hold a seat in the legislature.

Opening of Sessions. Rules, etc.

SEC. 7. The session of the legislature shall commence at twelve o'clock (noon) on the first Tuesday in January in the year next ensuing the election of members thereof, and at no other time, unless as provided by this constitution. A majority of the members elected to each house shall constitute a quorum. Each house shall determine the rules of its proceedings and be the judge of the election returns and qualifications o its members; shall choose its own officers; and the senate shall choose a temporary president to preside when the lieutenant-governor shall not attend as president, or shall act as governor. The secretary of state shall ca l the house of representatives to order at the opening of each new legislature, and preside over it until a temporary presiding officer thereof shall have been chos n and shall have taken his seat. No member shall be expelled by either house except by a vote of two-thirds of all the members elected to that house. and no member shall be twice expel ed for the same offense. Each house may punish by imprisonment any person, not a member thereof, who shall be guilty of disrespect to the house by disorderly or contemptuous behavior in its presence, but no such imprisonment shall extend beyond twenty-four hours at one time, u less the person shall persist in such disorderly or contemptuous behavior.

SEC. 8. Each house shall keep a journal of its proceedings and publish them (except such parts as may require secrecy) and the yeas and nays of the members on an question, shall, at the desire of any two of them, be entered on the journal. All votes in either house shall be *viva voce*. The doors of each house and of the committee of the whole shall be open, unless when the business shall be such as ought to be kept secret. Neither house shall, without the consent of the other, adjourn for more than three days.

Rules Concerning Bills.

SEC. 9. Any bill may originate in either house of the legislature, except bills appropriating money, which shall ori inate only in the house of representatives, and all bills passed by one house may be amended by the other.

SEC. 10. The enacting clause of a law shall be, "Be it enacted by the legislature of the state of Nebraska," and no law shall be enacted except by bill. No b ll shall be passed unless by assent of a majority of all the members elected to each house of the legislature. And the question upon the final passage shall be taken immediately upon it last reading, and the yeas and nays shall be entered upon the journal.

SEC 11. Every bill and concurr n resolution shall be read at large on three different days in each house, and the bill and all amendments thereto shall be printed before the vote is taken upon its final passage. No bill shall contain m re than one subject, and the same shall be clearly expressed in its title; and n law shall be amended, unless the new act contains the section or sections so amended, nd the section of sections so amended shall be repealed. The presiding officer of each house shall sign, in the presence of the house over which he presides, while the same is in session and capable of transacting business, all bills and concurrent resolutions passed by the legislature.

Members Privileged From Arrest.

SEC. 12. Members of the legislature, in all cases except treason, felony, or br ach of the peace, shall be privileged fr m arrest during the session of the legislature, and for fifteen days before the commencment and after the termination thereof.

Members Not to Receive any Civil Appointment or be Interested in any Contract.

SEC. 13. No person elected to the legislature shall receive any civil pointment within this state, from he governor and senate, during the term for which he has been elected. And all such appointments, and all votes given for any such member for any such office or appointment, shall be void. Nor shall any member of the legislature, or any state officer, be interested, either directly or indirectly, in any contract with the state, county, or city, authorized by any law passed during the term for which he shall have been elected, or within one year after the expiration thereof.

Of Impeachment.

SEC. 14. The senate and house of representatives, in join convention, shall have the sole power of impeachment but a majority of the members elected, must concur therein. Upon the entertainment of a resolution to impeach by either house, the other house shall at once be notified thereof, and the two houses shall meet in joint convention fo. the purpose of acting upon such resolution within three days of such notification. A notice of an impeachment of any officer, other than a justice of the supreme court, shall be forthwith served upon the chief justice by the secretary of the senate, who shall thereupon call a session of the supreme court to meet at the capital within ten days after such notice to try the impeachment. A notice of an impea-hment of a justice of the supreme court shall be served by the secretary of the senate upon the judge of the judicial district within which the capital is located, and he thereupon shall notify all the judges of the district court in the state to meet with him within thirty days at the capital, to sit as a court to try such impeachment, which court shall organize by electing one of its number to preside. No person shall be convicted without the concurrence of two-thirds of the members of the court of impeachment, but judgment in case of impeachment shall not extend further than removal from office and disqualification to hold and enjoy any office of honor, profit or trust in this state, but the party impeached, whether convicted or acquit ed, shall nevertheless be liable to prosecution and punishment according to law. No officer shall exercise his official duties after he shall have been impeached and notified thereof until he shall have been acquitted.

Local and Special Legislation Prohibited.

SEC. 15. The legislature shall not pass local or special laws in any of the following cases, that is to say:

For granting divorces.

Changing the names of persons and places.

Laying out opening, altering, and working roads and highways.

Vacating roads, town plats, streets alleys, and public grounds.

Locating or changing county seats.

Regulating county and township offices.

Regulating the practice of courts of justice.

Regulating the jurisdiction and duties of justices of the peace, police magistrates, and constables.

Providing for changes of venu in civil and criminal cases.

Incorporating cities, towns and villages, or changing or amending the charter of any town, city or village.

Providing for the election of officers in townships, incorporated towns or cities.

Summoning or empaneling grand or petit juries.

Providing for the bonding of cities, towns, precincts, school districts, or other municipalities.

Providing for the management of public schools.

Regulating the interest on money.

The opening and conducting of any election, or designating the place of voting.

The sale or mortgage of real estate belonging to minors or others under disability.

The protection of game or fish.

Chartering or licensing ferries or toll bridges.

Remitting fines, penalties, or forfeitures.

Creating, increasing, and decreasing fees, percentage, or allowances of public officers during the term for which said officers are elected or appointed.

Changing the law of descent.

Granting to any corporation, association, or individual the right to lay down railroad tracks, or amending existing charters for such purpose.

Granting to any corporation, association, or indivdual any special or exclusive privileges, immunity, or franchise whatever. In all other cases where a general law can be made applicable, no special law shall be enacted.

Extra Compensation to Public Officers Prohibited.

SEC. 16.   The legislature shall never grant any extra compensation to any public officer, agent, servant, or contractor after the services shall have been rendered, or the contract entered into.   Nor shall the compensation of any public officer be increased or dimished during his term of office.

Of Salt Springs.

SEC. 17.   The legislature shall never alienate salt springs belonging to this state.

State Lands not to be Donated.

SEC. 18.   Lands under the control of the state shall never be donated to railroad companies, private corporations, or individuals.

Appropriations.

SEC. 19.   Each legislature shall make appropriations for the expenses of the government until the expiration of the first fiscal quarter after the adjournment of the next regular session, and all appropriations shall end with such fiscal quarter.   And whenever it is deemed necessary to make further appropriations for deficiencies, the same shall require a two-thirds vote of all the members elected to each house, and shall not exceed the amount of revenue authorized by law to be raised in such time. Bills making appropriations for the pay of members and officers of the legislature, and for the salaries of the officers of the government shall contain no provision on any other subject.

Vacancies in State Offices.

SEC. 20.   All offices created by this constitution shall become vacant by the death of the incumbent, by removal from the state, resignation, conviction of a felony, impeachment, or becoming of unsound mind.   And the legislature shall provide by general law for the filling of such vacancy when no provision is made for that purpose in this constitution.

Lotteries Prohibited.

SEC. 21.   The legislature shall not authorize any games of chance, lottery, or gift enterprise, under any pretense, or for any purpose whatever.

Incidental Expenses.

SEC. 22.   No allowance shall be made for the incidental expenses of any state officer except the same be made by general appropriation, and upon an account specifying each item.

How Money Drawn From the Treasury.

No money shall be drawn from the treasury except in pursuance of a specific appropriation made by law, and on a presentation of a warrant issued by the auditor thereon, and no money shall be diverted from any appropriation made for any purpose, or taken from any fund whatever, either by joint or separate resolution.

Auditor to Publish Statement.

The auditor shall, within, sixty days after the adjournment of each session of the legislature, prepare and publish a full statement of all moneys expended at such session, specifying the amount of each item, and to whom and for what paid.   *State v. McBride*, 6 Neb., 506.

Members of Legislature not Liable for Words Spoken in Debate.

SEC. 23. No member of the legislature shall be liable in any civil or-criminal action whatever for words spoken in debate.

Act When Take Effect—How Published.

SEC. 24. No act shall take effect until three calendar months after the adjournment of the session at which it passed, unless, in case of emergency (to be expressed in the preamble or body of the act) the legislature shall, by a vote of two-thirds of all the members elected to each house, otherwise direct. All laws shall be published in book form within sixty days after the adjournment of each session, and distributed among the several counties in such manner as the legislature may provide.

ARTICLE IV.

Legislative Apportionment.

(Present apportionment given in another place.)

ARTICLE V.

Executive Department.

SECTION 1. The executive department shall consist of a governor, lieutenant-governor, secretary of state, auditor of public accounts, treasurer, superintendent of public instruction, attorney-general, and commissioner of public lands and buildings, who shall each hold his office for the term of two years, from the first Thursday after the first Tuesday in January next after his election, and until his successor is elected and qualified; *Provided, however*, that the first election of said officers shall be held on the Tuesday succeeding the first Monday in November, 1876, and each succeeding election shall be held at the same relative time in each even year thereafter. The governor, secretary of state, auditor of public accounts, and treasurer, shall reside at the seat of government during their terms of office, and keep the public records, books, and papers there, and shall perform such duties as may be required by law.

Governor—Eligibility.

SEC. 2. No person shall be eligible to the office of governor, or lieutenant-governor, who shall not have attained the age of thirty years, and been for two years next preceding his election a citizen of the United states and of this state. None of the officers of the executive department shall be eligible to any other state office during the period for which they shall have been elected.

Treasurer Ineligible for Third Term.

SEC. 3. The treasurer shall be ineligible to the office of treasurer for two years next after the expiration of two consecutive terms for which he was elected.

Election Returns—How Canvassed.

SEC. 4. The returns of every election for the officers of the executive department shall be sealed up and transmitted by the returning officers to the secretary of state, directed to the speaker of the house of representatives, who shall, immediately after the organization of the house, and before proceeding to other business, open and publish the same in the presence of a majority of each house of the legislature, who shall fo-that purpose assemble in the hall of the house of representatives. The person having the highest number of votes for either of said offices shall be declared duly elected; but if two or more have an equal and the highest number of votes, the legislature shall by joint vote, choose one of such persons for said office. Contested elections for all of said offices shall be determined by both houses of the legislature, by joint vote, in such manner as may be prescribed by law.

Liable to Impeachment.

SEC. 5. All civil officers of this state shall be liable to impeachment for any misdemeanor in office.

Supreme Executive Power.

SEC. 6. The supreme executive power shall be vested in the governor, who shall take care that the laws be faithfully executed.

Governor to deliver Message.

SEC. 7. The governor shall, at the commencement of each session, and at the close of his term of office, and whenever the legislature may require give to the legislature information by message of the condition of the state, and shall recommend such measures as he shall deem expedient. He shall account to the legislature, and accompany his message with a statement of all moneys received and paid out by him from any funds subject to his order, with vouchers, and, at the commencement of each regular session, present estimates of the amount of money required to be raised by taxation for all purposes.

Governor May Convene the Legislature..

SEC. 8. The governor may, on extraordinary occasions convene the legislature by proclamation, stating therein the purpose for which they are convened, and the legislature shall enter upon no business except that for which they were called together.

In Case of Disagreement May Adjourn the Legislature.

SEC. 9. In case of a disagreement between the two houses with respect to the time of adjournment, the governor may, on the same being certified to him by the house first moving the adjournment, adjourn the legislature to such time as he thinks proper, not beyond the first day of the next regular session.

Governor Appoint and Nominate Officers.

SEC. 10. The governor shall nominate and, by and with the advice and consent of the senate (expressed by a majority of all the senators elected voting by yeas and nays), appoint all officers whose offices are established by this constitution, or which may be created by law, and whose appointment and election is not otherwise by law or herein provided for; and no such officer shall be appointed or elected by the legislature.

In Case of Vacancy During the Recess of Senate.

SEC. 11. In case of a vacancy during the recess of the senate in any office which is not elective, the governor shall make a temporary appointment until the next meeting of the senate, when he shall nominate some person to fill such office; and any person so nominated, who is confirmed by the senate (a majority of all the senators elected concurring by voting yeas and nays), shall hold his office during the remainder of the term, and until his successor shall be appointed and qualified. No person, after being rejected by the senate, shall be again nominated for the same office at the same session, unless at request of the senate, or be appointed to the same office during the recess of the legislature.

Of Power to Remove.

SEC. 12. The governor shall have power to remove any officer whom he may appoint, in case of incompetency, neglect of duty, malfeasance in office; and he may declare his office vacant, and fill the same as herein provided in other cases of vacancy.

Of Power to Grant Reprieves, Pardons, etc.

SEC. 13. The governor shall have the power to grant reprieves, commutations, and pardons after conviction for all offenses, except treason and cases of impeachment, upon such conditions and with such restrictions and limitations as he may think proper, subject to such regulations as may be provided by law relative to the manner of applying for pardons. Upon conviction for treason, he shall have power to suspend the execution of the sentence until the case shall be reported to the legislature at its next session, when the legislature shall either pardon or commute the sentence, direct the execution of the sentence, or grant a further reprieve. He shall communicate to the legislature, at every regular session, each case of reprieve, commutation or pardon granted, stating the name of the convict, the crime of which he was convicted, the sentence and its date, and the date of the reprieve, commutation or pardon.

Commander-in-chief.

SEC. 14. The governor shall be commander-in-chief of the military and naval forces of the state (except when they shall be called into the service or the United States), and may call out the same to execute the laws, suppress insurrection, and repel invasion.

Of the Veto Power.

SEC. 15. Every bill passed by the legislature, before it becomes a law, and every order, resolution, or vote to which the concurrence of both houses may be necessary (except on questions of adjournment), shall be presented to the governor. If he approve he shall sign it, and thereupon it shall become a law; but if he do not approve he shall return it, with his objections, to the house in which it shall have originated, which house shall enter the objections at large upon its journal, and proceed to reconsider the bill. If then three-fifths of the members elected agree to pass the same, it shall be sent, together with the objections, to the other house, by which it shall likewise be reconsidered; and if approved by three-fifths of the members elected to that house it shall become a law, notwithstanding the objections of the governor. In all such cases the vote of each house shall be determined by yeas and nays, to be entered upon the journal. Any bill which shall not be returned by the governor within five days (Sundays excepted) after it shall have been presented to him, shall become a law in like manner as if he had signed it, unless the legislature by their adjournment, prevent its return; in which case it shall be filed, with his objections, in the office of the secretary of state within five days after such adjournment, or become a law. The governor may disapprove any item or items of appropriation contained in bills passed by the legislature, and the item or items so disapproved shall be stricken therefrom, unless repassed in the manner herein prescribed in cases of disapproval of bills.

In Case of Death.

SEC. 16. In case of the death, impeachment, and notice thereof to the accused, failure to qualify, resignation, absence from the state, or other disability of the governor, the powers, duties and emoluments of the office for the residue of the term, or until the disability shall be removed, shall devolve upon the lieutenant-governor.

Relating to the Lieutenant Governor.

SEC. 17. The lieutenant-governor shall be president of the senate, and shall vote only when the senate is equally divided.

SEC. 18. If there be no lieutenant-governor, or if the lieutenant-governor, for any of the causes specified in section sixteen of this article, become incapable of performing the duties of the office, the president of the senate shall act as governor until the vacancy is filled or the disability removed; and if the president of the senate, for any of the above named causes, shall become incapable of performing the duties of governor, the same shall devolve upon the speaker of the house of representatives.

Board of Public Lands and Buildings.

SEC. 19. The commissioner of public lands and buildings, the secretary of state, treasurer, and attorney-general, shall form a board, which shall have general supervision and control of all the buildings, grounds, and lands of the state, the state prison, asylums, and all other institutions thereof, except those for educational purposes; and shall perform such duties and be subject to such rules and regulations as may be prescribed by law. *State v. Bacon,* 6 Neb. 286.

Vacancies in the State Offices, How Filled.

SEC. 20. If the office of auditor of public accounts, treasurer, secretary of state, attorney-general, commissioner of public lands and buildings, or superintendent of public instruction, shall be vacated by death, resignation, or otherwise, it shall be the duty of the governor to fill the same by appointment; and the appointee shall hold his office until his successor shall be elected and qualified in such manner as may be provided by law

Accounts to be Kept and Semi-Annual Reports made to the Governor.

SEC. 21. An account shall be kept by the officers of the executive department, and of all the public institutions of the state, of all moneys received or disbursed by them severally from all sources, and for every service performed, and a semi-annual report thereof be made to the governor, under oath; and any officer who makes a false report shall be guilty of perjury, and punished accordingly.

Reports to be Made and Transmitted to the Legislature.

SEC. 22. The officers of the executive department and of all the public institutions of the state shall, at least ten days preceding each regular session of the legislature, severally report to the governor, who shall transmit such reports to the legislature, together with the reports of the judges of the supreme court, of defects in the constitution and laws, and the governor, or either house of the legislature, may at any time require information in witing, under oath, from the officers of the executive department and all officers and managers of state institutions, upon any subject relating to the condition, management, and expenses of their respective offices.

The Great Seal.

SEC. 23. There shall be a seal of the state, which shall be called the "Great seal of the state of Nebraska," which shall be kept by the secretary of state, and used by him officially, as directed by law.

Salaries.

SEC. 24. The salaries of the governor, auditor of public accounts, **and** treasurer shall **be two** thousand five hundred dollars ($2,500) each per annum, and of **the secretary** of state, attorney-general, superintendent of public instruction, **and** commissioner of public lands and buildings, two thousand dollars ($2,000) each per **annum.** The lieutenant-governor shall receive twice **the** compensation **of a** senator, and **after the** adoption of this **constitution** they shall not receive to their **own use any fees,** costs, interest **upon** public moneys in their hands or under their control, perquisites **of** office, or other compensation, and all fees **that may hereafter be payable** by law for services performed by any officer provided **for in this** article of the constitution, shall be paid in advance into the **state** treasury. There shall be no allowance for clerk hire in the offices **of the** superintendent of public instruction and attorney-general.

Officers to Give Bond.

SEC. 25. The officers mentioned in this article shall give bonds in not less than double the **amount of money** that may come into their hands, and in no case in less than **the sum of** fifty thousand dollars, with such provisions as **to sureties and the** approval thereof, and for the increase of the penalty of such bonds, as may be prescribed by law.

No new Offices to be Created.

SEC. 26. No other executive state office shall **be continued or created,** and the duties now devolving upon officers not provided **for by this** constitution shall **be performed** by the officers herein created. *State v. Weston, 4* Neb., 234.

ARTICLE VI.

The Judicial Department.

SEC. 1. **The judicial power of this state shall be vested in a** supreme **court, districts** courts, **county courts, justices of the peace, police** magistrates, **and in** such other courts inferior to the district courts **as may** be **created by** law for cities and incorporated towns.

The Supreme Court.

SEC. 2. The supreme court shall consist of three judges, a majority **of** whom shall be necessary to form **a** quorum or to pronounce a decision. It shall have original jurisdiction in **cases** relating to the revenue, civil cases in which the state shall **be** a party, mandamus, quo warranto, habeas corpus, and such appellate jurisdiction **as may** be provided by law.

SEC. 3. At **least two terms of the supreme** court shall be held each year at the seat of government.

SEC. 4. **The judges of the supreme court shall be** elected by the electors of the state at large, and their terms of office, except of those chosen at the first election, as hereinafter provided, shall be six years.

SEC. 5. The judges of the supreme court shall, immediately after the first election under this constitution, be classified by lot, so that one shall hold his office for the term of two years, one for the term of four years, **and one for** the term of six years.

SEC. 6. The judge of the supreme court having the shortest term to **serve, not holding his** office by appointment or elected to fill a vacancy, shall be the chief justice, and as such shall preside at all terms of the supreme court; **and in case of his** absence, the judge having in like manner the next **shortest term to serve shall preside** in his stead.

SEC. 7. No person shall be eligible to the office of judge of the supreme court unless he shall be at least thirty years of age, and a citizen of the United States; nor unless he shall have resided in this state at least three years next preceeding his election.

SEC. 8. There shall be appointed by the supreme court a reporter, who shall also act as clerk of the supreme court and librarian of the law and miscellaneous library of the state, whose term of office shall be four years, unless sooner removed by the court, whose salary shall be fixed by law, not to exceed fifteen hundred dollars per annum. The copyright of the state reports shall forever belong to the state.

District Court and Judges.

SEC. 9. The district courts shall have both chancery and common law jurisdiction, and such other jurisdiction as the legislature may provide, and the judges thereof may admit persons charged with felony to a plea of guilty, and pass such sentence as may be prescribed by law. *Turner v. Althaus*, 6 Neb., 54.

SEC. 10. The state shall be divided into six judicial districts, in each of which shall be elected by the electors thereof, one judge, who shall be judge of the district court therein, and whose term of office shall be four years.

SEC. 11. The legislature, whenever two-thirds of the members elected to each house shall concur therein, may, in or after the year one thousand eight hundred and eighty, and not oftener than once in every four years, increase the number of judges of the district courts, and the judicial districts of the state. Such districts shall be formed of compact territory, and bounded by county lines, and such increase, or any change in the boundaries of a district, shall not vacate the office of any judge.

SEC. 12. The judges of the district courts may hold courts for each other, and shall do so when required by law.

Salaries of Supreme and District Judges.

SEC. 13. The judges of the supreme and district courts shall each receive a salary of $2,500 per annum, payable quarterly.

SEC. 14. No judge of the supreme or district courts shall receive any other compensation, perquisite, or benefit for or on account of his office in any form whatever, nor act as attorney or counselor-at-law in any manner whatever, nor shall any salary be paid to any county judge.

County Courts and Judges.

SEC. 15. There shall be elected in and for each organized county one judge, who shall be judge of the county court of such county, and whose term of office shall be two years.

SEC. 16. County courts shall be courts of record, and shall have original jurisdiction in all matters of probate, settlement of estates of deceased persons, appointment of guardians and settlement of their accounts in all matters relating to apprentices; and such other jurisdiction as may be given by general law. But they shall not have jurisdiction in criminal cases in which the punishment may exceed six months imprisonment, or a fine of over five hundred dollars; nor in actions in which title to real estate is sought to be recovered, or may be drawn in question; nor in actions on mortgages or contracts for the conveyance of real estate; nor in civil actions where the debt or sum claimed shall exceed one thousand dollars.

Appeals.

SEC. 17. Appeals to the district courts from the judgments of county courts shall be allowed in all criminal cases, on application of the defendant; and in all civil cases, on application of either party, and in such other cases as may be provided by law.

Justices of the Peace and Police Magistrates.

SEC. 18. Justices of the peace and police magistrates shall be elected in and for such districts, and have and exercise such jurisdiction as may be provided by law; *Provided*, That no justice of the peace shall have jurisdiction of any civil case where the amount in controversy shall exceed two hundred dollars; nor in a criminal case where the punishment may exceed three months' imprisonment, or a fine of over one hundred dollars; nor in any matter wherein the title or boundaries of land may be in dispute.

Of Laws Relating to Courts.

SEC. 19. All laws relating to courts shall be general and of uniform operation, and the organization, jurisdiction, powers proceedings, and practice of all the courts of the same class of grade, so far as regulated by law and the force and effect of the proceedings, judgments and degrees of such courts severally, shall be uniform.

Term of Office.

SEC. 20. All officers provided for in this article shall hold their offices until their successors shall be qualified, and they shall respectively reside in the district, county, or precinct, for which they shall be elected or appointed. The terms of office of all such officers, when not otherwise prescribed in this article, shall be two years. All officers, when not otherwise provided for in this article, shall perform such duties and receive such compensation as may be provided by law.

Vacancies, How filled.

SEC. 21. In case the office of any judge of the supreme court or of any district court shall become vacant before the expiration of the regular term for which he was elected, the vacancy shall be filled by appointment by the governor, until a successor shall be elected and qualified, and such successor shall be elected for the unexpired term at the first general election that occurs more than thirty days after the vacancy shall have happened. Vacancies in all other elective offices provided for in this article shall be filled by election, but when the unexpired term does not exceed one year the vacancy may be filled by appointment, in such manner as the legislature may provide.

State May Sue and be Sued.

SEC. 22. The state may sue and be sued, and the legislature shall provide by law in what manner and in what courts suits shall be brought. *State v. Stout*, 7 Neb., 89.

Jurisdiction at Chambers.

SEC. 23. The several judges of the courts of record shall have such jurisdiction at chambers as may be provided by law.

Process Shall Run etc.

SEC. 24. All process shall run in the name of "The State of Nebraska," and all prosecutions shall be carried on in the name of "The State of Nebraska."

ARTICLE VII.

Right of Suffrage.

SEC. 1. Every male person of the age of twenty-one years or upwards, belonging to either of the following classes, who shall have resided in the state six months, and in the county, precinct, or ward for the time provided by law, shall be an elector.

First. Citizens of the United States.

Second. Persons of foreign birth who shall have declared their intention to become citizens conformably to the laws of the United States on the subject of naturalization, at least thirty days prior to an election.

SEC. 2. No person shall be qualified to vote who is *non compos mentis,* or who has been convicted of treason, or felony under the law of the state, or of the United States, unless restored to civil rights.

SEC. 3. Every elector in the actual military service of the United States or of this states, and not in the regular army, may exercise the right of suffrage at such place and under such regulations as may be provided by law.

SEC. 4. No soldier, seaman, or marine in the army and navy of the United States shall be deemed a resident of the state in consequence of being stationed therein.

SEC. 5. Electors shall in all cases except treason, felony, or breach of the peace, be privileged from arrest during their attendance at elections, and going to and returning from the same. and no elector shall be obliged to do military duty on the days of election except in time of war and public danger.

SEC. 6. All votes shall be by ballot.

ARTICLE VIII.

Education.

SEC. 1. The governor, secretary of state, treasurer, attorney general, and commissioner of public lands and buildings, shall, under the direction of the legislature, constitute a board of commissioners for the sale, leasing, and general management of all lands and funds set apart for educational purposes, and for the investment of school funds in such manner as may be presribed by law.

SEC. 2. All lands, money, or other property granted or bequeathed or in any manner conveyed to this state for educational purposes, shall be used and expended in accordance with the terms of such grant, bequest, or conveyance.

Perpetual Funds for School Purposes.

SEC. 3. The following are hereby declared to be perpetual funds for common school purposes, of which the annual interest or income only can be appropriated, to-wit:

First, Such percentum as has been or may hereafter be granted by congress on the sale of lands in this state.

Second. All moneys arising from the sale or leasing of sections number sixteen and thirty-six in each township in this state, and the lands selected or that may be selected in lieu thereof.

Third. The proceeds of all lands that have been or may hereafter be granted to this state, where by the terms and conditions of such grant the same are not to be be otherwise appropriated.

Fourth. The net proceeds of lands and other property and effects that may come to the state, by escheat and forfeiture, or from unclaimed dividends, or distributive shares of the estates of deceased persons. *State v. Reeder*, 5 Neb., 103.

Fifth. All moneys, stocks, bonds, lands, and other property now belonging to the common school fund.

Other Funds for the Support and Maintenance of Common Schools.

SEC. 4. All other grants, gifts, and devises that have been or may hereafter be made to this state, and not otherwise appropriated by the terms of the grant, gift, or devise, the interests arising from all the funds mentioned in the preceding section, together with all the rents of the unsold school lands, and such other means as the legislature may provide, shall be exclusively applied to the support and maintenance of common school in each school district in the state, *State v. McBride*, 5 Neb., 121.

SEC. 5. All fines, penalties, and license moneys arising under the general laws of the state shall belong and be paid over to the counties respectively where the same may be levied or imposed, and all fines, penalties, and license moneys arising under the rules, by-laws, or ordinances of cities, villages, towns, precincts, or other municipal subdivisions less than a county, shall belong and be paid over to the same respectively. All such fines, penalties, and license moneys shall be appropriated exclusively to the use and support of common schools in the respective subdivisions where the same may accrue. *State v. McConnel*, 8 Neb., 28

Free Instruction.

SEC. 6. The legislature shall provide for the free instruction in the common schools of this state of all persons between the ages of five and twenty-one years.

Equitable Distribution of School Funds.

SEC. 7. Provisions shall be made by general law for an equitable distribution of the income of the fund set apart for the support of the common schools, among the several school districts of the state, and no appropriation shall be made from said fund to any district for the year in which school is not maintained at least three months.

Lands not to be Sold For Less Than—

SEC. 8. University, agricultural college, common school, or other lands, which are now held or may hereafter be acquired by the state for educational purposes, shall not be sold for less than seven dollars per acre, nor less than the appraised value.

To be Deemed Trust Funds.

SEC. 9. All funds belonging to the state for educational purposes, the interest and income whereof only are to be used, shall be deemed trust funds held by the state, and the state shall supply all losses thereof that may in any manner accrue, so that the same shall remain forever inviolate and undimished; and shall not be invested or loaned except on United States or state securities, or registered county bonds of this state; and such funds, with the interests and income thereof, are hereby solemnly pledged for the purpose for which they are granted and set apart, and shall not be transferred to any other fund for other uses.

Six Regents.

SEC. 10. The general government of the university of Nebraska shall, under the direction of the legislature, be vested in a board of six regents, to be styled the board of regents of the university of Nebraska, who shall be elected by the electors of the state at large, and their term of office, except those chosen at the first election, as hereinafter provided, shall be six years. Their duties and powers shall be prescribed by law; **and they shall** receive no compensation, but may be reimbursed **their actual expenses** incurred in the discharge of their duties.

No Sectarian Instruction.

SEC. 11. No sectarian instruction shall be allowed in any school **or** institution supported **in** whole or in part by the public funds set apart for educational purposes, nor shall the state accept any grant, conveyance, or bequest of money, **lands, or other property,** to be used for sectarian purposes.

Reform School.

SEC. 12. **The legislature** may provide by law for the establishment of a school or schools for the **safe** keeping, education, employment, and reformation of all **children under** the age **of sixteen years, who,** for want of proper parental care or other cause, are growing up in mendicancy or crime.

ARTICLE IX.

Revenue and Finance.

SECTION 1. The legislature shall provide such revenue **as may be** needful by levying **a tax** by valuation, so **that** every person **and** corporation shall pay **a tax in** proportion to the **value** of his, her, **or its** property and **franchises, the** value to be ascertained in such manner as **the** legislature **shall** direct, **and** it shall have power to tax peddlers, **auctioneers,** brokers, hawkers, commission merchants, showmen, jugglers, innkeepers, **liquor** dealers, toll bridges, ferries, insurance, telegraph, and express **interests** or business, venders of patents, in such manner as it shall direct by general **law,** uniform as to the class **upon which it** operates. *State v. Lancaster county,* 4 Neb., 537.

Property Exempt from Taxation.

SEC. 2. **The** property of the state, counties, and municipal corporations both real and personal, shall be exempt from taxation, and such other **property as** may be used exclusively for agricultural and horticultural societies, for school, religious, cemetery, and charitable purposes, may be exempted **from taxation, but such exemptions shall be only** by general law. In the assessment of real estate encumbered by **public easement,** any depreciation occasioned by such easement **may** be deducted in the valuation of such property. The legislature may provide that the increased value of lands, by reason **of live** fences, fruit and forest trees **grown** and cultivated thereon, shall not be taken **into account in** the assessment thereof.

The Right of Redemption.

SEC. 3. The right of redemption from **all** sales of **real estate,** for the non-payment of taxes of special **assessment of any character** whatever, shall exist in favor of owners and persons interested in such real estate for a period of not less than two years from such sales thereof; *Provided,* That occupants shall in all cases **be** served with personal notice **before the time** of redemption expires.

The Legislature Shall Have No Power to Release, etc.

SEC. 4. The legislature shall have no power to release **or** discharge any county, city, township, town, or district, whatever, or the inhabitants thereof, or any corporation, or the property therein, from their or its proportionate share of taxes to be levied for state purposes, or due any municipal corporation, nor shall commutation **for** such taxes be authorized in any form whatever.

Limit of Taxation.

SEC. 5. County authorities shall never assess taxes, the aggregate of which shall exceed one and one-half dollar per one hundred dollars valuation, except for the payment of indebtedness existing at the adoption of this constitution, unless authorized by a vote of the people of the county.

Special Assessments and Taxation.

SEC. 6. The legislature may vest the corporate authorities of cities, towns, and villages with power to make local improvements by special assessments, or by special taxation of property benefitted. For all other corporate purposes, all municipal corporations may be vested with authority to assess and collect taxes, but such taxes shall be uniform in respect to persons and property within the jurisdiction of the body imposing the same.

Private Property Not Liable for Corporate Debts.

SEC. 7. Private property shall not be liable to be taken or sold for the payment of the corporate debts of municipal corporations. The legislature shall not impose taxes upon municipal corporations, or the inhabitants or property thereof, for corporate purposes.

Funding of Outstanding Warrants.

SEC. 8. The legislature at its first session shall provide a law for the funding of all outstanding warrants and other indebtedness of the state, at a rate of interest not exceeding eight per cent per annum. *The state v. McBride*, 6 Neb., 506.

Claims Upon the Treasury.

SEC. 9. The legislature shall provide by law that all claims upon the treasury shall be examined and adjusted by the auditor and approved by the secretary of state before any warrant for the amount allowed shall be drawn; *Provided*, That a party aggrieved by the decision of the auditor and secretary of state may appeal to the district court.

ARTICLE X.

Counties.

SECTION 1. No new county shall be formed or established by the legislature which will reduce the county or counties, or either of them, to a less area than four hundred square miles, nor shall any county be formed of a less area.

SEC. 2. No county shall be divided or have any part stricken therefrom without first submitting the question to a vote of the people of the county, nor unless a majority of all the legal voters of the county voting on the question shall vote for the same.

SEC. 3. There shall be no territory stricken from any organized county unless a majority of the voters living in such territory shall petition for such division, and no territory shall be added to any organized county without the consent of the majority of the voters of the county to which it is proposed to be added; but the portion so stricken off and added to another county, or formed in whole or in part into a new county, shall be holden for and obliged to pay its proportion to the indebtedness of the counties from which it has been taken.

SEC. 4. The legislature shall provide by law for the election of such county and township officers as may be necessary.

Township Organization.

SEC. 5. The legislature shall provide by general law for township organization, under which any county may organize whenever a majority of the legal voters of such county, voting at any general election, shall so determine; and in any county that shall have adopted a township organization, the question of continuing the same may be submitted to a vote of the electors of such county at a general election in the manner that shall be provided by law. *State v. Lancaster County*, 6 Neb., **474.**

ARTICLE XI.

CORPORATIONS.

Railroad Corporations.

SECTION. 1. Every railroad corporation organized or doing business in this state, under the laws or authority thereof, or of any other state, or of the United States, shall have and maintain a public office or place in this state for the transaction of its business, where transfers of stock shall be made, and in which shall be kept, for public inspection, books in which shall be recorded the amount of capital stock subscribed, and by whom, the names of the owners of its stock, and the amounts owned by them respectively, the amount of stock paid in and by whom, the transfers of said stock, the amount of its assets and liabilities, and the names and places of residence of its officers. The directors of every railroad corporation, or other parties having control of its road, shall annually make a report under oath to the auditor of public accounts, or some officer to be designated by law, of the amount received from passengers and freight, and such other matters relating to railroads as may be prescribed by law. And the legislature shall **pass** laws enforcing by suitable penalties **the provisions** of this section.

SEC. 2. The rolling stock and all other movable property belonging to any railroad company or corporation in this state shall be liable to execution and sale in the same manner as the personal property of individuals, and the legislature shall pass no law exempting any such property from execution and sale.

SEC. 3. No railroad corporation or telegraph company shall consolidate its stock, property, franchises or earnings, in whole or in part, with any other railroad corporation or telegraph company owning a parallel or competing line; and in no case shall any consolidation take place except upon public notice of at least sixty days to all stockholders in such manner as may be provided by law.

Declared Public Highways.

SEC. 4. Railways heretofore **constructed**, or that may hereafter be constructed, in this state, are hereby declared public highways, and shall be free to all persons for the transportation of their persons and property thereon, under such regulations as may be prescribed by law. And the legislature may from time to time pass laws establishing reasonable maximum rates of charges for the transportation of passengers and freight on the different railroads in this state. The liability of railroad corporations as common carriers shall never be limited.

Of Issuing Stocks or Bonds.

SEC. 5. No railroad corporation shall issue any stock or bonds **except** for money, **labor,** or property actually received and applied to the purposes for which such corporation was created, and all stock, dividends and **other fictitious** increase of the capital stock or indebtedness of any such corporation shall be void. The capital stock of railroad corporations shall not be increased for any purpose, except after public notice for sixty days in such manner as may be provided by law.

Eminent Domain.

SEC. 6. The exercise of the power and the right of eminent domain shall never be so construed or abridged as to prevent the taking, by the legislature, of the property and franchises of incorporated companies already organized or hereafter to be organized, and subjecting them to the public necessity, the same as of individuals.

Legislature to Correct Abuses and Extortion.

SEC. 7. The legislature shall pass laws to correct abuses and prevent unjust discrimination and extortion in all charges of express, telegraph, and railroad companies in this state, and enforce such laws by adequate penalties to the extent, if necessary for that purpose, of forfeiture of their property and franchises.

When not Entitled to the Right of Eminent Domain.

SEC. 8. No railroad corporation organized under the laws of any other state, or of the United States, and doing business in this state, shall be entitled to exercise the right of eminent domain, or have power to acquire the right of way or real estate for depot or other uses, until it shall have become a body corporate pursuant to and in accordance with the laws of this state.

MUNICIPAL CORPORATIONS.

SECTION. 1. No city, county, town, precinct, municipality, or other subdivision of the state, shall ever become a subscriber to the capital stock or owner of such stock, or any portion or interest therein, of any railroad or private corporation or association.

MISCELANEOUS CORPORATIONS.

SECTION 1. No corporation shall be created by special law, nor its charter extended, changed, or amended, except those for charitable, educational, penal, or reformatory purposes, which are to be and remain under the patronage and control of the state, but the legislature shall provide by general laws for the organization of all corporations hereafter to be created. All general laws passed pursuant to this section may be altered from time to time or repealed.

SEC. 2. No such general law shall be passed by the legislature granting the right to construct and operate a street railroad within any city, town, or incorporated village, without first requiring the consent of a majority of the electors thereof.

SEC. 3. All corporations may sue and be sued in like cases as natural persons.

SEC. 4. In all cases of claims against corporations and joint stock associations the exact amount justly due shall be first ascertained, and after the corporate property shall have been exhausted, the original subscribers thereof shall be individually liable to the extent of their unpaid subscription, and the liability for the unpaid subscription shall follow the stock.

SEC. 5. The legislature shall provide by law that in all elections for directors or managers of incorporated companies, every stockholder shall have the right to vote in person or by proxy for the number of shares of stock owned by him, for as many persons as there are directors or managers to be elected, or to cumulate said shares and give one candidate as many votes as the number of directors multiplied by the number of his shares of stock shall equal, or to distribute them upon the same principle among as many candidates as he shall think fit; and such directors or managers shall not be elected in any other manner.

SEC. 6. All existing charters or grants of special or exclusive privileges under which organization shall not have taken place, or which shall not be in operation within sixty days from the time this constitution takes effect, shall thereafter have no validity or effect whatever.

SEC. 7. Every stockholder in a banking corporation or institution shall be individually responsible and liable to its creditors, over and above the amount of stock by him held, for all its liabilities accruing while he remains such stockholder; and all banking corporations shall publish quarterly statements, under oath, of their assets and liabilities.

ARTICLE XII.
State, County and Municipal Indebtedness.

SECTION 1. The state may, to meet casual deficits or failures in the revenues, contract debts never to exceed in the aggregate one hundred thousand dollars: and no greater indebtedness shall be incurred except for the purpose of repelling invasion, suppressing insurrection, or defending the state in war; and provision shall be made for the payment of the interest annually, as it shall accrue, by a tax levied for the purpose, or from other sources of revenue, which law, providing for the payment of such interest by such tax, shall be irrepealable until such debt be paid.

SEC. 2. No city, county, town, precinct, municipality, or other subdivision of the state, shall ever make donations to any railroad or other work of internal improvement, unless a proposition so to do shall have been first submitted to the qualified electors thereof at an election by authority of law; *Provided,* That such donations of a county, with the donations of such subdivisions, in the aggregate shall not exceed ten per cent of the assessed valuation of such county; *Provided further,* That any city or county may, by a two-thirds vote, increase such indebtedness five per cent, in addition to such ten per cent, and no bonds or evidences of indebtedness so issued shall be valid unless the same shall have endorsed thereon a certificate signed by the secretary and auditor of state, showing that the same is issued pursuant to law. *Reineman v. C. C. B, H. R. R. Co.,* 7 Neb., 310.

SEC. 3. The credit of the state shall never be given or loaned in aid of any individual, association, or corporation.

ARTICLE XIII.
Militia.

SECTION 1. The legislature shall determine what persons shall constitute the militia of the state, and may provide for organizing and disciplining the same.

ARTICLE XIV.
Miscellaneous Provisions.

SECTION 1. Executive and judicial officers and members of the legislature, before they enter upon their official duties, shall take and subscribe the following oath or affirmation: "I do solemnly swear (or affirm) that I will support the constitution of the United States, and the constitution of the state of Nebraska, and will faithfully discharge the duties of——according to the best of my ability, and that at the election at which I was chosen to fill said office I have not improperly influenced in any way the vote of any elector, and have not accepted, nor will I accept or receive, directly or indirectly, any money or other valuable thing from any corporation, company, or person, or any promise of office for any official act or influence (for any vote I may give or withhold on any bill, resolution, or appropriation)." Any such officer or member of the legislature who shall refuse to take the oath herein prescribed, shall forfeit his office, and any person who shall be convicted of having sworn falsely to, or of violating his oath, shall forfeit his office, and thereafter be disqualified from holding any office of trust or profit in this state, unless he shall have been restored to civil rights.

SEC. 2. Any person who is in default as collector and custodian of public money or property, shall not be eligible to any office of trust or profit under the constitution or laws of this state; nor shall any person convicted of felony be eligible to office unless he shall have been restored to civil rights.

SEC. 3. Drunkenness shall be cause of impeachment and removal from office.

ARTICLE XV.

Amendments.

SECTION 1. Either branch of the legislature may propose amendments to this constitution, and if the same be agreed to by three-fifths of the members elected to each house, such proposed amendments shall be entered on the journals, with the yeas and nays, and published at least once each week in at least one newspaper in each county where a newspaper is published, for three months immediately preceding the next election of senators and representatives, at which election the same shall be submitted to the electors for approval or rejection, and if a majority of the electors voting at such election adopt such amendments, the same shall become a part of this constitution. When more than one amendment is submitted at the same election, they shall be so submitted as to enable the electors to vote on each amendment separately.

SEC. 2. When three-fifths of the members elected to each branch of the legislature deem it necessary to call a convention to revise, amend, or change this constitution, they shall recommend to the electors to vote at the next election of members of the legislature for or against a convention, and if a majority voting at said election vote for a convention, the legislature shall, at its next session, provide by law for calling the same. The convention shall consist of as many members as the house of representatives, who shall be chosen in the same manner, and shall meet within three months after their election, for the purpose aforesaid. No amendment or change of this constitution, agreed upon by such convention, shall take effect until the same shall be submitted to the electors of the state, and adopted by a majority of those voting for and against the same.

ARTICLE XVI.

Schedule.

SECTION 1. That no inconvenience may arise from the revision and changes made in the constitution of this state, and to carry the same into effect, it is hereby ordained and declared that all laws in force at the time of the adoption of this constitution, not inconsistent therewith, and all rights, actions, prosecutions, claims, and contracts of this state, individuals, or bodies corporate, shall continue to be as valid as if this constitution had not been adopted.

SEC. 2. All fines, taxes, penalties, and forfeitures owing to the state of Nebraska, or to the people thereof, under the present constitution and laws, shall inure to the use of the state of Nebraska under this constitution.

SEC. 3. Recognizances, bonds, obligations, and all other instruments entered into or executed upon the adoption of this constitution, to the people of the state of Nebraska, to the state of Nebraska, to any state or county officer, or public body, shall remain binding and valid, and rights and liabilities upon the same shall continue; and all crimes and misdemeanors shall be tried and punished as though no change had been made in the constitution of this state.

SEC. 4. All existing courts which are not in this constitution specifically enumerated, and concerning which no other provision is herein made, shall continue in existence, and exercise their present jurisdiction until otherwise provided by law.

SEC. 5. All persons now filling any office or appointment shall continue in the exercise of the duties thereof according to their respective commissions, elections, or appointments, unless by this constitution it is otherwise directed.

SEC. 6. The district attorneys now in office shall continue during their unexpired terms to hold and exercise the duties of their respective offices in the judicial districts herein created, in which they severally reside. In each of the remaining districts one such officer shall be elected at the first general election, and hold his office until the expiration of the terms of those now in office.

SEC. 7. This constitution shall be submitted to the people of the state of Nebraska, for adoption or rejection, at an election to be held on the second Tuesday of October, A. D. 1875, and there shall be separately submitted at the same time for adoption or rejection the independent article relating to "Seat of Government," and the independent article "Allowing electors to express a preference for United States senator."

SEC. 8. At said election the qualified electors shall vote at the usual places of voting, and the said election shall be conducted and the returns thereof made according to the laws now in force regulating general elections, except as herein otherwise provided.

SEC. 9. The secretary of state shall, at least twenty days before said election, cause to be delivered to the county clerk of each county blank poll-books, tally lists, and forms of return, and twice as many of properly prepared printed ballots for the said election as there are voters in such county, the expense whereof shall be audited and paid as other public printing ordered by the secretary is by law required to be audited and paid; and the several county clerks shall, at least five days before said election, cause to be distributed to the judges of election in each election precinct in their respective counties said blank poll-books, tally lists, forms of return, and tickets.

SEC. 10. At the said election the ballots shall be of the following form:

For the new constitution.

Against the new constitution.

For the article relating to "Seat of Government."

Against the article relating to "Seat of Government."

For the article "Allowing electors to express their preference for United States senators."

Against the article "Allowing electors to express their preference for United States senators."

SEC. 11. The returns of the whole vote cast, and the votes for the adoption or rejection of this constitution, **and for or against the articles respectively** submitted, **shall be made by the several county clerks to the** secretary of state, within fourteen days after the election, and the returns of said vote **shall, within** three days thereafter, be examined and canvassed by the president of this convention, and the secretary of state and **the governor, or any** two of them, and proclamation shall be made forthwith **by the governor, or** the president **of this** convention, of the result **of the canvass.**

SEC. 12. If it shall appear that a majority of the votes polled are "for **the new** constitution," then so much of this new constitution as was **not** separately submitted to be voted on by article shall be the supreme **law of the** state of Nebraska, on and after the first day of November, A. D. 1875. But if it shall appear that a majority of the **votes** polled were "against the new constitution," the whole thereof, including the articles separately submitted, shall be null **and void. If the votes** "for the new constitution" shall adopt the **same, and it shall appear that** a majority of the votes polled are **for the article relating to "the seat** of government," said article shall be a **part of the constitution of this state.** If the votes "for the **new** constitution" **shall adopt the same, and it shall appear that the** majority of the votes polled **are for the article "allowing electors to ex-**press their **preference for United States senator," said article shall be a** part of **the constitution of this state.**

SEC. 13. **The general election of this state shall be held on Tuesday suc-**ceeding the **first Monday of November of each year, except the first gen-**eral election, **which shall be on the second Tuesday in October, 1875. All** state, district, county, precinct, and township officers, by the constitution or laws made **elective by the people, except school district** officers, and municipal **officers in cities, villages, and towns,** shall be elected **at a** general election to be held as aforesaid. Judges of the supreme, district, and **county courts, all elective** county and precinct officers, and all other **elective officers, the time** for the election of whom is not herein otherwise provided for, and which are not included in the above exception, shall be elected at the first general election, and thereafter at the general election next preceding the time of the termination of their respective terms of office; *Provided,* That the office of no county commissioner shall **be** vacated hereby.

SEC. 14. The terms of office **of all state and** county officers, or judges of the supreme, district, and county courts, and regents **of** the university, shall begin on the first Thursday after the first Tuesday in January next succeeding their election. **The present state and county** officers, members of the legislature, and regents of the university, shall continue in office until their successors shall be elected and qualified.

SEC. 15. The **supreme,** district, and county courts established by this constitution shall be the successors respectively of the supreme court, the district, and the probate courts, having jurisdiction under the existing constitution.

SEC. 16. The supreme, district, and probate courts now **in** existence shall continue, and the judges thereof shall exercise the power and re**tain their present** jurisdiction until the courts provided for by this constitution shall **be organized.**

SEC. 17. All cases, matters, and proceedings pending and undetermined in the several courts, and all records, judgments, orders, and decrees remaining therein, are hereby transferred to and shall be proceeded and enforced in and by the successors thereof respectively.

SEC. 18. If this constitution be adopted, the existing constitution shall cease in all its provisions on the first day of November, A. D. 1875.

SEC. 19. The provisions of this constitution required to be executed prior to the adoption or rejection thereof, shall take effect and be in force immediately.

SEC. 20. The legislature shall pass all laws necessary to carry into effect the provisions of this constitution.

SEC. 21. On the taking effect of this constitution, all state officers hereby continued in office shall, before proceeding in the further discharge of their duties, take an oath or affirmation to support this constitution.

SEC. 22. The regents of the university shall be elected at the first general election under this constitution, and be classified by lot so that two shall hold their office for the term of two years, two for the term of four years, and two for the term of six years.

SEC. 23. The present executive state officers shall continue in office until the executive state officers provide for in this constitution shall be elected and qualified.

SEC. 24. The returns of the whole vote cast for the judges of the supreme and district courts, district attorneys, and regents of the university, under the first general election, shall be made by the several clerks to the secretary of state within fourteen days after the election; and the returns of the said votes shall, within three days thereafter, be examined and canvassed by the governor, secretary of state, and the president of this convention, or any two of them, and certificates of election shall forthwith be issued by the secretary of state to the persons found to be elected.

SEC. 25. The auditor shall draw the warrant of the state quartly for the payment of the salaries of all officers under this constitution whose compensation is not otherwise provided for, which shall be paid out of any funds not otherwise appropriated. *State v. Weston*, 4 Neb., 216. *State v. Weston*, 6 Neb., 16.

SEC. 26. Until otherwise provided by law, the judges of the district courts shall fix the time of holding courts in their respective districts.

SEC. 27. The members of the first legislature under this constitution shall be elected in the year 1876.

SEC. 28. This constitution shall be enrolled and deposited in the office of the secretary of state, and printed copies thereof shall be prefixed to the books containing the laws of the state, and all future editions thereof.

PROPOSITIONS SEPARATELY SUBMITTED.

ALLOWING ELECTORS TO EXPRESS THEIR PREFERENCE FOR UNITED STATES SENATOR.

The legislature may provide that at the general election immediately preceding the expiration of the term of a United States senator from this state, the electors may by ballot express their preference for some person for the office of United States senator. The votes cast for such candidates shall be canvassed and returned in the same manner as for state officers.

SEAT OF GOVERNMENT.

The seat of government of the state shall not be removed or re-located without the assent of a majority of the electors of the state voting thereupon at a general election or elections, under such rules and regulations as to the number of elections and manner of voting and places to be voted for as may be prescribed by law: *Provided,* The question of removal may be submitted at such other general elections as may be provided by law.

Done in convention at the capitol in the city of Lincoln, on the twelfth day of June, in the year of our Lord one thousand eight hundred and seventy-five, and of the independence of the United States of America the ninety-ninth.

JOHN LEE WEBSTER, President.

O. A. ABBOTT,
SAMUEL MAXWELL,
ANDREW HALLNER,
LUKE AGUR,
JOHN McPHERSON,
J. D. HAMILTON,
J. P. BECKER,
W. H. MUNGER,
JAMES HARPER,
J. E. BOYD,
J. H. PERRY,
ROBT. B. HARRINGTON,
CLINTON BRIGGS,
C. W. PIERCE,
J. B. HAWLEY,
JEFFERSON H. BROADY,
S. B. POUND,
M. L. HAYWARD,
CHARLES H. BROWN
ISAAC POWERS, JR.,
D. P. HENRY,
S. F. BURCH,
M. B. REES,
B. I. HINMAN,
S. H CALHOUN,
W. M. ROBERTSON,
M. R. HOPEWELL,
E. C. CARNS,
JOSIAH ROGERS,
C. E. HUNTER,
T. S. CLARK,
J. H. SAULS,
A. G. KENDALL,
S. H. COATS,

H. H. SHEDD,
S. M. KIRKPATRICK,
A. H. CONNER,
GEORGE S. SMITH,
JOHN J. THOMPSON,
W. B. CUMMINS,
W. H. STERNS,
L. B. THORNE,
JAMES W. DAWES,
R. F. STEVENSON,
JACOB VALLERY, SR.,
J. E. DOOM,
S. R. FOSS,
C. H. VAN WICK,,
W L. DUNLAP,
C. H. FRADY,
CHARLES F. WALTHERS,
R. C. ELDRIDGE,
JOSEPH GARBER,
A. M. WALLING,
J. G. EWAN,
C. H. GERE,
T. L. WARRINGTON,
JAMES LAIRD,
HENEY GREBE,
A. J. WEAVER,
CHAS. F. MANDERSON,
EDWIN N. GRENELL,
M. W. WILCOX,
FRANK MARTIN,
GEORGE L. GRIFFING,
J. F. ZEDIKER,
A. W. MATTHEWS,
WILLIAM A. GWYER.

ATTEST:
GUY A. BROWN, Secretary,
C. L. MATHER, Assistant Secretary.

STATUTORY PROVISIONS.

CHAPTER XXVII.

LEGISLATURE.

Clerks to File Certificates and Make Roll of Members.

2107. The clerks of each house shall file the certificates presented by members, each for his own house, and make a roll of the members who thus appear to be elected, and the persons thus appearing to be elected members shall proceed to elect such other officers as may be required for the time being.

Committee on Credentials.

2108. When the houses are temporarily organized they shall elect a committee of five on the part of the house and three on the part of the senate, by ballot, which committee shall examine and report upon credentials of those claiming to be elected members of their respective houses, and when such report is made, those reported as elected shall proceed to the permanent organization of their respective houses, and each house shall be the sole judge of the election returns and qualifications of its own members.

Any Member May Administer Oath.

2109. Any member may administer oath in the house of which he is a member and which acting on a committee may administer oaths on the business of such committee.

Freedom of Debate Guarranteed.

2110. No member of the legislative assembly, shall be questioned in any other place for any speech or words spoken in debate in either house.

Power to Punish Contempt, etc.

2111. Each house of the legislative assembly, has power and authority to punish as a contempt by fine and imprisonment, or either of them, the offense of knowingly arresting a member in violation of his privilege; of assaulting or threatening to do him any harm, in person or property, for anything said or done in either house, as a member thereof; of attempting, by menace or other corrupt means to control or influence a member in giving his vote or to prevent his giving it, of disorderly or contemptuous conduct tending to disturb its proceedings; of refusing to attend, or to be sworn, or to be examined as a witness before either house or a committee, when duly summoned; of assaulting or preventing any other person going to either house, or its committe by order thereof, knowing the same; of rescuing or attempting to rescue any person arrested by order of either house in the discharge of his duties as such.

Duration of Imprisonment and Where.

2112. Imprisonment for contempt of either house shall not be for more than six hours, and shall be in the jail of the county in which the legislative assembly may then be sitting, or if there be no jail, then in one of the nearest county jails.

Extent of Fine.

2113. Should a fine be enforced for any offense mentioned in section seven, it shall not exceed fifty dollars.

Fines and Imprisonment by Whom and How.

2114. Fines and imprisonment shall be only by virtue of an order of the proper house, entered on its journals, stating the grounds there for. Imprisonment shall be effected by a warrant, under the hand of the presiding officer, for the time being, of the house ordering it, countersigned by the clerk of the house, running in the name of the state and directed to the sheriff of the proper county; and under such warrant, the officer of the house, sheriff, **and jailer will be authorized to arrest and detain** the person.

Fines How Collected.

2115. **Fines shall** be collected by virtue of a similar warrant, directed to any proper officer of the county in which the offender has property, **and executed** in the same manner as executions for fines issued by courts **of justice,** and the proceeds shall be paid into the state treasury.

Punishment No Bar to Other Proceedings.

2116. Punishment for contempt, as in this chapter provided, is no bar to any other proceedings, **civil or** criminal, for the same offense.

Officers and Employees of the Senate.

2117. That the **officers** and employees of the senate shall consist of a president, secretary, assistant secretary, sergeant-at-arms, door keeper, enrolling clerk, engrossing clerk, **chaplain,** and **such** other officers and employees, not to **exceed sixty-six in number,** as may be deemed necessary for the proper **transaction of business. Such** other officers **or** employees to be elected **by the senate.**

Officers and Employees of the House.

2118. **The officers and employees of the house of representatives** shall consist **of a speaker, chief clerk, assistant clerk, sergeant-at-arms,** door keeper, **enrolling clerk, engrossing clerk, chaplain, and such other** officers and **employees, not exceeding** seventy-five **in number, as may be** deemed **necessary for the transaction of business. Such other officers or employees to be elected by the house.**

Pay of Officers and Employees.

2119. **There shall be** paid **to** each of the several officers and employees **named in** this act, for the official services rendered by them under the **provisions** of this act, the following sums, and no more: The president **of the senate** and speaker of the house of representatives shall each be en**titled** to receive the sum of three dollars per day; the secretary and chief clerk the sum of four dollars per day; the assistant clerks, the sum of four **dollars** per day, the sergeant-at-arms, the sum of three dollars per day; the chaplains, the sum of three dollars per day; the door keepers, the sum of three dollars per day; and the pages, the sum of one dollar and fifty **cents** per day; enrolling and engrossing clerks, three dollars per day.

Duties.

2120. It shall be the duty of the president of the senate and the speaker of the house of representatives to preside over their respective houses, to keep and maintain order during the session thereof, and to do and perform the duties devolving upon them by general parliamentary usage, and the rules adopted by the two houses. It shall be **the** duty of the chief clerk of the house of representatives, and the secretary of the senate, to attend **the sessions of the respective** houses, to call the rolls, read **the** journals, bills, memorials, resolutions, petitions, and all other papers or **documents** necessary to be read in either house, to keep a correct journal of the proceedings in each house, and to do and perform such other duties as may be imposed upon them by the two houses, or either of them. The assistant clerk and assistant secretary shall be under the control **and direction of the chief clerk and secretary** respectively, and shall assist **them in the proper discharge** of their duties and shall do and perform such other services as may be directed by the two houses or either of them. **It shall be** the duty of the sergeant-at-arms to enforce the attendance **of absent members,** when directed properly so to **do; to** arrest all members, or **other persons, when lawfully** authorized so **to do; to** keep and preserve **order** during the **session** of each house; to convey to the postoffice the mail matter sent by the respective members, and to deliver the same to them on each morning of the session; to obey and **enforce** the orders of the presiding officers, and to **do and** perform such other duties **as may** be enjoined on them by law and the respective houses. **It shall** be the duty of the door-keeper to **prepare and keep in order the senate chamber** and hall **of the** houses, including **cleaning and warming the same; to** attend **to and keep** closed the door **and bar of the respective** houses, **unless otherwise directed by** the presiding **officers therof; and to** perform such other **duties as may be** enjoined **on them by** either **house.** It shall be **the duty of the engrossing** clerk to **correctly** engross **such bills** as may be **required** to be engrossed **by** the committee on engrossed and enrolled bills, and to perform such **other** duties as may be required **by** either house. It shall **be the duty of the** enrolling clerk **to** correctly **and** neatly enroll all such **bills as may** be placed **in his hands therefor, and to perform** such other duties as may be enjoined **on him by** either house. **It shall be the duty** of the chaplains to open the sessions of each **house with prayer, and to** perform such other duties as **may be** imposed **on** them. **And it shall be** the duties of the pages **to act under** and as directed **by the presiding** officers of the respective houses. **It** shall also be the duty of the sergeant-**at-arms** to procure a **national flag,** and to place the same on the top of **the capitol** building, **there to be kept** during the time each or either of **the two houses shall** be **in session,** and **after** the adjournment of the two **houses, the said flag shall** be taken down **and kept down until** the opening **of the session of one of the two** houses.

The Secretary of State to Distribute Laws and Journals.

2121. The **secretary of state is** hereby authorizad to distribute the laws and journals of the state, **as hereinafter prescribed.**

The County Clerks to Make Requisition on Secretary of State for Laws and Journals.

2122. The county clerk of each organized county shall make a requisition upon the secretary of state for six copies (or as many less than that amount as he shall find necessary for the county) of the laws, and fourteen copies of the journals of each branch of the legislative assembly, for the use of the county of which he is clerk; and he shall name the conveyance and means of transportation, and shall also specify to whom they shall be directed, and to whose care, and upon the receipt of such requisition the secretary shall at once forward the required number of laws and journals as specified in the requisition of such county clerk, and the county clerk shall receipt for the same to the secretary, which receipt shall be filed in the office of the secretary of state.

Laws and Journals, How Distributed.

2123. The county clerk shall distribute one copy of the laws to each of the officers of the county, as follows: The probate or county judge; each member of the board of county commissioners; the sheriff; the county

treasurer; the county surveyor; **the prosecuting attorney; each notary**
public; each justice **of the peace; each constable; each road supervisor:**
and each precinct **assessor in said county. He shall also reserve one for**
himself, and give two copies each of the laws and journals **to every coun-**
cilman and representative who was a member of the legislative assembly
by which the **laws were enacted.**

Each Officer to Deliver up to his Successor.

2124. **Each officer** shall deliver up **to his** successor in office **all** statutes
which shall have come into his possession under the provisions of this
chapter, as soon after his successor shall have been qualified **as** such suc-
cessor or the county clerk may require.

Surplus to be Sold.

2125. After the above distribution the copies remaining in the hands
of the county clerk shall be sold at auction (ten days' notice having been
given in three public places in such county) to the highest bidder, no
person, however, to purchase more than two copies; and the proceeds of
such sale **shall go, first, to defray the** cost of transportation from the secretary **of state to the** county clerk, and the remainder, if any shall exist,
shall be **paid over to the** state librarian, and to be by him held **subject to**
the order **of the legislative** assembly.

Secretary of State Authorized to Sell Copies of Laws.

2126. After having so distributed the laws and journals of each legislative **assembly, the secretary is** authorized to sell **copies of the laws at a**
price **at least equal to cost, and** the amount **so received shall be applied**
to the **library fund of the state. The secretary of state shall deliver all**
copies **of the laws and journals yet in his possession to** the state librarian,
who **shall** officially **receipt therefor.**

Resident United States Officers Provided for.

2127. **The librarian shall, upon the order of** either of the judges **of the**
supreme court, issue one copy each to the district attorney, United
States Marshal, each register and **receiver of** all United States land offices in the state, each United States commissioner residing in the state,
and such other officers as the judges in their discretion may direct; *Pro-*
vided always, That the librarian shall permit no person to take away a
copy or copies of the laws and journals without taking a receipt therefor.

Each Incoming Legislature to be Provided for With Laws and Journals.

2128. The members of each succeeding legislative assembly shall be
furnished by the state librarian, at the commencement of each session
for which they are elected, with one copy each of the **laws** and journals
of the preceding session.

CHAPTER LI.
STATE PRINTING.

The Printing of Bills, Laws and Journals.

4423. The printing of all bills for the legislature, with such matters as
may be ordered by either house thereof, to be printed in bill form, shall
be let in **one contract.** The printing and binding in one contract.
The printing and binding **of** reports of state officers authorized by law to
be printed, and all other reports and documents ordered by **the** legislature, except such as enter into and form **a part** of the journals, shall be
let in another contract. The printing and binding of the laws, joint resolutions, and memorials enacted by the legislature shall be let in anoth-

er contract. And the printing and binding of all **blanks, blank books,** and **circulars required to** be furnished **by** the officers of the **executive department of the state** shall be let in another contract.

The Printing of Bills Shall be Executed Promptly.

4133. The **contractor for the printing of** bills or any matter printed in **bill form shall promptly, and without** unnecessary delay, execute all orders **of the legislature, or** either house thereof, for such printing, and **for each failure to complete** said printing within three days after receiving **the order for the same the** contractor shall **forfeit** and pay a penalty of **twenty-five dollars, to be deducted from his account** on settlement; and all **contractors under the provisions of this act shall without** unnecessary delay **execute all orders issued to them by the printing board, and the** contractor **for printing and binding the laws shall deliver the same** to the secretary **of state within sixty days after the adjournment of each** session **of the** legislature, and **the contractor for printing and binding** of the journals **shall** deliver the same **to the secretary of state within ninety** days after receiving the copy thereof.

Copy to be Furnished Without Unnecessary Delay.

4434. The secretary of state shall furnish a true and accurate **copy of** the laws and journals as they may be demanded by the printer **thereof,** and the clerks **of the respective branches of the** legislature shall each furnish **to the** printer, who **is bound** by his contract **to print the same,** copies of the journals, bills, reports, and other papers and documents, **without** unnecessary delay, and **no contractor shall be accountable for any delay** occasioned by the want of such **copy.**

MISSCELANEOUS PROVISIONS.

Votes Canvassed by the Legislature.

1633. **The votes** cast for governor, lieutenant governor, members of congress, secretary of state, auditor of public accounts, **state** treasurer, state superintendent of public instruction, attorney general, commissioner of public **lands and buildings, and district attorneys, and votes** cast expressing choice **for United States senators shall be** canvassed by the legislature at its next regular session. A **copy of the** abstract of votes cast for such officers shall be sealed up by the county clerk immediately upon the completion of the canvass, endorsed "abstract of votes cast for officers of the executive department, from ———— county," **or,** "abstract of votes cast expressing the choice of electors for United States senator from ———— county," and addressed to "the speaker of the house of representatives."

Duplicate Abstracts to the Secretary of State.

1634. **The** county clerk shall at the **same time envelope and seal up a duplicate copy of** the same abstracts directed to **the** secretary **of state, and all** the abstracts shall be placed in **one** envelope and addressed to **the secretary of state,** who shall preserve the ones addressed **to "the speaker of the house** of representatives" unopend, until the meeting of the legislature, and **from** the duplicate copies prepare a tabulated sheet of the votes cast for such officers and preserve the same for use of the legislature in making the official canvass as required by the constitution.

Shall Hear and Determine Contested Election Cases.

1649. The legislature in joint meeting shall hear and determine cases of contested election for all officers of the executivee department. The meeting of the two houses, to decide upon such elections, shall be held in the hall of the house of representatives, and the speaker of the house shall preside.

Contest of Members.

1650. The senate and house of representatives shall severally hear and determine contests of the election of their respective members.

DECISIONS OF THE SUPREME COURT.

Bill to have but one general object which must be fairly expressed in the title 5, 311,5, 516.

Amendatory act valid if not inconsistant with title and subject matter of amended one, though there be apparent confusion in application to provisions sought to be amended. 27, 764,8 (43 N. W. 1140) 29, 149.

A provision in an amendatory act repealing an act not connected with the subject of the amendment is void. Where title has two subjects, act may be sustained as to one, 17. 85 (22 N. W. 228).

Part of an act may be valid and part not. 16, 239 (20 N. W. 312). 25 457 (41 N. W. 280).

One house cannot amend title of bill originating in the other. 17, 394 (23 N. W. 3).

It is sufficient if subject is farily expressed in the title. 16, 683 (21 N W. 398).

Title an index to legislative intent. 6 485.

Title of amendatory act cannot be broader than the original. 9, 511 (4. N, W. 240.)

An act broader than its title may be declared void as to the excess, but valid as to the rest. 25, 676 (41 N. W.) 638).

An act to prohibit the fraudulent tranfer of property and to declare the same a crime and to prescribe the punishment thereof held constitutional the act having but one subject. 21, 53 (31 N. W. 258).

The title of the act of June 6, 1871. Amending sections 50, 51, 71 and 105 of revenue act valid. 13, 17 (12 N. 832).

Section 3 of "An act to exempt homesteads from Judicial Sale," approved February 19, 1877, is within the title and is valid. 13 122 (12 N. W. 831).

The title of the act which took effect September 1, 1879. "Counties and County Officers" is not open to the constitutional objection of containing more than one subject. 15, 387 (11 N. W. 495).

When title of act is to amend a particular section of the statute, the proposed amendment must be germane to the subject matter of the section sought to be amended. 11, 377 (9 N. W. 477.) The title of an "Act regulating the herding and driving of stock," approved February 26, 1879, is not comprehensive enough to authorize the provision in section four giving damages for the castration of animals. 13, 253 (13 N. W. 276.)

Where an act not complete in itself, but amendatory of a former, statute is void. 7, 413

Old section need not be recited in amendatory act. 1, 199.

Law complete and repealing the provisions under which acts were formerly done is valid. 6, 36.

Where the new act is in the very words of the act it repeals, and the evident intention was to continue it in force (with a lesser penalty), this intention **will be given effect,** and **will not** prevent the prosecution for a crime committed before the repeal. **15,** 448 (19 N. W. 686).

Rule as to repeal of statutes by implication. **18,** 140 (24 **N. W. 447**).

Two amendments to same same act **on** succeeding days, how **interpreted. 23,** 134 (36 N. W. 348).

A later statute, which contains provisions clearly repugnant to a **former** **repeals** the former **as completly** as though **it** contained express **words to** **that effect. 14, 31 (14 N. W.** 660).

Legislature cannot pass law to legalize bonds already issued. **6,** 234.

Does not require **the** printing of amendments after the bill has been put upon its final **passage. 9,** 494 (4 N. W. 75).

Failure of the presiding officer of the senate to sign a bill which the **journal shows** passed does not effect the validity of the **act. 9,** 129 (1 N. W. 100). **17,** 88 (22 N. W. 119).

The certificate of the presiding officers that the bill has passed **is** only *prima facie* evidence of the fact. The journals are higher evidence. **18,** **237 (25 N. W. 77).**

In amending an act it may be designated by its title or chapter in the **statutes. 20,** 377 (30 N. W. 267). **25,** 817 (41 N. W. 796).

Fiscal quarter means the legislative quarter **in which the session is to** **be held** 5, 570.

Fiscal year begins December 1st. **Appropriations extend to the end of** first quarter **after** adjournment of next regular session. **22,38(33 N. W.-** **711).**

Where entire amount derived from **sale of state lots and lands,** was appropriated, and sale was made partly on credit, held that warrants could be drawn upon the whole amount of purchase price **at** once, and without waiting **for full** payment thereof. 24, 790 (40 N. W. 316)

See note to the section 22 citing **14,** 444 (16 N. W. 481).

As to what constitute a vacancy. **17,** 599 (24 N. W. 282).

Intended to establish a permanent **rule in regard to future payments** of expenditures **of the** state. **6,** 513.

A specific appropriation is one **expressly providing funds for a** particular purpose. **15, 609** (19 N. W .596).

No appropriation necessary to pay salary **of officers** fixed by constitution. Officers whose salaries are not fixed by the constitution depend upon legislative appropriation. **4,** 218 6, 17.

The voucher of the officers of the senate will not authorize **the auditor** to draw a warrant in favor **of a party,** unless the **claim is authorized by** **law. 14,** 444 (16 N. W. 481).

An appropriation for "conveying convicts to the penitentiary" **cannot** **be** drawn **against** for "conveying juvenile offendors to the reform school." **12, 408** (11 N. W. 860).

Money **due county** treasurer as fees cannot be paid except where their **is** a specific appropriation. **18,** 222 (24 N. W. 683).

Appropriation of $95,000.00 to **provide for** the salaries of **nineteen** judg**es is** an appropriation in gross. **21,** 662 (33 N. W. 426).

Each appropriation contained **in** the general appropriation bill must be a specific appropriation for the purpose named and the account must be itemized. **22,** 45 (33 N. W. 711). **See 4,** 507. **9,** 470 **(4 N. W. 61).**

DECISIONS OF THE HOUSE OF REPRESENTATIVES ON POINTS OF ORDER.*

ADJOURN SINIE DIE.

In Order.

During the third day of the session, a motion was made to adjourn *sinie die*. The speaker ruled the motion out of order, but upon an appeal the decision of the chair was reversed, but when the motion to adjourn *sinie die* was put to the house it failed by one vote. Journal H. R. 1866, p. 11.

AMENDMENTS.

Can not Amend a Senate Message.

The speaker ruled that the house can not amend a senate message. (Journal H. R. 1881, p. 108).

Former Action can only be Reached by a Reconsideration.

Point of order raised that when a substance of an amendment has been decided by a former action of the house, it could only be reached by a motion to reconsider, sustained by the chair. (Journal H. R. 1887, p. 502).

BALLOTING FOR CANDIDATES.

Dropping Candidates from the List.

While balloting for candidates a motion was made to drop from the list the candidates having received the least number of votes, against which a point of order was raised. Sustained. (Journal, H. R. 1876-7, p. 47).

BILLS.

To take a Bill out of its place in the File on Third Reading takes a Two-Thirds Majority.

The speaker ruled that it takes a two-thirds majority to take a bill out of its place on third reading. An appeal was taken, and the chair was sustained. (Journal H. R. 1883, p. 885.)

Not in Order to Table a Bill on its Second Reading.

Upon a point of order raised the speaker ruled that it was out of order to table a bill on its second reading. (Journal H. R. 1879, p. 136.)

The House can Take Action on Bills Still in the Hands of Standing Committees.

Point of order raised "that as the resolution contained house rolls which were still in the possession of the standing committees, and not reported with favorable recommendation, therefor the resolution was not in order," Over ruled by the speaker. (Journal H. R. 1885, p. 861.)

In Making a Special Order for Several Bills.

A resolution suspending the rules and making a number of bills on the general file a special order, a division of the subject was called for, and a motion made "that a vote be taken on each bill seperately." The motion ruled out of order by the speaker, and on an appeal, the chair was sustained. (Journal H. R. 1885 p. 860.)

A Bill on its Third Reading Cannot be Discussed.

While a bill was on its third reading a member obtained the floor and proceeded to discuss the objects of the bill. The speaker ruled discussion

---

* [These decisions are published as found in the journals of the house of representatives. Their correctness as ruling is left to the judgment of the reader.]

out of order, on an appeal, the chair was sustained. (Journal H. R. 1885 p. 1271.)

Not in Order to Recommit a Bill on its Final Passage.

After the reading and pending the vote on the passage of a bill a motion was made to recommit the bill. The speaker ruled the motion out of order. An appeal was taken and the chair was sustained. [Journal 1887, p. 1275.]

Cannot Have Vote Recorded on the Passage of a Bill after the Fate of the Bill is decided.

A point of order raised that it was not in order for a member of the house to vote upon the question of the final passage of a bill after a yea and nay vote had been taken and the fate of the bill decided. Sustained by the speaker. [Journal H. R. 1885, p. 626.

When a Bill has Passed a Motion to Recommit is out of Order.

After a bill had passed and received a constitutional majority, a motion was made to recommit the bill to the committee of the whole. A point of order was raised that the motion to recommit, under rule 47, was out of order, sustained by the speaker. (Journal H. R. 1885, p. 882).

Held that Bills can be Considered out of their Regular Order.

A point of order raised "that the house having just adopted a special order file of bills for consideration it was not in order to consider house rolls out of their regular order," not sustained by the chair. (Journal H. R. 1885, p. 949.

Any Motion Out of Order.

A point of order raised "that after a bill has been read the third time any motion is out of order." Sustained by the chair. (Journal H. R. 1887, p. 1137).

Amendments in Order After Bill has Passed to a Third Reading.

The speaker ruled after a bill has passed to a third reading amendments are in order. On an appeal the chair was sustained. (Journal H. R 1873, p. 330, 346).

The Order of Bills on Third Reading.

Upon a point of order raised "that it would require a two-thirds majority to suspend the order of bills on third reading." Sustained by the speaker, but over-ruled by the house. [Journal H. R. 1891, p. 530].

Call of the House May be Made at any Time.

Point of order raised.
"That there has been no intervening business since the last call of the house, therefore a renewal of the call was out of order." The speaker ruled that under rules 33 and 36 the call of the house may be made at any time when seconded by two members, and the absentees must be sent for at any time when demanded by five members. [Journal H. R. 1889, p. 515].

Joint Committee.

House Can Not Discharge Committee After Being Appointed.

A motion being made to discharge the members on the part of the house on a joint committee, a point of order was raised, that the action of the house in the appointment of the committee had passed from the house to the senate, and therefore it was not competent for the house to take action in the matter. The speaker sustained the point of order, and on an appeal the house sustained the chair. [Journal H. R. 1883, p. 176.

COMMITTEE OF THE WHOLE.
Not Competent for the House to Adopt Rules Governing the Committee of the Whole.

A resolution being offered "that when the house is in committee of the whole, no member shall speak more than once on the same subject; nor longer than five minutes;" declared out of order by the speaker. [Journal H. R. 1885, p. 737 and 981.]

COMMITTEE REPORTS.
Minority Report can not be Entertained Until Majority Report Is Made.

Point of order: "That the report of the minority can not be entertained until the majority has reported. Sustained by the speaker. [Journal II. R. 1881, p. 162,169].

A Motion in Conflict With an Adopted Committee Report out of Order.

The speaker ruled that a motion in conflict with the report of a committee already adopted, is out of order. [Journal II. R. 1889, p. 1123].

A Report not to be Considered Twice.

Upon a point of order raised, the speaker decided it incompetent for the house to again consider a report upon which action has once been passed upon and settled by the house this day. [Journal II. R. 1889, p. 669).

Recommendation to Recommit Takes The Precedence.

Upon a point of order raised "that the recommendation of the commitee of the whole to recommit, took the precedence of a motion to order the bill engrossed to a third reading." Sustained. [Journal II. R. 1889, p. 1128.]

A Minority Report not an Amendment of the Majority Report.

Upon the point of order that an amendment proposed, be put to the house before the main question, and that a minority report of a committee by the usages and rules of parlimentary law, is an amendment to the majority report, and should therefore be first considered, the chair ruled adversly, and upon an appeal was sustained by the house. (Journal H. R. 1886, p. 32.)

Can Not be Tabled.

Upon a point of order raised "that a report of committee acting under instruction of the house could not be tabled." Sustained. [Journal H. R. 1891, p. 219.

CONTEST CASES.
Interested Parties May Vote.

Point of order raised "that in a contest case before the house the interested members could not vote upon a question refering to said contest." Over ruled by the speaker, and on an appeal the chair was sustained. [Journal H. R. 1866, p. 8.]

INDEFINITE POSTPONEMENT.
A Motion to Indefinently Postpone Cannot be Amended.

A motion being made to indefinitely postpone a bill, a motion was made to amend that the bill be ordered engrossed for a third reading. The point of order was raised, "that a motion to indefinitely postpone cannot be amended." Sustained by the chair. [Journal H. R. 1887 p. 1435.]

A motion to Indefinitely Postpone, Once Decided can not be Renewed.

Point of order raised "that a motion to indefinitely postpone having once been decided, could not be again made at the same **stage of proceedings.** (Journal H. R. 1889. p. 1535.)

READING OF THE JOURNAL.
Can not be Dispensed with.

"Pending the reading," of the journal, a motion was made to dispense with the further reading of the journal. Motion ruled out of order by the **speaker. (Journal H. R. 1866, p. 9.)**

RECONSIDER.
Motion For need not be made the Same day.

Point of order raised "that a motion to reconsider must be made the same day the resolution is adopted." The speaker over-ruled the point of order (Journal H. **R. 1881, p. 68.)**

Part of a Subject Matter once Acted upon can not be Reconsidered.

Point of order raised "that a motion to reconsider a part of a subject matter that has been acted upon by a deliberate body, is out of order. The speaker sustained the point of order. [Journal H. R. 1881, p. 69.

REFERENCE.
Refer takes Precedence.

Point of order raised "that a motion to refer takes precedence over a substitute." Sustained by the speaker. Journal **H.** R. 1881 p. 101.

RESOLUTIONS.
Not a Concurrent Resolution.

Upon a resolution asking the senate to concur in an adjournment, **the** point of order was raised "that being a concurrent resolution under rule 43 it should be read at large on three different days." The point of order over-ruled. **[Journal H. R. 1885, p. 432.**

ROLL CALL.
Can not be Interrupted by a call of the House.

The speaker ruled that roll call could not be interrupted by a call of the house. (Journal H. R. 1866, p. 1192).

During roll call a Motion out of Order.

The speaker ruled that pending a call for the ayes and nayes a motion is out of order. Upon an appeal the chair was sutained. [Journal H. R. 1866, p. 11).

Sergeant-at-arms, Assistant, Provided for in Statutes.

Point of order raised "that the position of assistant sergeant-at-arms was not provided for in the general statutes." The speaker decided the point of order not well taken. [Journal H. R. 1876, p. 46].

TO TABLE.
A Defeated Motion to table can not again be Entertained.

A point of order was raised "that when a motion to table has been defeated, it can not again be entertained upon the same suject." Sustained [Journal H. R. 1889, p. 1123].

MANUAL OF PARLIAMENTARY PRACTICE.

[A condensed summary of Cushing's mannual as applicable to the every day questions arising in all legislative bodies, compiled by Eric Johnson, chief clerk, 1891-3].

Importance of Rules.

It is highly important to the preservation of order, decency, and regularity, in a numerous assembly, and not least essential to its power of harmonious and efficient action, that its proceedings should be regulated by established forms and methods; and, with a view to these purposes, it is more material, perhaps, that there should be rules established, than that they should be founded upon the firmest basis of reason and argument; the great object being to effect a uniformity of proceeding in the business of the assembly, securing it at once against the caprice of the presiding officer, and the captious disputes of members. It is to the observance of regularity and order among the members, that the minority look for protection against the power of the majority; and in the adherence to established forms, between the different branches, that each finds its security against the encrochments of the other.

QUORUM.

The number necessary to constitute a quorum of any assembly may be fixed by law, as in the case with most of our legislative assemblies; but if no rule is established on the subject, a majority of the members composing the assembly is the requisite number.

No business can regularly be entered upon until a quorum is present; nor can any business be regularly proceeded with when it appears that the members present are reduced below that number; consequently the presiding officer ought not to take the chair until the proper number is ascertained to be present; and if at any time, in the course of the proceedings notice is taken that a quorum is not present, and, upon the members being counted by the presiding officer, such appears to be the fact, the assembly must be immediately adjourned.

Rules and Orders.

When a code of rules is adopted beforehand, it is usual also to provide therein as to the mode in which they may be amended, repealed, or dispensed with. Where there is no provison, it will be competent for the assembly to act at any time, and in the usual manner, upon questions of amendment or repeal; but in reference to dispensing with a rule or suspending it, in a particular ease, if there is no express provision on the subject, it seems that it can only be done by general consent.

The terms "general consent" as used in parliamentary practice, denote the unanimous opinion of the assembly when their opinion is expressed informally, and not by means of a vote. Whenever, therefore, it is said that the "general consent of the assembly is necessary to the adoption of any measure it is to be understood, that if the question is proposed informally, no objection must be made to it, or that, if proposed in a formal manner, the vote in its favor must be unanimous.

When any of the rules adopted by the assembly or in force, relative to its manner of proceeding, is disregarded or infringed, every member has the right to take notice thereof, and to require that the presiding officer, or any other whose duty it is, shall carry such rule into execution; and in that case the rule must be enforced at once, without debate or **delay**. It is then too late to alter, repeal, or suspend the rule: so long as **any** one member insists upon its execution, it must be enforced.

The Presiding Officer.

The principal duties of this officer are the following:—

To open the **sitting at** the time to which the assembly is adjourned.

To announce the business before the assembly, **in the** order in which **it** is to be acted upon;

To receive and submit in the proper manner, **all** motions and propositons presented by the members;

To put to vote all questions which are regularly moved, or necessarily arise in the course of the proceedings, and to announce the result;

To restrain the members, when engaged in debate, within the rules of order;

To enforce on all occasions the observance of order and decorum **among the members;**

To **receive** all messages and other communications, and announce them to the assembly.

The presiding officer may read sitting but should rise to state a motion **or put a question to** the assembly.

The Recording Officer.

He is to enter what is done and past, but not what is said or moved.

It is also the duty of the secretary **to read** all papers, etc., which **may**, be ordered to be read.

The clerk is also charged with the custody of all the papers and documents of every description, belonging to the assembly, as well as the journal of its proceedings, and is to let none of them be taken from the table by any member or other person, without the leave or order of the assembly.

OF THE RIGHTS AND DUTIES OF MEMBERS.

Ever **member,** however humble he may be, has the same right with every other, **to submit his** propositions to the assembly, **to** explain and recommend **them in** discussion, and to have them **patiently** examined and deliberately decided upon by the assembly; and, on the other hand, it is the duty of every one so to conduct himself, both in debate and in **his** general deportment in the assembly, as not to obstruct any other member in the enjoyment of his equal rights.

The observance of decorum by the members of a deliberative assembly is not only due to themselves and to one another as gentlemen assem**bled together to** deliberate on matters of common importance and interest, **but** is also essential to the regular and satisfactory proceeding of **such an** assembly. No member is to disturb another or the assembly itself by hissing, coughing, or spitting; by speaking or whispering to other members; by standing up to the interruption of others; by passing between the presiding officer and a member speaking; going across the assembly-room, or walking up and down in it.

Assaults by one member upon another, threats, challenge, affrays, etc. **are** also high breaches of decorum.

The only punishments which can be inflicted upon its members, by a deliberative assembly of the kind now under consideration, consist of reprimanding, to which are to be added such other forms of pun ishment, as by apology, begging pardon, etc., as the assembly may see fit to impose.

OF THE INTRODUCTION OF BUSINESS.

When a member has occasion to make any communication whatever to the assembly,————whether to present a petition **or other** paper, or to make or second a motion of any kind, or merely to make a verbal statement,————as well as when one desires to address the assembly in the de**bate, he** must in the first, place as the expression is, "obtain the floor" for **the purpose** he has in view. In order to do this, he must rise in his place **and,** standing uncovered address himself to the presiding officer by his **title,** the latter on hearing himself thus addressed, calls to the members by his county, and the member may then, but not before proceed with his business.

If two or more members rise and address themselves to the presiding officer at the same time, or nearly so, he should **give** the floor to the member whose voice he first heard.

A petition, in order to be received, should be subscribed by the petitioner himself, with his own hand, either by name **or** mark.

Whenever **a** member introduces a proposition of his **own,** for **the con**sideration of the assembly, he puts it into the form he **desires** it should have, and then moves that it be adopted as the resolution, order **or vote** of the assembly. If this proposition so far meets approbation of other members that one of them rises in his place, and seconds it, it may then be put to the assembly; and the result, whether affirmative **or negatively** becomes the judgement of the assembly.

A motion must **be submitted in writing; otherwise the presiding** officer will be justified in refusing to receive it.

When a motion **has been** made and received, it is then to be stated by **the** presiding officer **to** the assembly, and thus becomes a question for its decision; and, **until so** stated, **it is** not in order for any member to speak to it, but when moved, seconded, and stated from the chair, a motion is in the possession of the assembly and cannot be withdrawn by the mover, but by special leave of the assembly, which must be obtained by a motion made and seconded as in other cases.

Previous Question.

This motion was introduced into the House of Commons in England more than **two** centuries ago, and for the purpose of suppressing subjects of a delicate nature relating to high personages, or the discussion of which might call forth observations of an injurious tendency. When first made use of, the form of the motion was, "shall the main question be put?" and the effect of a decision of it in the negative was to suppress the main question for the whole session. The form of it was afterwards changed to that which it has at present, namely, "shall the main question be now put?" and the effect of a negative decision of it now is to suppress the main question for the residue of the day only. This is the **purpose** for which the previous question was originally invented, and for **which it is still used in** the British Parliament. But the previous ques**tion may** be decided in the affirmative, **as** well as the negative; that is, that the main question shall now be **put** immediately, without any further debate, and the form in which it then exists. **This** operation of the previous question, when decided affirmatively, has **led** to the use of it for the purpose of surpressing debate on a principal question, and coming to a vote upon it immediately; and this is ordinarly the only object of the previous question, as made use of in the legislative assemblies of the United States.

Indefinite Postponement.

In order to suppress a question altogether, without coming to a direct vote upon it, in such a manner that it cannot be renewed, the proper motion is for indefinite postponement; that is, a postponement or adjournment of the question, without fixing any day for resuming it. The effect of this motion, if decided in the affirmative, is to quash the proposition entirely. A negative decision has no effect whatever.

OF MOTIONS TO POSTPONE.

The assembly is willing to entertain and consider a question, but not at the time when it is moved, the proper course is either to postpose the subject to another day, or to order it to lie on the table.

When the members individually want more information than they possess at the time a question is moved, or desire further time for reflection and examination, the proper motion is, to postpone the subject to such future day as will answer the views of the assembly.

OF MOTIONS TO COMMIT.

The third case for the use of a subsidiary motion, occurs when the subject-matter of a proposition is regarded with favor, but the form in which it is introduced is so defective, that a more careful and deliberate consideration is necessary than can conveniently be given to it in the assembly itself, in order to put it into a satisfactory form. The course of proceeding then is, to refer the subject to a committee, which is called a commitment; or, if the subject has already been in the hands of a committee, a recommitment, a part only of a subject may be committed, without the residue; or different parts may be committed to different committees.

OF MOTIONS TO AMEND.

The last case, for the introduction of subsidiary motions, is when the assembly is satisfied with the subject-matter of a proposition, but not with the form of it, or with all its different parts or desires to make some addition to it. The course of proceeding then is to bring the proposition into the proper form, and make its details satisfactory by means of amendments.

Division of a Question.

When a proposition or motion is complicated, that is, composed of two or more parts which are so far independent of each other as to be susceptible of division into several questions, and it is supposed that the assembly may approve of some but not of all these parts, it is a compendious mode made of amendment to divide the motion into separate questions, to be separately voted upon and decided by the assembly, a proposition, to be divisible, must comprehend points so distinct and entire, that, if one or more of them be taken away, the others may stand entire and by themselves.

FILLING BLANKS.

It often happens that a proposition is introduced with blanks purposely left by the mover to be filled by the assembly, either with times and

numbers, or with provisions analogous to those of the **proposition itself**
In the latter case, blanks are filled in the same way that other amendments
by the insertion of words are made. In the former propositions **to fill**
blanks are not considered as amendments to the question, but **as original.**
motions, to be **made** and decided before the principal **question.**

The rule is, that if the larger comprehends the lesser, **as in question to**
what day a postponement shall take **place, the number, of which a** com-
mittee shall consist, the amount of a fine to be imposed. The question
must begin *a maximo* and be first taken upon the greatest or farthest
and so on to the least or nearest, until the assembly comes to a vote; but if
the lesser include the greater, as in questions on the limitation of the rate
of interest, on the amount of a tax, on what day the session of a legislative
assembly shall be closed by adjournment, or what day the next session
shall commence, the question must first be taken on the least or nearest,
and so on to the greatest or most remote until the assembly comes to a vote.

GENERAL RULES RELATING TO AMENDMENTS.

All amendments of which a proposition is susceptible, as far as form **is**
concerned, may be effected in one of three ways: namely, either by inserting **or** adding certain words; or **by** striking out certain words; or
striking out certain words, and inserting or adding others.

Amendments by Striking Out.

If an amendment is proposed by striking out a particular paragraph or
certain words, and the amendment is rejected, it cannot **be** again moved
to strike out the same words **or a** part of them.

If an amendment **by** striking **out** is agreed to, it cannot **be** afterwards
moved to insert the same words struck **out,** or a part of **them.**

Amendment by Inserting.

If an amendment is proposed by inserting **or adding a** paragraph or
words and the **amendment is** rejected, it cannot **be moved** again **to** insert
the same words or a part of them.

If it is proposed to amend by inserting a paragraph, and the amendment
prevails, it cannot be afterwards moved to strike out the same words **or a**
part of them.

Amendment by Striking out and Inserting.

The third form of amending a proposition, namely by striking out
certain words and inserting others in their place.

If the motion is divided, the question is first **to be** taken on striking
out, and, if that **is** decided in **the** affirmative, **then** on inserting; but if
the former is decided **in** the negative, the **latter falls,** of course

If the motion to strike out and insert is put **to** the question undivided
and is decided in the negative, the same **motion** cannot be made again.

If the motion **to** strike out and insert **is** decided in the affirmative, it
cannot be then moved to insert the words struck out or a part of them,
or to strike out the words inserted or a part of them.

Amendments Changing the Nature of a Question.

It is allowable to amend a proposition in such a manner **as** entirely to
alter its nature, and to make it bear a sense different from what it was
originally intended to bear; so that the friends of it, as it was first introduced, may themselves be forced to **vote** against it **in its** amended
form.

The Order and Succession of Questions.

It is a general rule, that when a proposition is regularly before a deliberative assembly, for its consideration, no other proposition or motion can regularly be made or arise so as to take the place of the former, and be first acted upon, unless it be either, first, a privileged question; secondly, a subsidiary question; or, thirdly, an incidental question or motion.

All these motions take the place of the principal motion, or main question as it is usually called, and are to be first put to the question; and among themselves also, there are some which, in like manner, take the place of all the others. Some of these questions merely supersede the principal question, until they have been decided, and when decided, whether affirmatively or negatively, leave that question as before. Others of them also supersede the principal question until they are decided; and, when decided one way, dispose of the principal question, but, if decided the other way, leave it as before.

Privileged Questions.

There are certain motions or questions which, on account of their superior importance attributed to them, either in consequence of a vote of the assembly, or in themselves considered, or of the necessity of the proceedings to which they lead, are entitled to take the place of any other subject or proposition which may then be under consideration, and to be first acted upon and decided by the assembly. These are called privileged questions, because they are entitled to precedence over other questions though they are of different degrees among themselves. Questions of this nature of three kinds: namely, first, motions to adjourn; secondly, motions or questions relating to the rights and privileges of the assembly, or of its members individually; and thirdly, motions for the orders of the day.

Adjournment.

A motion to adjourn takes the place of all other questions whatsoever; for otherwise the assembly might be kept sitting against its will; and for an indefinite time; but, in order to entitle this motion to precedence, it must be simply to "adjourn."

The reason why a motion to adjourn moved for the purpose of superseding or suppressing a pending question, is not susceptible of amendment, is, that if amended, it would at once become inadmissable, in point of order, on the ground of its being introductory to a second question, having no privilege to take the place of a question already pending, and entitled to be first disposed of.

Questions of Privilege.

The questions next in relative importance, and which supersede all others for the time being, except that of adjournment, are those which concern the rights and privileges of the assembly or of its individual members.

When settled, the question interrupted by it is to be resumed at the point where it was suspended.

Orders of the Day.

When a consideration of a subject has been assigned for a particular day, by an order of the assembly, the matter so assigned is called the order of the day for that day.

A question which is thus made the subject of an order for its consideration on a particular day is thereby made a privileged question for that day.

Orders of the day, unless proceeded in and disposed of on the day assigned, fall, of course, and must be renewed for some other day.

Questions of Order.

It is the duty of the presiding officer of a deliberative assembly, to enforce the rules and orders of the body over which he presides, in all its proceedings; and this without question, debate or delay, in all cases in which the breach or order, or the departure from rule, is manifest. It is also the right of every member, taking notice of the breach of a rule, to insist upon the enforcement of it in the same manner.

When any question of this nature arises in the course of any other proceeding, it necessarily supersedes the further consideration of the subject out of which it arises, until that question is disposed of; then the original motion or proceeding revives, and resumes its former position, unless it has been itself disposed of by the question of order.

When a question of order is raised, as it may be by any one member, it is decided by the presiding officer. If the decision of the presiding officer is not satisfactory, any one member may object to it, and have the question decided by the assembly, this is called appealing from the decision of the chair.

Withdrawal of a Motion.

A motion when made, seconded and stated, cannot be withdrawn without the general consent, or, if put formally to the question, the unanimous vote of the assembly.

If this motion is decided in the affirmative, the motion to which it relates is thereby removed from before the assembly, as if it had never been moved; if in the negative, the business proceeds as before.

Suspension of a Rule.

It is usual in the code of rules adopted by deliberative assemblies, and especially legislative bodies, to provide that a certain number exceeding a majority, as two-thirds or three-fourths, shall be competent to the suspension of a rule in a particular case; where this is not provided, there seems to be no other mode of suspending or dispensing with a rule than by general consent.

Amendment of Amendments.

It is allowable to amend a proposed amendment, and that the question or such sub-amendments must necessarily be put and decided before putting the question on the amendment.

Subsidiary Question Lie on the Table.

This motion takes precedence of and superceeds all the other subsidiary motions. If decided in the affirmative, the principal motion, together with all the other motions, subsidiary and incidental, connected with it, is removed from before the assembly, until it is again taken up.

Previous Questions.

If first moved, is not subject to be superseded by a motion to postpone, commit, or amend.

If the previous question is moved before the others above mentioned, and put to the question, it has the effect to prevent those motions from being made at all.

Postponement.

The motion to postpone is either indefinite or to a day certain, and, in both these forms, may be amended.

This motion stands in the same degree with motions for the previous question, to commit, and to amend and if first made, is not susceptible of being superseded by them.

Commitment.

May be amended by the substitution of one kind of committee for another, or by enlarging or diminishing the number of the members of the committee as originally proposed, or by instructions to the committee.

This motion stands in the same degree with the previous questions, and postponement, and, if first made is not superseded by them.

Amendment.

A motion to amend, as has been seen, may be itself amended. It stands in the same degree only with the previous question and indefinite postponement; and neither, if first moved, is superseded by the other.

But this motion is liable to be superseded by a motion to postpone to a day certain; so that, amendment and postponement competing, the latter is to be first put.

A motion to amend may also be superseded by a motion to commit.

Of the Order of Proceeding.

In considering and amending any paper which consists of several distinct propositions begin at the beginning and proceed through it by paragraphs.

To this natural order of beginning at the beginning, there is one exception according to parliamentary usage, where a resolution or series of resolutions, or other paper, has a preamble or title; in which case, the preamble or title is postponed until the residue of the paper is gone through with.

When a paper has been referred to committee, and reported back to the assembly, is taken up for consideration, the amendments only are first read, in course, by the clerk. When the amendments reported by the committee have been thus disposed of, the presiding officer pauses, and gives time for amendments to be proposed in the assembly; when through the whole, he puts the question on agreeing to or adopting the paper.

When the paper referred to a committee is reported back, as amended, in a new draft, the new draft is to be considered as a substitute for the original paper, and then to treat it as such.

The regular course of proceeding requires the motion to lie on the table, to be first put; if this is negatived, the question of privilege is then settled; after that comes the question of order; then the question of commitment; if this is negatived the question of amendment is taken; and, lastly the main question.

When a member has obtained the floor, he cannot be cut off from addressing the assembly on the one question before it; nor, when speaking, can he be interrupted in his speech by any other member rising, and moving an adjournment, or for the orders of the day, or by making any other privileged motion of the same kind, a member in possession of the floor, or proceeding with his speech, cannot be taken down or interrupted but by a call to order; and the question of order being decided, he is still to be heard through.

When, therefore, a member rises whilst another is speaking, and addresses the chair, he should inform the presiding officer that he rises to a point of order, or the orders of the assembly, or to a matter of privilege. It will then be the duty of the presiding officer to direct the member speaking to suspend his remarks or to resume his seat, and the member rising, to proceed with the statement of his point or other matter of orderer of privilege. If the latter, on proceeding, discloses matter which shows that the interruption was proper, the subject so introduced must first be disposed of; and then the member who was interrupted is to be directed to proceed with his speech. If it appears that there was no sufficient ground for the interruption, the member rising is to be directed to resume his seat; and the member interrupted, to proceed with his speech.

OF ORDER IN DEBATE.

As to the Manner of Speaking.

When a member desires to address the assembly on any subject before it (as well as to make a motion), he is to rise and stand up in his place, uncovered, and to address himself not to the assembly or any particular member, but to the presiding officer.

No person, in speaking, is to mention a member then present by his name, but to describe him by his seat in the assembly, or as the member who spoke last, or last but one, or on the other side of the question, or by some other equivalent expression.

As to Time of Speaking.

No member can speak more than once to the same question; but he may speak to the same subject as often as it is presented in the form of a different question.

A member may also be permitted to speak a second time in the same debate, in order to clear a matter of fact, or merely to explain himself in some material part of his speech.

It is sometimes supposed, that, because a member has a right to explain himself, he therefore has a right to interrupt another member while speaking, in order to make the explanation; but this is a mistake: he should wait until the member speaking has finished; and if a member, on being requested, yields the floor for an explanation, he relinquishes it altogether.

As to Stopping Debate.

The only mode in use in this country, until recently, for the purpose of putting an end to an unprofitable or tiresome debate, was by moving the previous question

The other mode of putting an end to debate is for the assembly to adopt beforehand a special order in reference to a particular subject, that, at such a time specified, all debate upon it shall cease, and all motions or questions pending in relation to it shall be decided.

Another rule which has lately been introduced for the purpose of shortening rather than stopping debate is, that no member shall be permitted to speak more than a certain specified time on any question.

OF THE QUESTION.

When any proposition is made to a deliberative assembly, it is called "a motion," when it is stated or propounded to the assembly for their acceptance or rejection, it is denominated "a question," and, when adopted, it becomes "the order," "resolution," "or vote," of the assembly.

OF RECONSIDERATION.

It is a principal of parliamentary **law,** upon which many **of the rules
and** proceedings previously stated **are** founded, that when **a question
has been once put to a** deliberative **assembly,** and decided **whether affirmative or negative, that decision is the judgment** of the assembly **and**
cannot be again **brought into question.**

It has now come **to be a** common practice **in** all deliberative assemblies
and may consequently be considered as a principal of the common parliamentary **law of** this country, **to** reconsider a vote already passed, whethe
affirmatively **or** negatively.

It is usual in legislative bodies, **to regulate by a special rule the** time
manner, and **by whom, a motion to reconsider may be** made, **but** where
there is no special rule on the subject, a motion to reconsider must **be
considered in the same light as any other motion and as subject to** no
other rules. On the motion to **reconsider, the whole subject is as much
open** for debate as if it had not been discussed at all; and, if **the motion
prevails,** the subject **is again open** for debate on the original motion, **in
the same manner as** if that motion had never been put to the question.

COMMITTEE OF THE WHOLE.

The proceedings in **a committee of the whole,** though in general simi-
**lar to those in the assembly itself and in other committees are yet differ-
ent in** some **respect, the** principal of which **are the following:**

First, The previous question cannot be **moved in a committee of the**
whole. The only means of avoiding an **improper discussion is, to move**
that the committee **rise.**

Second, A committee **of the whole cannot** adjourn to some other time
or place, for the **purpose of going on with** and completing the consideration of the **subject referred to them; but,** if their business is unfinished at
the usual time for the assembly to adjourn, or for any other reason they
wish to **proceed** no **further at a particular time, the form** of proceeding is,
for some member **to move that the committee rise,** report progress and
ask leave to sit again.

Third, In a **committee of the whole, every member may speak as often**
as he pleases, **provided he can obtain the floor.**

Fourth, A committee **of the whole, cannot refer any matter to** another
committee.

Fifth, In a committee **of the whole, the preciding officer of the assem-**
bly has a right to take a part in **the debate and proceedings in the same**
manner as any other member.

Sixth, A committee of the whole, like a select committee, has no author-
ity to punish a breach of order, **whether of** a member **or stranger; but
can only rise** and report the **matter to the** assembly.

A Bill Having Been Read the **Third Time** may be **Recommitted**
for Some Special Purpose.

After a bill has been ordered to be read **a** third time, or has been read a
third time it is then to late to recommit **it** generally, but it may then,
nevertheless, **be** recommitted for some special purpose, **as to receive**
some particular **clause** or proviso, **or for the purpose o** being divided into
two bills. When a bill after being **thus recommitted is** reported to the
house and again taken up for consideration, **it is resumed** at the point at
which the proceedings upon it where **interrupted by** the recommitment.

CONCLUDING REMARKS.

A presiding officer will often find himself embarrassed by the difficulty, as well as the delicacy, of deciding points of order, or giving directions as to the manner of proceeding. In such cases it will be useful for him to recollect that—

"THE GREAT PURPOSE OF ALL RULES AND FORMS IS TO SUBSERVE THE WILL OF THE ASSEMBLY, RATHER THAN TO RESTRAIN IT; TO FACILITATE, AND NOT TO OBSTRUCT, THE EXPRESSION OF THEIR DELIBERATE SENSE."

A CHAPTER ON LEGISLATIVE PRACTICE.

ORGANIZATION OF THE LEGISLATURE.

Temporary Organization.

The Legislature convenes at 12 o'clock M., on the first Tuesday in January, biennally.

At the hour appointed the secretary of the state calls the house of
representatives to order, and the lieutenant-governor the senate.

Clerk Protem.

It has of late years become the custom for the secretary of state to
select some one to act as clerk *pro tem*, formerly on motion of some
person claiming to be elected, a clerk *pro tem* was selected, and the roll
of members, as prepared by the Secretary of State from the official returns, is called over to see who of the regularly elected members of
the legislature are present and entitled to participate in the organization. After this roll call the next thing in order is the election of a

Speaker Pro Tem.

As soon as the *speaker pro tem* is elected, the secretary of state selects a
committee of two members to conduct the *speaker pro tem* to the chair.

Chief Clerk Pro Tem.

The next thing in order is the election of a Chief Clerk *pro tem*

Committee on Credentials.

Now committee of five on credentials should be appointed, on motion of some member whose seat is not contested, and the speaker *pro
tem*. should select for such committee only those whose right to act is un-
questioned by any contest.

The Representatives Districts will be called over and the credentials
should be handed to the clerk as the numbers are called.

Recess.

The House should now take a recess long enough to allow the committee on credentials to make up its report.

No business can be transacted until the Legislature is organized, therefore the committee on credentials should report back to the House as
soon as possible the names of all who are entitled to seats, as all contested cases must go before the standing committee of the House after
it is permantly organized.

After Recess.

When the House is called to order the committee on credentials makes
a report, and when adopted, a committee of three should be appointed
to wait on the chief justice or one of the associate judges of the supreme
court, and request him to administer the oath of office to the members
elect.

The Oath of Office.

The following oath must be sworn to and subscribed by each member:
"We and each of us do solemnly swear [or affirm] that we will support
the constitution of the United States and the constitution of the state of
Nebraska, and will faithfully discharge the duties of members of the
legislature according to the best of our ability, and that at the election
at which we were chosen to fill said office, we have not improperly influ-

enced in any way the vote of any elector, and have not accepted, nor will we accept **or** receive, directly or indirectly, any money or other valuable thing from any corporation, **company, or person or any** promise of office [for any **vote** we may give or **withhold on any** bill, resolution, or appropriation.]"

The house is now ready for

Permanent Organization.

A motion should now be made "to proceed to a permanent organization." which being agreed to, nominations will be in order for speaker.

The roll will be called by the clerk, and each member will announce his choice for speaker. A majority of all the votes cast is necessary for a choice. Upon the election of a speaker, a committee of two should be appointed to escort him to the chair.

Upon taking the chair, the speaker-elect usually delivers a short address.

Other Officers Elected.

The following officers should then be elected:

Chief clerk, assistant clerks, sergeant-at-arms, door-keeper, enrolling clerk, engrossing clerk, and chaplain.

Other officers and employes, as may be deemed necessary for the proper transaction of business, may then be elected or appointed by resolution. [See page 55, Sec. 2118.]

The speaker has no authority to appoint officers or employes, except a resolution of the house give him that authority.

Oath of Office for Officers.

All officers elected or appointed must take and subscribe the following oath:

"We, and each of us, do solemnly swear that we will support the constitution of the United States, and the constitution of the state of Nebraska, and faithfully discharge the duties of our respective offices. So help us God."

Organization of the Senate.

The organization of the senate proceeds in like manner, except it is called to order by the lieutenant-governor, voting only when the senate is equally divided. [Const., Sec. 17, Art. V.] A president of the senate is, however, chosen, who presides over the senate when the lieutenant-governor shall not attend or shall act as governor. [Const., Sec. 7, Art. III.]

The senate also elects a secretary, assistant secretary, sergeant-at-arms, door-keeper, enrolling clerk, engrossing clerk, chaplain, and such other officers and employes as may be elected or appointed by resolution of the senate. (See page 55, Sec. 2117.)

PERMANENT ORGANIZATION OF BOTH HOUSES.

As soon as a permanent organization is effected, a committee of three is then appointed to wait upon the senate and inform it that the house is organized and ready for business.

As soon as the senate and house are organized, a joint committee of both houses, consisting of two senators and three representatives, is appointed to wait on the governor and inform him that the legislature is organized and in readiness to receive any communication from him.

FIRST BUSINESS.

The first business of the legislature is to meet in joint convention and canvass the vote for state officers. (Con., Sec. 4, Art. 5. See page 35.) This is usually done on the second day of the session,and on the third day the officers elect are brought before the bar of the house and the oath of office administered to them in the presence of both houses assembled in joint convention. It is customary for the newly elected governor to deliver his inaugural message at this time.

GOVERNOR'S MESSAGE.

The senate and house have usually assembled in joint convention, in the representative chamber, upon some day and hour suggested by the governor during the first week of the session, generally on the afternoon of the second day, to hear his annual message.

At the first opportunity after hearing the message read, the various recommendations therein contained should be referred by resolution to appropriate standing committees.

STANDING COMMITTEES.

The standing committees are appointed by the speaker at as early a day in the session as possible, in accordance with rules of the house. In the senate no uniform custom of appointing committees exists. In 1877, 1883, 1891 and 1893 the committees were appointed by the senate. In 1879 and 1881 they were appointed by the lieutenant governor.

RULES.

A committee on rules should be appointed early in the session, and pending its report it has been customary to adopt the rules of the preceding legislature.

SEATS.

Seats in the house have generally been selected by members in advance of the session.

STATIONERY.

It has been the custom to furnish every member with the necessary stationery required in his official capacity, which will be issued by the direction of the chief clerk as needed.

MAIL FACILITIES.

The legislative mail will be taken from the U.S. post-office to the capitol building as soon as distributed, and will be opened by the post-master of the house immediately.

All mail matter deposited with the post-master at the capitol will be taken to the U.S. post-office in time to make connections with the regular mail trains leaving Lincoln.

Of Letters, Petitions, Memorials, etc.

If a letter, petition, bill, memorial or remonstrance be sent to a member to be by him presented to the house or senate, his first duty is to fold it in a neat form and endorse on the back of it, in brief, the subject on which it treats, and immediately below this he signes his name and county. For example, a member has a petition for the passage of a bill, etc., he endorses it in this way.

"A petition signed by 100 citizens of Phelps county praying for the passage of House Roll No. 33." E. SODERMAN, of Phelps county.

In presenting it, the member rises in his place, when the order of "petetions and memorials" is reached and says:

"Mr. Speaker (or Mr. President) I present the petition of the citizens of ———praying, etc." He then hands it to one of the pages, to be handed to the chief clerk, who also reads the indorsement, by way of information to the house or senate, after which the speaker refers it to the appropriate committee. The same course is pursued in regard to memorials and remonstrances.

Of Resolutions.

The parliamentary meaning of "resolution" is the expression of the will or sympathy of the house in regard to any subject before it, public or private, as for example, that the use of the hall be granted for a particular purpose; that certain companies be required to furnish statements, etc., that the house extends its sympathy to the Typographical Union, etc. If information is desired from any of the departments, or from the executive, the resolution assumes the form of a request as for example:

Resolved, "That the auditor be requested to furnish the house with a statement," etc.

When a member is desirous of bringing before the house any proposition for its determination, he writes it out in the form of a resolution, in a plain, legible hand, and as soon as the speaker announces the order of "Resolutions" he rises in his place and says:

"Mr. Speaker (or president), I offer the following resolution and move its adoption." He then delivers it to one of the pages, to be handed to the chief clerk. The speaker then directs the clerk to read the resolution, which is then put to the house for its adoption or rejection.

Joint resolutions, being in the nature of bills, cannot be submitted to the house under the order of "resolutions." The proper time to offer them is under the order of "Introduction of bills."

Concurrent resolutions are those on which action of both Senate and House are required, and are treated, in each house, the same as resolutions.

Of Bills.

Too much care in the preparation and passage of bills cannot be taken. The decisions of our courts whereby laws are held unconstitutionl merely on account of some slight defect in title or want of proper observance of constitutional requirements in their passage, are growing in frequency. Our present constitution throws numerous safe-guards around the passage of bills with a view of preventing hasty and improvident legislation. See Const. Art. III. Sec's. 9, 10, 11.

All bills should be written in black ink on legal cap paper, or type-written; folded up in neat form and the title of the bill endorsed on the upper end of the back of it and the member sign his name and the county immediately under the title in this way:

House Roll No. 33.

A bill for an act to regulate railroads, to classify freights etc.

BY FRED NEWBERRY,
Hamilton Co.

When the order of introduction of bills "is reached, the member rises in his place and says: "Mr. Speaker, I ask leave to introduce a bill," when he hands it over to one of the pages to be handed to the Chief Clerk, when it is read the first time and ordered to a second reading. On the next or a subsequent day, when the order of "bills on the second reading," is reached the bill is read the second time, ordered to be printed, and referred to a committee.

Action of Committees.

When a committee, to whom has been referred a bill for their consideration, make amendments to it, they should be careful to make them in such a way as to be readily comprehended by the clerks. But no part of any bill should be mutilated, nor any interlineations made, and no amendments made in pencil should be entertained. They should be written plainly and pinned to the bill. The Chief Clerk furnishes proper blanks upon which to make the reports to the House.

Reports of Committees.

A bill reported from a committee should be accompanied by a written report and whether "with amendments," or "without amendments." If reported favorably and concurred in by the House the bill goes on "general File."

COMMITTEE OF THE WHOLE.

The committee of the whole is an expedient to simplify the business of legislative bodies. No record is made of its proceedings, and it has no officer except of its own creation for temporary purposes. It is liable to instant dissolution in case of disorder when the speaker takes the chair to suppress it; in case of lack of quorum when the speaker takes the chair for a call of the house or an adjournment, and in case of a message from the senate or governor when the speaker takes the chair to receive it.

Either house may resolve itselfs into a committee of the whole on some particular bill, resolution, or subject; or it may go into committee of the whole upon the general file of bills. In the first case the motion is,

"That the house do now resolve itself into a committee of the whole upon [bill No....., a bill....], or [joint resolution No....., providing, etc,], or [upon all bills relating to...., as the case may be."

In the second case it is,

"That the house do resolve itself into a committee of the whole upon the general file of bills."

Bills, resolutions, and general matters which have been once considered in committee of the whole, in which progress has been made and leave granted for further consideration, have the preference. The motion of the committee of the whole for their further consideration, must be made under the head of "bills in which the committee of the whole made progress and obtained leave to sit again;" and in which case the member who presided when the same matter was previously considered in committee of the whole, resumes the chair, unless the speaker name a different member.

The motion of the committee of the whole upon the general file must be made under the order of "bills not yet considered in committee of the whole."

When the house resolves itself into committee of the whole the speaker selects a chairman, as follows:

"The gentleman from......, Mr................., will take the chair."

The appointed chairman advances to the speaker's desk, and, having taken the chair, receives from the clerk the papers indicated by the motion for the committee, when the chairman announces:

"Gentlemen:—The committee have under consideration bill No......... entitled—(reading the title from the back of the bill), or (in case of consideration of the general file) the committee have under consideration the general file of bills; the first in order is bill No... ..,entitled......

The clerk will read the first section.

The section read, the chairman asks:

"Are there any amendments proposed to the first section? If none, and no objections heard the section will be considered approved."

This process is continued **through the whole bill, when at the close** of the reading the chairman **says:**

"The....th section and the whole bill have now been **read, and are open** to amendments."

At this point, after the friends of the bill have **perfected it,** it is customary for the opponents of the bill to open their attack.

After **the** discussion of the bill to such an extent as may **be desired,** if no amendments are made, the final vote is generally upon a motion:

"That **the bill** be reported back to the house without amendment."

If any other bills are before the committee, they are proceeded with in the same manner.

If it is desired to have a further consideration of any matter before the committee, or if the general file has not been gone through with, the motion is,

"That the committee rise, report progress, and ask leave to sit again."

If the committee has completed its duties, **the motion is,**

"That the committee rise and report."

Which being analogous to a motion to adjourn, is not debatable. The chairman states the matter as follows:

"It is moved that the committee do now rise and report" [or *otherwise as the case may be.*]

Is the committee ready for the question?

"Gentlemen:—Those who are of the opinion that this committee do now arise and report [or *as the case may be*],say aye; those of the contrary opinion, say no."

In case **of doubt, a division** must be had, as the ayes and noes cannot be called **in committee of the whole.**

When the **committee** rises, the speaker resumes his seat, and the chairman, **through the chief clerk, reports as** follows:

"**Mr. Speaker.**"

"The committee of the whole have had under consideration bill No..... entitled......, and have instructed me to report the same to the house with amendments," [or *as the case may be*].

When the general file has been under consideration, the report is as follows:

"The committee of the whole have had under consideration the general file of bills, have gone through the same, and have directed me to report to the house the bills contained therein, with sundry amendments and recommendations, as follows, to-wit:" (Here follow the title of bills considered, with action taken upon them.)

In case the file has been left untouched the **report is—**

"The committee of the whole have under consideration the general file of bills, and have made some progress therein. I am directed to report back the following bills with the amendments and recommendations hereinafter specified, **and** ask leave for the committee to sit again. (Here follows the report **of** amendments, etc., as **above.)**

On the latter report the question is—

"Shall **leave be granted?**"

When, upon a count, it is ascertained that **a** quorum is not present, the **report is—**

"The committee of the whole have had under consideration..... and after some progress therein, find there is no quorum present: that fact I herewith report to you."

In case of confusion or disorder, the speaker of his own accord **resumes the chair temporarily and without any** formality, for the **purpose of suppressing it.** When order is restored, the chairman resumes the **chair and the business proceeds.**

Upon the coming in of a report, the recommendations are at once acted on by the house.

When, in committee of the whole, any **member** desires to offer an amendment, it must be reduced in writing and **sent** to the clerk, who reads it, and asks—

"**Is the** committee ready for the question upon **the** amendment?"

And if no further amendment or debate, he puts the question in the usual **manner.**

After a section is once passed, with an unsuccessful effort to amend it, no further amendments are in order. The strictness of this rule, is, however, not always adhered to—an amendment once made, **may, however, be reconsidered.** Such a motion is—

"**That the** amendment offered by the gentleman from....to the....th section **be** reconsidered;"

And it is stated as follows:

"**The gentleman from....moves that the amendment offered by the** gentleman from....to the....th second be reconsidered."

"Is the committee ready for the question?"

"Those who are of the opinion that said **amendment be reconsidered, say** aye; those of a contrary opinion, **say no.**"

In case the amendment is reconsidered, the chairman says:

"The motion **is carried.** The amendment is reconsidered. The question now recurs upon the adoption of the amendment. Is the committee **ready for** the question?" etc.

Passage of Bills.

When the **order of business entitled** "**Bills** on third reading" is reached, **at the conclusion of the** reading **of each bill,** the speaker says: "This **bill has been read** at large on three seperate days, and printed with all the amendments thereto. Agreeably to **the constitution the** yeas and nays will be taken on the final passage of the **bill.**"

Upon the passage of a bill the presiding officer **reads its title** and says: "The bill is passed; the question is as to the title. Is the **title** agreed **to?**" The title is generally agreed to, though it may be changed if the **house so order.**

Forms.

The following forms are used when bills have become laws, as provided **by the** constitution other than by approval of the executive.

When a bill has not been returned **by** the executive within five days (Sundays excepted) after it has been presented to him for approval, the following certificate **is** attached, **signed,** and sent with the bill to the secretary **of** state.

"We hereby certify that the bill **(here** insert title) was presented to the governor on the........day of........A. D...., and the same not having been returned by him within five days (Sundays excepted) after such presentation, it has become a law agreeably to the constitution of this **state.**

"ATTEST:. ....

....Lieutenant-Governor

Secretary of the Senate." ....

"............... ....Speaker of the House.

Chief Clerk of the House."

Or in case the legislature, by their adjournment, prevent the return of the bill, the following certificate should be made:

"We hereby certify that the bill (here insert title) was presented to the Governor on the........day of.........A. D.....,that the legislature have this....day of........adjourned, and that said bill has become a law agreeably to the constitution of this state unless the Governor shall, within five days after such adjournment, file his objections thereto in the office of the secretary of state.

"ATTEST: ".................................... ....

".. .Lieutenant-Governor

Secretary of the Senate"...

"................... ....Speaker of the House

Chief Clerk of the House.".

When a bill has been passed over the vote of the governor by a three-fifths vote of all the members elected to each house, the certificates attached are as follows:

"We hereby certify that the bill entitled (here insert title) which has been disapproved by the governor, and returned with his objections to the senate (or house of representatives), in which it originated, was passed by three-fifths of the members elected to the senate on the........day of ....A. D....., and the foregoing is the act so passed by the senate.

"............. ....,"

LIEUTENANT GOVERNOR.

"...... ....•.."

"Lincoln, (date)."   SECRETARY OF THE SENATE.

"We hereby certify that the bill entitled (here insert title) which has been disapproved by the governor, and returned with his objections to the house of representatives (or senate) in which it orginated, was passed by three-fifths of all the members elected to the house of representatives on the........day of........A. D. ...., and the forgoing is the act so passed by the house of representatives.

"............................"

SPEAKER OF THE HOUSE.

"............................"

CHIEF CLERK OF THE HOUSE

STANDING RULES OF THE SENATE.

Quorum Necessary; What Constitutes.

1. The President having taken the chair, and a quorum being present the journal of the preceding day shall be read, to the end that any mistake may be corrected that shall be made in the entries. A quorum shall consist of a majority of the members of the senate.

On Decorum.

2. No member shall speak to another, or otherwise interrupt the business of the senate, or read any newspapers while the journals or other public papers are being read, or when any member is speaking in any debate.

3. Every member when he speaks shall address the president, and shall speak standing in his place, and when he has finished shall sit down.

Restrictions on Debate.

4. No member shall speak more than twice in any one debate, on the same day, without leave of the senate.

When two Members Rise at the Same Time.

5. When two members rise at the same time, the president shall name the person to speak, but in all cases the member who shall first rise and address the president shall be entitled to the floor.

When a Member is Called to Order.

6. When a member shall be called to order by the president or a senator, he shall sit down; and every question of order shall be decided by the president, without debate, subject to an appeal to the senate.

7. If a member be called to order for words spoken, the exceptional words shall be immediately taken down in writing, that the president may be better enabled to judge the matter.

On Compelling the Attendance of Absentees.

8. No member shall absent himself from the service of the senate without leave of the senate being first obtained. And in case a less number than a quorum of the senate shall convene, they are hereby authorized to send the sergeant-at-arms, or any other person or persons by them authorized, for any or all absent members, as a majority of such members present shall agree, at the expense of such absent members respectively, unless such excuse for non-attendance shall be made as the senate, when a quorum is convened, shall judge sufficient; and that case the expense shall be paid out of the contingent fund.

On Motions.

9. No motion shall be debated till the same shall be seconded, and the question stated by the chair.

10. When a motion shall be made and seconded, it shall be reduced to writing, if desired by the president or any member, delivered at the table and read before the same shall be debated.

On Debate.

11. When a question is under debate, no motion shall be received but to adjourn, for the previous question, to lay on the table, to postpone indefinitely, to postpone to a certain day, to commit or amend, which

several motions shall have precedence in the order they stand arranged. Any motion may be withdrawn by the mover at any time before a decision, amendments, or ordering of the yeas and nays, except a motion to reconsider, which shall not be withdrawn without leave of the senate. A motion to adjourn shall always be in order, that, and the motion to lay on the table, shall be decided without debate.

12. If a question in debate contain several points, any member may have the same divided: but on a motion to strike out and insert, it shall not be in order to move for a division of the question; but the rejection of a motion to strike out and insert one proposition shall not prevent a motion to strike out and insert a different proposition; nor prevent a subsequent motion to simply strike out: nor shall the rejection of a motion simply to strike out prevent a subsequent motion to strike out and insert.

On Filling Blanks.

13. In filling up blanks, the largest sum and the longest time shall be first put.

Unfinished Business.

14. The unfinished business in which the senate was engaged at the last preceding adjournment shall have the preference in the special orders of the day.

The Ayes and Nays.

15. When the ayes and nays shall be called for by two of the members present, each member called upon shall, unless for the special reason be excused by the senate, declare openly and without debate his assent or dissent to the question. In taking the ayes and nays, and upon the call of the house, the names of the members shall be taken alphabetically.

16. When the ayes and nays, shall be taken on any question, in pursuance of the above rule, no member shall be permitted to vote after the decision is announced from the chair.

On Secret Sessions.

17. On a motion made and seconded to shut the doors of the Senate on the discussion of any business which may, in the opinion of a member, require the secrecy, the president shall direct the senate to be cleared of all persons, as provided in Rule 32, and during the discussion of such motion, the doors shall remain shut.

18. No motion shall be deemed in order to admit any person or persons whatsoever within the doors of the senate chamber, to present any petition, memorial, or address, or to hear any such read.

On Reconsideration.

19. When a question has been once made and carried in the affirmative or negative, it shall be in order for any member of the majority to move for the reconsideration thereof; but no question for the reconsideration of any vote shall be in order after a bill, resolution, message or report, amendment or motion upon which the vote was taken, shall have gone out of possession of the senate announcing their decision; nor shall any motion or reconsideration be in order unless made on the same day on which the vote was taken or within the next two days of actual session of the senate thereafter.

On Calling Members to the Chair.

20. The president of the senate, or the temporary president, **shall have the** right to name a member to perform the duties of the chair, but such substitution shall not extend beyond an adjournment.

Memorials and Petitions.

21. Every petition, or memorial, or other paper, shall be referred, of course, without putting a question for that purpose, unless the reference is objected to **by a member at the time such** petition, memorial, or other paper is presented. And before any **petition or** memorial addressed to the senate shall be received and **read at the** table, whether the same shall be introduced by the president or a member, a brief statement of the contents of the petition or memorial may verbally **by** made bo the introducer.

Order of Business.

22. The following shall be the order of busines;
   1. Roll call.
   2. Prayer by the chaplain.
   3. Reading journal.
   4. Petitions and memorials.
   5. Reports from standing committees.
   6. Reports of select committees.
   7. Resolutions.
   8. **Notices and** introduction of bills,
   9. Bills **on** first reading.
   10. Bills on second reading.
   11. Special order.
   12. Bills on third reading,
   13. Bills on their passage.
   14. Unfinished **business.**
   15. Special order of **the day.**

On Printing Papers and Documents.

23. No paper **or document, except** bills, shall be printed for the use of the Senate without special **order.**

ON BILLS.

Reading, Printing and Recommitment.

24. Every bill shall receive three readings **previous to** its being passed, and the president shall give notice at each **whether it** be first, second, or third, which reading shall be on different **days.** And all resolutions to which the approbation and signature of the governor may **be requisite, or** which may **grant** money **out** of the contingent or any other **fund, shall be treated** in all respects, in the introduction and from of proceedings on them in the senate, in a similar manner with bills; and all other resolutions shall lie on the table one day for consideration, and also reports of all committees, except a committee of the whole, and engrossed and enrolled bills.

25. No bills shall be committed or amended until it shall have been twice read. It shall then be printed, unless otherwise ordered by the senate, and then **referred** to its appropriate standing committee or the special committee. After which it may be amended, and all amendments thereto shall be printed before the vote is taken on its final **passage.**

26. All bills, after they have been referred to their appropriate standing or special committees, and reported back to the senate and printed, shall first be considerded by the senate in the committee of tho whole before they shall first be taken up and proceeded on by the senate, agreeably to the standing rules, unless otherwise ordered. And when the senate shall consider a bill or resolution, as a committee of the whole, the president or temporary president shall call a member to fill the chair during the time the senate shall remain in committee of the whole; and the chairman so called shall, during such time, have the power of a temporary president.

27. The final question, upon the second reading of every bill, resoluion or motion orignating in the senate, and requiring three readings previous to its being passed, shall be: Whether it shall be engrossed and read a third time?" and no amendment shall be received for discussion at a third reading of any bill, resolution, or motion, unless by unanimous consent of the members present; but it shall at all times be in order, before the final passage of any bill, resolution, or motion, to move its commitment; and should such commitment take place and any amendment be reported by the committee, the said bill, resolution, or motion shall be again read the second time, and considered in committee of the whole, and then the aforesaid question shall be again put.

28. The titles of bills and such parts thereof only as shall be affected by proposed amendments, shall be inserted on the journal.

The Proceedings Shall be Entered on the Journal.

29. The proceedings of the senate, when not acting as in committee of the whole, shall be entered on the journal as concisely as possible, care being taken to detail a true and accurate account of the proceedings; but every vote of the senate shall be entered on the journal, and a brief statement of the contents of each petition, memorial, or paper presented to the senate, shall also be inserted on the jouranal.

On Reference.

30. When motions are made for reference of the same subject to a select committee and to a standing committee the question on reference to the standing committee shall be first put.

Nominations by the Governor.

31. When nominations shall be made in writing by the governor to the senate, a future day shall be assigned, unless the senate unanimously direct otherwise, for taking them into consideration.

Confidential Communications by the Governor to be Kept Secret.

32. All confidential communications made by the Governor to the senate shall be by the members thereof kept secret. All information or remarks touching or concerning the character or qualification of any person nominated by the governor to office, shall be kept secret. When acting on confidential or executive business, the senate shall be cleared of all persons except the secretary and assistant secretary of the senate sergeant-at-arms, and door-keeper. The legislative proceedings, the executive proceedings, and the confidential legislative proceedings of tho senate shall be kept in seperate and distinct books.

Messages.

33. Messages shall be sent to the house by the secretary, sergeant-at-

arms, or door-keeper, the secretary having previously endorsed the final determination thereon.

34. Messages are introduced in any state of business, except when a question is being put, while the yeas and nays are being called, or while the ballots are being counted.

The Presiding Officer Shall Have Supervision Of—

35. The presiding officer of the senate shall have the regulation of such parts of the capitol and its passages as are or may be set apart for the use of the senate and its officers.

Rules Governing Committee of the Whole.

36. The rules of the senate shall be observed in the committee of the whole, so far as they may be applicable, except limiting the time of speaking, and except the yeas and nays shall not be taken.

37. A motion that a committee rise shall always be in order, and shall be decided without debate.

Punishment for Disclosing Secrets.

38. Any officer or member of the senate convicted of disclosing any matter directed by the senate to be held in confidence, shall be liable, if an officer, to dismissal from the service of the senate, and in case of a member, to suffer expulsion from that body.

Jefferson's Manual Shall Govern Except—

39. The rules of parliamentary practice comprised in Jefferson's manual shall govern the senate in all cases in which they are applicable, and in which they are not inconsistent with the standing rules and orders of the senate, and the joint rules of the senate and house of representatives.

Reporters Admitted.

40. Reporters may be admitted to the floor of the senate under the direction of the president, and are required to inform him what paper they report for.

No Smoking.

41. No smoking shall be allowed in the senate chamber or galleries during the session of the senate.

Rules how Amended or Suspended.

42. These rules may be altered, amended, or suspended, two-thirds of the members present voting therefor

Who Priveleged to the Floor.

43. No person shall be admitted to the floor of the senate except as follows: members of the house of representatives and its officers, state officers and their clerks, judges of the supreme and district courts, senators and representatives in congress.

Emergency Clause.

44. When an emergency is expressed in the preamble or body of an act, as a reason why such act should take effect from and after its passage, or some day less than three calendar months after the adjournment of the session, the question shall be, "Shall the bill pass?" and if decided affirmatively by a vote of two-thirds of all the members elected to the senate, then the bill shall be deemed passed; but if upon such vote a majority of less than two-thirds of said members vote affirmatively on said question, then the vote on said bill shall be deemed reconsidered, and the bill subject to amendment by striking out such part thereof as expresses an emergency and the time of taking effect, and then said bill shall be under consideration upon its third reading, with the emergency clause and the time of taking effect stricken out.

Time of Meeting.

45. The hours of meeting of the senate shall be at 10 o'clock A. M. and at 2 o'clock P. M. of each day, unless otherwise specially ordered by a vote of the senate.

Formula for Amendments to Bills.

46. If a section is to be amended, the formula should be after the enacting clause:

That section....of chapter....of the code of civil procedure, of the state of Nebraska, (or the statutes as the case may be) be amended so as to read as follows: Then follow the sections desired as amended, full and complete in themselves, and the last section of the new act should repeal the section which has been amended.

Committees to Report Bills.

47. Every bill and resolution referred to any special or standing committee, shall be reported to the senate by such committee within four days after such referrence, unless further time is specially granted by the senate.

Standing Committees to be Appointed by the Senate.

48. All standing committees of the senate shall be appointed by the senate.

STANDING COMMITTEES.

49. The senate shall have the following standing committees: A committee of

Nine on judiciary.
Seven on finance, ways, and means.
Seven on agriculture.
Five on highways, bridges, and ferries.
Five on accounts and expenditures.
Five on military affairs.
Five on municipal affairs.
Seven on public lands and buildings.
Five on internal improvements.
Five on school lands and school funds.
Five on federal relations.
Five on public printing.
Seven on enrolled nnd engrossed bills.
Five on counties and county boundaries.
Five on education.
Five on library.
Five on claims.
Five on banks and currrency.
Nine on railroads.
Five on miscellaneous corporations.
Five on state prison.
Five on university and normal school.
Seven on constitutional amendments.
Five on public charities.
Five on privileges and elections.
Five on live stock and grazing interests.
Seven on miscellaneous subjects.
Five on medical legislation.
Three on insane hospital.
Three on deaf, dumb, and blind asylum.

Three on reform school and home for the friendless.
Nine on re-districting and apportionment.
Five on immigration.
Five on mines and minerals.
Five on manufactures and commerce.
Five on labor.
Five on revenue.
Five on rules.
Seven on standing committees.
Five on industrial home and institute for feeble minded youth.
Five on fish culture and game.

The duties of the committees on insane hospital, the deaf and dumb and blind asylum, and reform school and home for the friendless, shall be confined to a visit of the committee to the institutions herein named, and a report thereon to the senate during the seession, unless otherwise ordered by the senate.

Members to be Reported Present When on Committee Work.

50. All members of the senate shall be reported present by the secretary when absent on committee work, **except** when the "ayes and nays" are called. At such time, absentees shall be notified **to appear.**

Call of the House.

51. The call of the house shall be seconded by five members, and the proceedings under the call shall not be suspended unless all the members who are not excused are present, while five or more members object.

On Pairs.

52. **Whenever a** senator desires **to be** a absent he may make a pair **with** any senator who may agree to the same; the president of the senate to be notified **of such** pair.

RULES OF THE HOUSE OF REPRESENTATIVES.

OF THE DUTIES OF THE SPEAKER.

1. He shall take the chair every day precisely at the hour to which the house shall have adjourned on the preceding day; shall immediately call the members to order, and on the appearance of a quorum, shall cause the journal of the preceding day to be read.

2. He shall preserve order and decorum; may speak to points of order in preference to other members, rising from his seat for that purpose; and shall decide questions of order, subject to an appeal to the house by any two members, on which appeal no member shall speak more than once, unless by leave of the house.

3. He shall rise to put a question, but may state it sitting.

4. Questions shall be distinctly put in this form, to-wit: "As many as are of the opinion that (as the question may be), say, aye," and after the affirmative voice is expressed, "As many as are of the contrary opinion, say no." If the speaker doubts, or a division is called for, the house shall divide; those in the affirmative of the question shall first rise from their seats, and afterwards those in the negative.

5. The speaker shall examine and correct the journal before it is read. He shall have general direction of the hall, and permit no smoking therein. He shall have a right to name any member to perform the duties of the chair, but such substitutes shall not extend beyond the adjournment, and in case of absence of the speaker the chairman of the judiciary committee shall act as speaker.

6. All committees shall be appointed by the speaker unless otherwise especially directed by the house, in which case they shall be appointed by a *viva voce* vote; and if the number required shall not be elected by a majority of the votes given, the house shall proceed to a second vote in which a plurality of votes shall prevail; and in case a greater number than is required to compose or complete a committee shall have an equal number of votes, the house shall proceed to a further choice.

7. In all cases of election by the house, the speaker shall vote, and in other cases he shall vote when the yeas and nays are demanded, when the house is equally divided, or when his vote, if given to the minority, will make the division equal, and in case of equal division the question shall be lost.

8. In all cases where other than a member of the house shall be eligible to an office by the election of the house, there shall be a previous nomination.

9. All votes shall be taken *viva voce*.

10. All acts, memorials, and joint resolutions passed by the legislature shall be signed by the speaker in the presence of the house, while in session and capable of transacting business, and all writs, warrants, and subpœnas issued by order of the house shall be under his hand and seal attested by the clerk.

Who Admitted to the Privileges of the Floor.

11. No person shall be admitted into the hall of the house of representatives except the members and the officers of the senate, the judicial and state officers, the officers of the house, and such other persons as the house may deem proper to admit.

Order of Business.

12. Order of business of the day:
1. Prayer by the chaplain.
2. Roll call.
3. Reading the journal.
4. Petitions and memorials.
5. Reports of standing committees.
6. Reports of select committees.
7. Resolutions.
8. Introduction of bills.
9. Bills on first reading.
10. Bills on second reading.
11. Bills on third reading.
12. Bills not yet considered in the committee of the whole.
13. Special order of the day.
14. Unfinished business and messages on speaker's desk.
15. Miscellaneous business.

13. *Provided, however*, that after the reading of the journal each day, the house shall proceed with the regular orders, commencing in the order upon which it was last engaged at the time of adjournment of the preceding day, first disposing of the particular business of the order which may have been pending at adjournment, and as soon as the regular orders have been called through the call shall be resumed, commencing with the first order and proceeding in the same manner.

On Decorum and Debate.

14. When any member is about to speak in debate or deliver any matter to the house, he shall arise from his seat and respectfully address himself to "Mr. Speaker," and shall confine himself to the question under debate, and avoid personalities.

15. If a member be called to order for words spoken in debate, the person calling him to order shall repeat the words excepted to, and they shall be taken down in writing at the clerk's table; and no member shall be held to answer or subject to the censure of the house for words spoken in debate, if any member has spoken or other business intervened after the words spoken, and before exception to them shall have been taken.

No Member Shall Speak More Than Once Except—

16. No member shall speak more than once on the same question without leave of the house, except in explanation, unless he be the mover, or proposer, or introducer of the matter pending, in which case he shall be permitted to speak in reply, but not until every member choosing to speak shall have spoken.

17. If a question pending be lost by adjournment of the house and revived on the succeeding day, no member who shall have spoken on the preceding day shall be permitted again to speak without leave, except it be the mover, proposer, or introducer of the matter pending, who shall have the same right as in the last preceding rule.

No Member Without the bar Shall be Counted.

18. Upon a division and count of the house on any question, no member without the bar shall be counted.

Every Member Shall Vote Unless Excused.

19. Every member who shall be in the house when the question is put shall give his vote, unless the house, for special reasons, shall excuse him. All motions to excuse a member from voting shall be made before the

house divides, or before **the** yeas and nays are commenced; and any member requesting to **be excused** from voting may make a brief verbal statement of the reasons for making such request, and the question shall then be taken without further debate.

Motions to be stated by the speaker Before Being Debated.

20. When a **motion is made and seconded, it shall be stated by the** speaker, **or being in writing, shall be read aloud by** the clerk before being debated.

Every Motion to be Reduced to Writing.

21. Every motion shall be reduced **to** writing, if the speaker or **any** member desires it.

Motion may be Withdrawn by Consent.

22. After the motion is stated by the speaker, or read by the clerk, it shall be deemed in possession of the house, but may be withdrawn at any time before a decision **or amendment, by consent.**

The Order of Motions.

23. When a question is under debate, no motion shall be received but to adjourn, to lie **on** the table, for the previous question, to postpone indefinitely, to postpone to a day certain, to commit or amend; which several motions shall have precedence in the order in which they are arranged; and no motion to postpone to a day certain, to commit, or to postpone indefinitely, being decided, shall again be allowed on the same **day** at the same stage of the bill or proposition. A motion to **strike out the** enacting words of **a bill shall** have precedence of a motion **to amend, and** if carried, **is equivalent to its** rejection.

The Order of Commitment.

24. **When a resolution shall be** offered or a **motion made to refer any subject, and different committees proposed, the question shall be taken in the following order: The committee of the whole; a standing committee;** a select committee.

Motion to Adjourn Always in Order.

25. A motion to adjourn, a motion to fix **the day** to which the house shall adjourn, shall always be in order; these motions and a motion to lie on the table shall be decided without debate.

Hour of Adjournment to be Entered on Journal.

26. The hour at which every motion to adjourn is **made,** shall **be entered** on the journal.

The Previous Question.

27. The previous question shall be in this form: "Shall the debate now close?" It shall be admitted when demanded by five or more members **and** must be sustained by a majority vote, and until decided shall preclude further debate and all amendments and motions except one motion **to** adjourn and one motion to lie on the table.

No Debate on Previous Questions.

28. On a previous question there shall be no debate. All incidental questions of order, arising after a motion is made for the previous question, and pending such motion, shall be **decided,** whether on appeal or otherwise, **without debate.**

Any Member may Call for a Division of the Question.

29. Any member may call for a division of the question, which shall be divided if it comprehend propositions in substance so distinct, that one being taken away, a substantive proposition shall remain for the decision of the house. A motion **to** strike out and insert shall be deemed inadvis-

able; but a motion to strike out being lost, shall preclude **neither amend-ment** nor a motion, to strike out or insert.

Different Propositions Under Color of Amendment not Admissible.

30. No motion **or** proposition, or a subject different from **that** under consideration, shall be admitted under color of amendment. **No** bill **or** resolution shall at any time be amended by annexing thereto, or incorporating therewith, any other bill or resolution pending before the house.

On Reconsideration

31. When **a** motion has been once made and carried in the affirmative or negative, **it** shall be in order for any member of the majority to move a reconsideration thereof on the same or succeeding day; and such motion shall take precedence of all other questions except a motion **to** adjourn.

Reading of Papers Must Have Consent.

32. **When the reading of** a paper is called for, and the same **is objected to by any member, it** shall be determined by vote of the **house.**

Any two Members may Call for the Yeas and Nays.

33. Any two members may call for the yeas and nays upon any question and may demand a call of the house; a majority of the members present may compel the presence of all members subject to a call of the house.

Names of Members to be Called Alphabetically.

34. Upon a call of the house, or upon taking the yeas and nays upon any question, the names of the members shall be called alphabetically.

No Member to be Absent Without Leave.

35. No member shall absent himself from the service of the house, unless he have leave, or be sick, or unable to attend.

Call of the House.

36. Upon the call of the house, the names of the members shall be called over by the **clerk** and the absentees noted, after which the names of the absentees shall be again called over; the doors shall then be shut, and those for whom no excuse is made may, **by** order of those present, if five in number, be taken into custody, as they appear, or may be sent for and taken into **custody** wherever found, by the sergeant-at-arms or special messenger to be appointed for that purpose.

House May Remit Penalty.

37. **When** a person shall be discharged from custody and admitted to his seat the house shall determine whether such discharge shall be without paying fees; and in like manner, whether a delinquent member taken into custody by a special messenger shall or shall not be liable to defray the expenses of such messenger.

Sergeant-at-Arms.

38. **A** sergeant-at-arms shall be elected, to hold his office during the pleasure of the house, whose duty it shall be to attend the house during its sittings, to execute the commands of the house from time to time, together with all such process issued by authority thereof, as shall be directed to him by the speaker.

All Officers to be Sworn.

39. All officers shall be sworn to keep the secrets of the house.

Standing Committees.

40. Forty-two standing committees shall be appointed by the speaker, who shall name one member of each committee to be the chairman, and

said committee to consist of the following number of members, and to be known and designated by the following names:

Eleven on the judiciary.
Eleven on **finance, ways,** and means.
Seven on agriculture.
Seven on roads and bridges.
Nine on **militia.**
Thirteen on public lands and buildings.
Seven on internal improvements.
Seven on federal relations.
Nine on engrossed and enrolled bills.
Nine on accounts and expenditures.
Eleven on constitutional amendments.
Nine on county boundaries, county seats, and township organization.
Fifteen on railroads.
Eleven on privileges and elections.
Nine on state penitentiary.
Nine on insane hospital.
Nine on other asylums.
Seven on corporations.
Seven on library.
Nine on cities and towns.
Seven on banks and currency.
Seven on public schools.
Nine on university and normal schools.
Nine on public printing.
Seven **on mines and** minerals.
Eleven on immigration.
Seven on manufactures and commerce.
Nine on school lands and funds.
Seven on miscellaneous subjects.
Eleven on claims.
Nine on live stock and grazing interests.
Eleven on revenue and taxation.
The speaker and six on rules.
Thirteen on labor.
Fifteen on apportionment.
Seven **on** benevolent institutions.
Seven **on** fish culture and games.
Nine on insurance.
Nine on telegraph, telephone and electric companies.
Seven on medical societies, Sunday laws and regulations.
Nine on fees and salaries.
Seven on soldiers home.

41. The several **standing** committees of **the** house shall have leave to **report by bill or** otherwise.

On Bills.

42. Every bill shall be introduced on the report of the committee, or **by** any member, when the introduction **of** bills is for, or at any time by leave.

43. Every bill and concurrent resolution shall be read at large on three different days, and the bill and all amendments thereto shall be printed before the **vote** is taken upon its final passage.

44. Fvery **bill, joint and** concurrent resolution shall, upon its introduction, **be read the first** time. The question shall then be, "Shall the **bill be ordered to a** second **reading?" If not so** ordered it shall be deemed **equivalent to its rejection.**

45. **Upon the second** reading of **the** bill, the speaker **shall** state it as **ready for commitment or** engrossment; and if committed, then the question **shall be, whether to** a select or standing committee, or to a committee **of the whole house, if no motion** be made **to** commit, the question shall be stated **on its engrossment; and if not ordered** to be engrossed on the day **of its being reported, it shall** be placed on the general file on the speaker's **table to be taken up in** its order.

46. **Five hundred copies of every bill shall be printed, after a second reading, unless otherwise** ordered; and all bills. **resolutions, and** memorials that **shall be printed, shall** remain at least one day on the files after being printed, **before being considered.**

47. After **commitment and report thereof** the house, or any time before **a** bill **is ordered to a third** reading, it **may be** recommitted,

48. After **a bill shall have been ordered** to a third reading, five hundred copies of **the amendments thereto shall** be printed, unless the house orders the entire bill **printed as amended, and no amendments thereto shall be afterwards allowed.**

49. All bills **ordered to be engrossed shall** be executed in a fair, round **hand.**

50. Upon the passage of every bill **or** joint resolution, the vote shall be **yea or** nay, and this rule shall not be suspended.

51. The question after the third reading of every bill shall be stated as follows: "This bill having been read at large on three different days, and **the same, with all its** amendments, having been printed, the question is **'Shall the bill pass!' "**

Message to the Senate.

52. All messages from **the house to the senate shall be transmitted by** the clerk or assistant clerk of **the house, or by** a special **committee appointed** for that purpose.

Rules, how Changed.

53. No standing rule or order of the house **shall** be rescinded, changed or suspended, except **by a vote of at** least a majority of the members elected; nor shall the order **of** business, as established by the rules of **the house, be** postponed or changed, except by a vote of at least a majority of the members elected.

A Privileged Committee.

54. It shall **be in** order for the committee on engrossed and enrolled bills to report **at any** time.

Cushing's Manual shall Govern Except—

55. **The rules of** parliamentary practice comprised **in** Cushing's Manual shall govern the house in all cases to which they are applicable, and in which they are not inconsistent with standing rules and orders of the house, and the joint rules of the senate and house of representatives.

Reconsideration.

56. No bill or question which has been **once passed** or rejected shall be

called up for reconsideration during the same session, unless two-thirds of the house shall be in favor of taking the same.

General Laws Take Precedence.

57. **All bills for general** laws shall take **precedence on the speaker's** table **to local bills and** special enactments.

Emergency Clause.

58, When an emergency is expressed in the preamble or body of an act **as a** reason why such act should take effect prior to the expiration of the three caleuder months **after** the adjournment of the session at which it passed, the question shall be, "Shall the bill pass?" and if decided affirmatively by a vote of two-thirds of all the members elected to the house, then the bill shall be deemed passed; but if, upon such vote, a majority of less than two-thirds of said members vote affirmatively on said question then the vote on said bill shall be deemed reconsidered, and the bill subject to amendment by striking out such part thereof **as expresses an emergency** and the time of taking effect, **and then said** bill shall be under consideration **upon** its third reading, **with an** emergency clause and the **time of taking effect** stricken out.

Committees Entitled to Clerks.

59. There shall be a clerk to each of the following committees, who shall **be** appointed and removed by the chairman of the committee:

Committe on judiciary.
Committee on finance, ways and means.
Committee on railroads.
Committee on public lands and buildings.
Committee ou engrossed and enrolled bills.
Committee ou clains.

Hours For Convening.

60. The **hours** for convening shall be 10 o'clock A. M. and 2 o'clock P. M. each day, unless otherwise specially ordered.

Changes.

The house in 1897 made the following changes:
Rule 19 to read as follows :
19, Every member who shall be in the house when the question is put shall give his vote.
Rule 44 to read as follows:
44. Every bill, joint and concurrent resolution shall, upon its first introduction, be read the first time.
Rule 45 was amended by striking out **the words** "select or" between the words "a" and "standing."
Rule 53 was amended by striking out all after **the word "members"** at **the end of second line.**
Rule 59 was amended by striking out "Committee on Railroads," and **"Committee on Public Lands** and Buildings," and inserting "Committee **on Accounts** and Expenditures," and "Committee on Privileges and Elections."
Rule 61 was stricken out.

JOINT RULES OF THE SENATE AND HOUSE OF REPRESENTATIVES.

Conference Committees.

1.   In every case of an amendment of a bill agreed to in one house and dissented to in the other, if either house shall request a conference, and appoint a committee for that purpose, and the other house shall appoint a committee to confer, such committee shall, at a convenient hour, to be agreed upon by their chairman, meet and state to each other verbally, or in writing, as either shall choose, the reasons of their respective houses for and against the amendment, and confer freely thereon.

Messages from the Senate.

2.   When a message shall be sent from the senate to the house of representatives, it shall be announced at the door of the house by the sergeant-at-arms, and shall be respectfully communicated to the chair by the person by whom it may be sent.

Messages to the Senate.

3.   The same ceremony shall be observed when a message shall be sent from the house of representatives to the senate.

When Messages may be Transmitted.

4.   Messages may be transmitted from one house to the other at any time while the house to which the message is sent is in session; provided neither house shall have adjourned for a longer period than one day.

All Bills Shall be Signed.

5.   All bills shall be signed by the secretary or chief clerk of the house in which they originated, before the transmission to the other house.

Bills that have Passed to be Enrolled.

6.   After a bill shall have passed both houses, it shall be duly enrolled by the enrolling clerk or of the house in which it orignated, before it shall be presented to the governor.

Duty of Joint Committee on Enrolled Bills.

7.   When a bill is duly enrolled, it shall be examined by the committees of the two houses on enrolled bills, acting jointly, who shall carefully compare the enrolled bill with the engrossed bill as passed by the two houses. Said commitee shall correct any errors that may be discovered in the enrolled bill, and make their report forthwith to their respective houses.

8.   After examination and report each bill shall be signed in their respective house, first by the speaker of the house of representatives, then by the president of the senate, there being endorsed on the roll a certificate of the secretary or chief clerk of the house in which the same originated.

9.   After a bill shall have thus been signed in each house, it shall be presented by said committee to the governor for his approval, and the said committee shall report the day of presentation to the governor, which time shall be carefully entered on the journal of each house.

10.   All orders, resolutions, and votes which are to be presented to the governor for his approval, shall also, in the same manner, be enrolled, ex-

amined, and signed, **and** shall be presented in the **same manner** and by the same committee **as** provided in the case of bills

Joint Address to the Governor.

11. **When the** senate and house of representatives shall **judge it proper to** make **a joint** address to the governor, it shall be presented **to him by the** president **of the** senate, in the presence of the **speaker** and both houses.

A Measure once Rejected in one House can be renewed by a two-thirds Vote.

12. **When a** bill or resolution, which has been **passed in** one house, **shall** be rejected in the other, it shall not be brought in during the same session, without leave of two-thirds of **that** house within which **it shall** be renewed.

Each House shall Transmit Papers when Demanded.

13. Each house shall transmit to the other, in case they are demanded, all papers on **which any** bill or resolution shall be founded.

Each House to give Notice to the Other.

14. When a bill or resolution, which has been passed in one house, **shall be rejected** in the other, notice thereof shall be given **to the house** in which the same originated; and after each house shall have adhered to its disagreement, a bill or resolution shall be lost.

Joint Convention.

15. Whenever there shall be a joint convention **of the two** houses the proceedings shall be entered at length on the journal of each house. The president of the senate shall preside over such joint convention, and **the secretary of the senate** shall act as clerk thereof, assisted by the chief clerk of the house.

No Adjournment Longer than Three Days.

16. **Neither house** shall adjourn during any session thereof, without the consent of the other, for a longer period than three days.

Call of the House.

17. A call of the house may be made when in joint session on motion seconded by five members, and the proceedings under the call shall not be suspended while **five members object, unless** all members are present who **are** not excussed

APPORTIONMENT.

CONGRESSIONAL DISTRICTS.

FIRST DISTRICT.

Consists of the counties of Cass, Otoe, Nemaha, Richardson, Pawnee, Johnson, and **Lancaster.**

SECOND DISTRICT.

Consists of the counties of Sarpy, Douglas, and Washington.

THIRD DISTRICT.

Consists of the counties of Burt, Thurston, Dakota, Dixon, Cuming, Dodge, **Colfax,** Stanton, Wayne, Cedar, Knox, Pierce, **Madison, Platte,** Nance, Boone, Antelope, and **Merrick.**

FOURTH DISTRICT.

Consists of the counties of Saunders, Butler, Seward, Saline, Gage, Jefferson, Thayer, Fillmore, York, Polk and Hamilton.

FIFTH DISTRICT.

Consist of the counties of Hall, **Adams, Webster, Franklin, Kearney,** Phelps, Harlan, **Gosper,** Furnas, Red **Willow, Frontier, Hitchcock, Hayes,** Perkins, Chase, Dundy, Nuckolls **and Clay,**

SIXTH DISTRICT.

Consists of the counties of Sioux, Scotts Bluff, Banner, Kimball, Dawes, Box Butte, Cheyenne, Sheridan, Deuel, Cherry, Grant, Arthur, Keith, Lincoln, McPherson, Hooker, Thomas, Logan, Dawson, Custer, Blaine, **Brown,** Keya Paha, Rock, Loup, **Holt,** Garfield, Valley, Sherman, Buffalo, Harvard, Greely, Wheeler and Boyd.

SENATORIAL DISTRICTS.

FIRST DISTRICT.

Consists **of the counties** of Richardson and Pawnee and are entitled to one senator.

SECOND DISTRICT.

Consists of the counties of Nemaha and Johnson and are entitled to one **senator.**

THIRD DISTRICT

Consists of the county of Otoe and is entitled to one senator.

FOURTH **DISTRICT.**

Consists **of the** county of Cass and **is** entitled to one senator.

FIFTH DISTRICT.

Consists of the counties of Saunders and Sarpy and are entitled to one senator.

SIXTH DISTRICT.

Consists of the county of Douglas and is entitled to three senator.

SEVENTH DISTRICT.

Consists of the **counties** of Cuming **and** Burt and are entitled to one senator.

EIGHTH DISTRICT.

Consists of the **counties** of Dixon, Dakota, **Knox, Cedar, and, Thurston** and are entitled **to one** senator.

NINTH DISTRICT.

Consists **of the** counties of Antelope, **Boone,** and Greeley **and are entitled to one senator.**

TENTH DISTRICT.

Consists of the counties of Washington and Dodge **and are entitled to one senator.**

ELEVENTH DISTRICT.

Consists of the counties of Wayne, Stanton, Madison, and Pierce and are entitled to one senator.

TWELFTH DISTRICT.

Consists of the counties of Platte and Colfax and **are** entitled to one senator.

THIRTEENTH **DISTRICT.**

Consists of the counties of Holt, Garfield, Wheeler, and the **unorganized territory north of Holt** and Keya Paha **and be entitled** to one senator.

FOURTEENTH DISTRICT.

Consists **of the** counties of Brown, Keya Paha, Cherry, Sheridan, **Dawes** Box Butte, **and Sioux** and is entitled to one senator.

FIFTEENTH DISTRICT.

Consists **of the** counties of **Custer, Valley, Loup, and Blaine and are entitle to one senator.**

SIXTEENTH DISTRICT.

Consists of the counties of Buffalo **and Sherman and** are entitled to one senator.

SEVENTEENTH DISTRICT.

Consists of the counties of Hall and Howard and are entitled to one senator.

EIGHTEENTH DISTRICT.

Consists of the counties of Polk, Merrick, and Nance and are entitled to one senator.

NINETEENTH **DISTRICT.**

Consists of the counties of Butler and **Seward** and are entitled to one senator.

TWENTIETH DISTRICT.

Consists of the county **of Lancaster and are** entitled to two senators.

TWENTY-FIRST DISTRICT.

Consists of the county **of Gage** and is entitled to one senator.

TWENTY-SECOND DISTRICT.

Consists of the **county of** Saline and is **entitled** to one senator.

TWENTY-THIRD DISTRICT.

Consists of the counties **of** Jefferson and Thayer and are entitled to one senator.

TWENTY-FOURTH DISTRICT.

Consists of the counties of York and Fillmore and are entitled to one senator.

TWENTY-FIFTH DISTRICT.

Consists of the counties of Clay and Hamilton and is entitled to **one senator.**

TWENTY-SIXTH DISTRICT

Consists of the counties of Nuckolls, Webster, and Franklin and is entitled to one senator.

TWENTY-SEVENTH DISTRICT.

Consists of the county of Adams and is entitled to one senator.

TWENTY-EIGHTH DISTRICT.

Consists of the counties of Kearney, Phelps, **and Harlan** and is entitled **to one senator.**

TWENTY-NINTH DISTRICT.

Consists of the counties of Furnas, Red Willow- Hitchcock Dundy, Gosper, Frontier, Chase and Hayes and is entitled to **one senator.**

THIRTIETH DISTRICT.

Consists of the counties of Dawson, Lincoln, Keith, Cheyenne, Logan, and the unorganized territory west of Blaine and Logan and is entitled to one senator.

REPRESENSATIVE **DISTRICTS.**

FIRST DISTRICT.

Consists of the counties of Richardson and is entitled to three representatives.

SECOND DISTRICT.

Consists of the county of Pawnee and is entitled to two representatives.

THIRD DISTRICTS.

Consists of the county of Nemaha and is entitled to two representatives.

FOURTH DISTRICT.

Consists of the county of Johnson and **is entitled to one** representative.

FIFTH DISTRICT.

Consists of the counties of Nemaha and Johnson and is entitled to one representative.

SIXTH DISTRICT.

Consists of the county of Otoe and is entitled to two representatives.

SEVENTH DISTRICT.

Consists of the county of Cass and is entitled to two representatives.

EIGHTH DISTRICT.

Consists of the counties of Cass and Otoe and is entitled to one representative.

NINTH DISTRICT.

Consists of the county of Sarpy and is entitled to one representative.

TENTH DISTRICT.

Consists of the county of Douglas and is entitled to nine representatives.

ELEVENTH DISTRICT.

Consists of the county **of** Washington and is entitled to one representative.

TWELFTH DISTRICT.
Consists of the county of Burt and is entitled to one representative.

THIRTEENTH DISTRICT.
Consists of the counties of Burt and Washington and is entitled to one representative.

FOURTEENTH DISTRICT.
Consists of the county of Dodge and is entitled to two representatives

FIFTEENTH DISTRICT.
Consists of the county of Cuming and is entitled to one representative.

SIXTEENTH DISTRICT.
Consists of the counties of Cuming, Dakota and Thurston and are entitled to one representative.

SEVENTEENTH DISTRICT.
Consists of the counties of Wayne and Stanton and is entitled to one representative.

EIGHTEENTH DISTRICT.
Consists of the county of Dixon and is entitled to one representative.

NINETEENTH DISTRICT.
Consists of the counties of Cedar and Pierce and is entitled to one representative.

TWENTIETH DISTRICT.
Consists of the county of Knox and is entitled to one representative.

TWENTY-FIRST DISTRICT.
Consists of the county of Antelope and is entitled to one representative.

TWENTY-SECOND DISTRICT.
Consists of the county of Boone and is entitled to one representative.

TWENTY-THIRD DISTRICT.
Consists of the county of Madison and is entitled to one representative.

TWENTY-FOURTH DISTRICT.
Consists of the county of Platte and is entitled to one representative.

TWENTY-FIFTH DISTRICT.
Consists of the counties of Platte and Nance and is entitled to one representative.

TWENTY-SIXTH DISTRICT.
Consists of the county of Colfax and is entitled to one representative.

TWENTY-SEVENTH DISRTICT.
Consists of the county of Saunders and is entitled to two representatives.

TWENTY-EIGHTH DISTRICT.
Consists of the county of Butler and is entitled to two representatives.

TWENTY-NINTH DISTRICT.
Consists of the county of Seward and is entitled to two representatives

THIRTIETH DISTRICT.
Consists of the county of Lancaster and is entitled to five representatives.

THIRTY-FIRST DISTRICT.

Consists of the county of Saline and is entitled to two representatives,

THIRTY-SECOND DISTRICT.

Consists of the county of Gage and is entitled to three representatives

THIRTY-THIRD DISTRICT.

Consists of the counties of Gage and Saline and are entitled to one representative.

THIRTY-FOURTH DISTRICT.

Consists of the county of Jefferson and is entitled to one representative.

THIRTY-FIFTH DISTRICT.

Consists of the county of Thayer and is entitled to one representative.

THIRTY-SIXTH DISTRICT.

Consists of the counties of Thayer and Jefferson and are entitled to one representative.

THIRTY-SEVENTH DISTRICT.

Consists of the county of Fillmore and is entitled to two representatives.

THIRTY-EIGHTH DISTRICT.

Consists of the county of York and is entitled to two representatives.

THIRTY-NINTH DISTRICT.

Consists of the county of Polk and is entitled to one representative.

FORTIETH DISTRICT.

Consists of the county of Merrick and is entitled to one representative.

FORTY-FIRST DISTRICT.

Consists of the county of Hamilton and is entitled to two representatives.

FORTY-SECOND DISTRICT.

Consists of the county of Clay and is entitled to two representatives.

FORTY-THIRD DISTRICT.

Consists of the county of Nuckolls and is entitled to one representative.

FORTY-FOURTH DISTRICT.

Consists of the county of Webster and is entitled to one representative

FORTY-FIFTH DISTRICT.

Consists of the county of Adams and is entitled to one representative.

FORTY-SIXTH DISTRICT.

Consists of the counties of Webster and Adams and is entitled to one representative.

FORTY-SEVENTH DISTRICT.

Consists of the county of Hall and is entitled to two representatives.

FORTY-EIGHTH DISTRICT.

Consists of the county of Howard and is entitled to one representative.

FORTY-NINTH DISTRICT.

Consists of the counties of Garfield, Greely, Wheeler, Loup, and Blaine and the unorganized territory west of Blaine and is entitled to one representative.

FIFTIETH DISTRICT.

Consists of the **county** of Holt and is entitled to two representatives.

FIFTY-FIRST DISTRICT.

Consists of **the** county of Brown and is entitled to one representative.

FIFTY-SECOND DISTRICT .

Consists of the counties of Cherry and **Keya** Paha and is **entitled to** one representative.

FIFTY-THIRD DISTRICT.

Consists of the counties of Sheridan, **Dawes,** Box Bute, and Sioux and **is** entitled to one representative.

FIFTY-FOURTH DISTRICT.

Consists of the counties of Lincoln, Cheyenne, and Keith and the unorganized territory west of Logan **and** is entitled **to** one representative.

FIFTY-FIFTH DISTRICT.

Consists of the county of Valley and is entitled to one representative.

FIFTY-SIXTH DISTRICT.

Consists of the counties of Custer and Logan and are entitled to two representatives.

FIFTY-SEVENTH DISTRICT.

Consists of the county of Sherman and is entitled **to one representative.**

FIFTY-EIGHTH DISTRICT.

Consists of the county **of** Buffalo and is entitled to two representatives.

FIFTY-NINTH DISTRICT.

Consists **of the county of** Dawson and **is** entitled to one representative.

SIXTIETH DISTRICT.

Consists of the county of Kearney and is entitled to one representative.

SIXTY-FIRST DISTRICT.

Consists of the county of Franklin and is entitled to one representative.

SIXTY-SECOND DISTRICT.

Consists of the county of Harlan and is entitled to one representative.

SIXTY-THIRD **DISTRICT.**

Consists of the county of Phelps **and is** entitled to one representative.

SIXTY-**FOURTH** DISTRICT.

Consists of the county of Furnas and is entitled to one representative.

SIXTY-FIFTH DISTRICT.

Consists of the county of Red Willow and **is** entitled **to one** representative.

SIXTY-SIXTH DISTRICT

Consists of the counties of Frontier and **Gosper** and is **entitled** to one Representative.

SIXTY-SEVENTH DISTRICT.

Consists of the counties **of** Hitchcock, Dundy, Hayes, and Chase, and are entitled to one representative.

STATE AND TERRITORIAL GOVERNMENT.

SENATORS FROM NEBRASKA SINCE THE ADMISSION OF THE STATE INTO THE UNION.

John M. Thayer............ 1867-71	Alvin Saunders.............**1877-83**
Thomas W. Tipton.........1867-75	C. H. Van Wyck.............1881-87
Phineas W. Hitchcock......1871-77	Chas. F. Manderson..........1883-95
Algernon S. Paddock...... 1875-81	Algernon S. Paddock.......1887-93
William **V.** Allen..............1893-1899	John M. Thurston............1895-1901

DELEGATES TO CONGRESS FROM THE TERRITORY OF NE-
BRASKA.

Napoleon B. Gidding..Dec. 12, 1854	Experience Estabrook.Oct. 11, 1859
Bird B. Chapman.......Nov. 6, 1855	Samuel G. Daily.........Oct. 9, 1860
Fenner Ferguson.......Aug. 3. 1857	Phineas W. Hitchcock.Oct. 11, 1864

REPRESENTATIVES TO CONGRESS SINCE THE ADMISSION
OF THE STATE INTO THE UNION.

XXXX Congress, 1865-67.
T. M. Marquett.
    XL Congress, 1867-69.
John Taffe.
    XLI Congress, 1869-71.
John Taffe.
    XLII Congress, 1871-73.
John Taffe.
    XLIII Congress, **1873-75.**
Lorenzo Crounse.
    XLIV Congress, 1875-77.
Lorenzo Crounse.
    XLV Congress, 1877-79
Frank Welch.
Thos. J. Majors [to fill vacancy.]
    XLVI Congress, 1879-81.
E. K. Valentine.
    XLVII Congress, 1881-83.
E. K. Valentine.
    XLVIII Congress, 1883-85.
First District..........A. J. Weaver
Second District.......James Laird
Third District......E. K. Valentine

XLIX Congress, 1885-87.
First District.........A. J. Weaver
Second District.......James Laird
Third District...Geo. W. E. Dorsey
    L Congress, 1887-89.
First District....John A. McShane
Second District........James Laird
Third District...Geo. W. E. Dorsey
    LI Congress, 1889-91.
First District.........W. J. Connell
Second District.......James Laird
          Gilbert L. Laws*
Third District. Geo. W. E. Dorsey
    LII Congress, 1891-93.
First District..........W. J. Bryan
Second District..W. A. McKeighan
Third District......... O. M. Kem
    LIII Congress. 1893-95
First District..........W. J. Bryan
Second District.......H. D Mercer
Third District.....Geo. Meiklejohn
Fourth District.......E. J. Hainer
Fifth District....**W. A.** McKeighan
Sixth District...........O. M. Kem

*To fill vacancy caused by the death of Congressman Laird.

OFFICERS OF THE TERRITORY AND STATE OF NEBRASKA
SINCE ITS ORGANIZATION.

GOVERNORS

Francis Burt (a)...... .Oct. 16, 1854	Silas Garber............Jan. 11, 1875
Mark W. Izard.........Feb. 20, 1855	Albinus Nance......... Jan. 9, 1879
W. A. Richardson (b)...Jan. 12, 1858	James W. Dawes........Jan. 4, 1883
Samuel W. Black.......May 2, 1858	John M. Thayer..........Jan. 6, 1887
Alvin Saunders........May 15, 1861	James E. Boyd.........Jan. 8, 1891
David Butler (c)........Feb. 21, 1867	Lorenzo Crounse.......Jan. 13, 1893
Robert W. Furnas.....Jan. 13, 1873	Silas A. Holcomb...........Jan. 3, 1895

LIEUTENANT GOVERNORS.

Othman A. Abbott..... Jan. 4, 1877	H. H. Shedd............Jan. 8, 1885
Edmund C. Carns.......Jan. 9, 1879	Geo. D. Meiklejohn....Jan. 3, 1889
A. W. Agee..............Jan. 4, 1883	Thomas J. Majors......Jan. 6, 1891

SECRETARIES OF STATE.

Thos. B. Cuming (e)...Aug. 13, 1854	Bruno Tzschuck........**Jan.** 11, 1876
John B. Motley (f)...March 23, 1858	S. J. Alexander..........**Jan.** 9, 1879
J. Sterling Morton (g)..July 12, 1858	Edward P. Roggen......**San.** 4, 1883
Alg. S. Paddock (h).... May 6, 1861	Gilbert L. Laws...... ..**Jan.** 6, 1887
Thos. P. Kennard......Feb. 21, 1867	Ben. **R.** Cowdery (k)...**Nov. 20,** 1889
Wm. H. James (i)......Jan. 10, 1871	John **C. Allen**..........**Jan. 8,** 1891
John J. Gosper........Jan. 13, 1873	

AUDITORS.

Charles B. Smith... .**March 16,** 1855	Jefferson B. Weston...Jan. 13, **1873**
Samuel L. Campbell...Aug. 3. 1857	F. W. Liedtke............Jan. 9, 1879
William E. Moore......June 1, 1858	John Wallichs.........Nov. 12, 1880
Robert C. Jordan........Aug. 2, 1858	H. A. Babcock..........Jan. 8. 1885
William E. Harvey......Oct. 8, 1861	Thos. H. Benton........Jan. 3, 1889
John Gillespie..........Oct. 10, 1865	Eugene Moore..........Jan. 13, 1893

TREASURERS.

B. **P.** Rankin........March 16, 1855	Geo. M. Bartlett........**Jan. 9, 1879**
Wm. W.Wyman........Nov. 6, 1855	Phelps D. Sturdevant...**Jan. 4, 1883**
Augustus Kountze......Oct. 8, 1861	Charles H. Willard......**Jan. 8. 1885**
James **Sweet**.........Jan. 11, 1869	John E. Hill............**Jan. 3, 1889**
Henry A. Koenig......Jan. 10, 1871	**Joseph** S. Bartley......**Jan. 13. 1893**
J. C. McBride..........Jan. 11, 1875	

ATTORNEY GENERALS.

Champion **S. Chase**............1867	C. J. Dilworth..........**Jan. 9,** 1879
Seth Robinson..................1869	Isaac Powers, Jr.......**Jan. 4,** 1883
Geo. H. Roberts........**Jan.** 10, 1871	William Leese........ ..**Jan. 8,** 1885
J. R. Webster..........**Jan.** 13, 1873	George H. Hastings (b)..**Jan. 8,** 1891
Geo. H. Roberts........**Jan.** 11, 1875	

SUPERINTENDENTS OF PUBLIC INSTRUCTION.

Seth W. Beals.................1869	W. W. W. Jones..........Jan 6, 1881
J. M. McKenzie........**Jan.** 10, 1871	Geo. B. Lane.............Jan. 6, 1887
S. R. Thompson........**Jan.** 4, 1877	A. K. Goudy ....Jan. 8, 1891

COMMISSIONERS OF PUBLIC LANDS AND BUILDINGS.

F. M. Davis............Jan. 4, 1877	John Steen.............**Jan. 3, 1889**
A. G. Kendall..........Jan. 6, 1881	A. R. Humphrey ....**Jan. 8, 1891**
Joseph Scott..........Jan. 8, 1885	

(a) Died Oct. 18, 1854, the office being **filled by T. B.** Cuming, Secretary, until the appointment of Gov. Izard.

(b) Resigned, the office being **filled by** J. Sterling Morton until the arrival of Gov. Black.

(c) **Elected in** 1866, but did not enter upon the duties **of the** office **until** the admission of the state into the Union, in Feb., 1867. Re-elected **Oct.** 8, 1868. **Re-elected Oct.** 18, 1870. Succeeded **June 2,** 1871, by W. H. James, Secretary of State, until the inauguration of Gov. Furnas.

(e) Acting Governor from Oct. 18, 1854, to Feb. **20, 1855,** and from Oct. 25, 1857, to Jan. **12, 1858. Died** March 12, 1858.

(f) Acting Secretary until the arrival of Secretary J. Sterling Morton.

(g) Acting Gov. from Dec. 5, 1858, to May 2, 1859, and from Feb. 24, 1860, to 1861.

(h) Acting governor from May 15, 1861, and during the greater portion of the period to 1867. U. S. Senator from 1875 to 1881.

(i) Acting Governor until Jan. 13, 1873.

(k) Appointed by Gov. Thayer to fill vacancy caused by **resignation of** Gilbert L. Laws.

JUDGES SUPREME COURT—CHIEF JUSTICES.

Fenner Ferguson.......Oct. 12, 1854 | Daniel Gantt (a) ....Jan. 1, **1872**
Augustus Hall.......March 15, 1858 | Samuel Maxwell......May 29, **1878**
William Pitt Kellogg..May 27, 1861 | George B. Lake..........Jan. 5, **1888**
William Kellogg.......May 8, 1865 | Amasa Cobb............Jan. 3, 1884
William A. Little (a)...........1866 | Samuel Maxwell.......Jan. 4, 1886
Oliver P. Mason................1866 | M. B. Reese... ....Jan. 1888
George B. Lake........**Jan. 16**, 1873 | Amasa Cobb..................1890

Samuel Maxwell, 1892,

ASSOCIATE JUSTICES AND JUDGES.

Edward R. Harden.. ..Dec. 4, 1854 | Lorenzo Crounse.......Feb. 21, 1867
James Bradley. ....Oct. 25, 1854 | Daniel Gantt ....**Jan.** 16 1873
Samuel W. Black................ | Samuel Maxwell.......**Jan.** 16, 1873
Eleazer Wakely......April 22, 1857 | Amasa Cobb............**May** 29, 1878
Joseph Miller.... .....April 9, 1859 | M. B. Reese..........**Jan.** 3, 1884
William F. Lockwood..May 16, 1861 | T. L. **Norval**............**Jan.** 1890
Elmer S. Dundy......June 22, 1863 | A. M. **Post**...............**Jan.** 1892
George B. Lake........Feb. 21, 1867 |

CLERKS OF THE SUPREME COURT.

H. C. Anderson...... ....1856 | William Kellogg, Jr........ 1865
Charles L. Salisbury.......... 1858 | George Armstrong.............1867
E. B. Chandler..................1859 | Guy A. Brown (a).......Aug. 8, 1868
John H. Kellom..............1861 | D. A. Campbell.......July 14, 1890

REPORTERS OF THE SUPREME COURT.

J. M. Woolworth.............1878 | Guy A. Brown (a)..............1875
Lorenzo Crounse..............1873 | D. A. Campbell................1890

LIBRARIANS.

James S. Izard......March 16, 1855 | Thos. P. Kennard.....June 22, 1867
H. C. Anderson........Nov. 6, 1855 | Wm. H. Jones..........Jan. 10, 1871
John H. Kellon....... Aug 3, 1857 | Guy A. Brown.... .....March 3, 1871
Alonzo D. Luce........Nov. 7, 1859 | D. A. Campbell...... July 14. 1891
Robert S. Knox... ....1861 |

(a) Died in office.

PRESIDENTS

Of the Territorial Council.

JOSEPH L. SHARP................(1st Session,) 1855
B. R. FOLSOM ....(2d Session,)......................... 1855
L. L. BOWEN....................(3d Session,)...... 1857
GEORGE L. MILLER............(4th Session,)......................1857
L. L. BOWEN ....(5th Session,)......................1858
E. A. DONELAN.................(6th Session,)......................1859
W. H. TAYLOR..................(7th Session,) 1860
JOHN TAFFE.. ....(8th Session,)......................1861
E. A. ALLEN....................(9th Session,)......................1864
O. P. MASON...................(11th Session,)......................1866
E. H. ROGERS................(12th Session,)......................1867

PRESIDENTS

Of the Senate of the State of Nebraska.

FRANK WELSH..................1st Session,......................1866
E. H. ROGERS...................2d Session,......................1867
E. H. ROGERS...................3d Session,.... 1867
E. H. ROGERS......... ....4th Session,......................1868
E. B. TAYLOR..... ....5th Session,......................1869
E. B. TAYLOR.............. ......6th Session,......................1870

E. B. TAYLOR......................7th **Session,**......................1870
E. E. CUNNINGHAM............8th Session,........ 1871
W. A. GWYER......................9th Session,......................1873
W. A. GWYER..................10th Session,......................1873
N. K. GRIGGS.............11th Sessson,......................1875
GUY C. BARTON............12th Session,......................1876
GUY C. BARTON...........13th Session,......................1876

SPEAKERS
Of the Territorial House of Representatives.

ANDREW J. HANSCOM..............1st Session,......................1855
P. C. SULLIVAN...................2d Session,...... 1855
L. L. GIBBS... ....3rd Session,......................1857
J. H. DECKER.....................4th Session,...... 1857
H. P. BENNET...................5th Session,......................1858
S. A. STRICKLAND..................6th Session,......................1859
HENRY W. DE PUY,...............7th Session,...... 1860
A. D. JONES.....................8th Session,......................1861
Geo. B. LAKE...........9th Session,......................1861
S. M. KIRKPATRICK............10th Session,......................1865
JAMES G. MEGEATH.............11th Session,......................1866
W. P. CHAPIN....................12 Session,......................1865

SPEAKERS
Of the House of Representatives of the State of Nebraska.

W. F CHAPIN............1st, 2d, 3d, and 4th Sessions............1867-68-69
W. McLENNAN..............5th, 6th and 7th Session.............1868-69-70
HON. GEORGE W. COLLINS...1871
HON. M. SESSIONS...1873
HON. EDWARD S. TOWLE..1875
HON. ALBINUS NANCE...1877
HON. C. P. MATHEWSON..1879
HON. H. H. SHEDD 1881
HON. GEO. M. HUMPHREY..1883
HON. ALLEN W. FIELD..1885
HON. N. V. HARLAN..1887
HON. JOHN C. WATSON.............. 1889
HON. S. M. ELDER..1891
HON. J. N. GAFFIN...1893

CHIEF CLERKS
Of the Territorial Council.

G. L. MILLER.......................1st Session,......................1855
E. G. MCNEELEY...................2d Session,...... 1855
O. F. LAKE.....................3d Session,......................1857
WASHBURN SAFFORD.............4th Session,......................1857
S. M. CURRAN.....................5th Session, ...1858
S. M. CURRAN............. ......6th Session, ...1859
E. P. BREWSTER.. ....7th **Session,**......................1860
R. W. FURNAS....................8th Session,......................1861
J. W. HOLLINGSHEAD...... ....9th **Session,**......................1864
JOHN L. BOWEN.................10th Session,......................1865
WM. E. HARVEY....... ....11th Session,......................1866
O. B. HEWETT.................12th Session,......................1867

SECRETARIES
Of the Senate of the State of Nebraska.

C. E. YOST...........................1st Session,...... 1866
O. B. HEWETT.....................2d Session,............................1867
I. L. HOLBROCK...................3rd Session,...........................1867
L. L. HOLBROCK..................4th Session,............................1868
SAMUEL M. CHAPMAN........... ...5th Session,...... 1867
SAMUEL M. CHAPMAN..............6th Session,.........................1879
SAMUEL M. CHAPMAN..............7th Session,.........................1870
C. H. WALKER.....................8th Session,.........................1871
D. H. WHEELER...................9th Session,.........................1873
D. H. WHEELER............. ...10th Session,.........................1873
D. H. WHEELER..................11th Session,.. 1875
D. H. WHEELER..................12th Session,.........................1876
D. H. WHEELER..................13th Session,...... 1876
D. H. WHEELER..................14th Session,.........................1877
SHERWOOD BURR.................15th Session,.................. 1879
SHERWOOD BURR.................16th Session,.........................1881
SHERWOOD BURR.................17th Session,...... 1882
GEO. L. BROWN....................18th Session,. 1883
SHERWOOD BURR.................19th Session,.........................1885
WALT M. SEELEY.................20th Session,.. 1887
WALT M. SEELEY.................21st Session,...... 1889
C. H. PIRTLE.....................22d Session,...........................1891
H. A. EDWARDS...................23d Session,...........................1893

CHIEF CLERKS
Of the Territorial House of Representatives.

JOSEPH W. PADDOCK..............1st Session,...........................1855
I. L. GIBBS..........................2d Session,.......................1855
J. H. BROWN........................3d Session,..........................1857
S. M. CURRAN.......... ....4th Session,..........................1857
E. A. MCNEELEY... ... .5th Session,...... 1858
JAMES W. MOORE..................6th Session,.. 1859
GEORGE L. SEYBOLT.... ....7th Session,........................1859
GEORGE L. SEYBOLD.............8th Session,........................1861
RIENZI STREETER................9th Session,..........................1864
JOHN TAFFE.....................10th Session,.........................1865
GEORGE MAY....................11th Session,..........................1866
J. S. BOWEN...................12th Session,.........................1867

CHIEF CLERKS
Of the House of Representatives of the State of Nebraska.

J. S. BOWEN.............1st, 2d, 3d, 4th and 5th Sessions.........1867-68-69
C. H. WALKER...............6th and 7th Sessions.......................1870
F. M. MCDONAH...................................... 1871
LOUIS E. CROSPSEY................................... 1871
I. W. ELLER..1873
GEORGE L. BROWN............................. 1875
B. D. SLAUGHTER...1877
B. D. SLAUGHTER...... 1879
B. D. SLAUGHTER..1881
B. D. SLAUGHTER...... 1883

James F. Zeidker...1885
B. D. Slaughter..1887
B. D. Slaughter...................... 1889
Eric Johnson..1891
Eric Johnson...1893

MARSHALS OF THE UNITED STATES.

Mark W. Izaard........Oct. 28, 1854	J. T. Hoile..............July 1, 1861
Eli R. Doyle...........April 7, 1855	William Daily...................1870
Benjamin P. Rankin March 29, 1856	Ellis Bierbower.. 1855
Phineas W. Hitchcock Sept. 19, 1861	Brad D. Slaughter............1889
Casper E. Yost........April 1, 1869	F. E. White...................1893

MEMBERS OF NEBRASKA LEGISLATURE, 1855 TO 1893, INCLUSIVE.

Council and Senate.

(Up to and inclusive of the 17th session each member is credited with the session of which he was a member, "T" standing for "Territorial," and "S" for "State" session. Commencing with the 18th session, 1883, each member is credited with the year he served. From and after that year there were no special sessions. Ed.)

NAMES.	SESSIONS.	NAMES.	SESSIONS.
Abbott, Rufus........	S. 11, 12, 13	Bunnell, A. T...........	S. 15
Albertson, Isaac......	T. 10, 11	Burnham, S. W.........	1887
Allen, Edwin A.......	T. 9, 10, 11	Burns, J. F...........	S. 16, 17
Allen, Samuel S	T. 3, 4	Burns, Martin........	S. 16, 17
Ambrose, Geo. W......	S. 14	Burr, C. C............	S. 11, 12, 13
Arnold, E. W.........	S. 15		1885
Ashton, T.............	S. 5, 6, 7	Burton, Geo. W........	1889
Aten, John...........	S. 14	Butler, David...... ..T. 9, 1883
Babcock, Wm. H.......	1893	Cady, H. F...........	S. 16, 17
Baird, Cyrus N.......	S. 14	Cadman, John.........	S. 1
Baird, Harlan..........	2, 3, 4	Calhoun, S H.........	S. 1
Baker, Sydney........	S. 16, 17	Calkins, Elisha C......	S. 14
Ballentine, D. C....	S. 16, 17	Calkins, D. K....	1887
Barker, L. D........	1883	Campbell, Jacob N......	1893
Barnum, E. W........	S. 9, 10	Campbell, J. E.........	1887
Barnum, Guy C........	S. 5, 6, 7, 8, 9	Campbell, John C.....	T. 9
	10, 11, 12, 13	Canfield, George.......	1883
Bates, Barnabas.......	T. 12	Carns, Edmund C.....	S. 14
Barnum, William....	T. 12	Case, O. C...........	1883
Bayne, Oliver F......	T. 10, 11	Casper, C. D.	1887
Bear, Alexander......	S. 11, 12, 13	Chapin, Wm. P........	S. 5
Beardsley, S. W......	1889	Chapman, John W...	T. 10, 11
Beck, William B......	S. 15, 1891	Chapman, Sam M.....	S. 11, 12, 13
Belden, David D.....	T. 7, 8		14
Bennett, Hiram P.....	T. 1	Cheever, John H......	T. 5, 6
Bennett, John B......	T. 7, 8, 10, 11	Cherry, A. B.........	1885
Birkhouser, P. W......	S. 14, 15	Cheney, M. B.........	S. 15
Blanchard, Carrington	T. 8, 10, 11	Christofferson, George	1891
Blanchard, Geo. F....	S. 14	Clancy, William.......	T. 3, 4
Bomgardner, D. D......	1883	Clark, Chas. H........	1893
Bowen, A	S. 9, 10	Clarke, Harry F........	1885
Bowen, L. L...........	T. 3, 4, 5	Clarke, Henry T.......	S. 9
Bonesteel..........	1887	Clark, Munson H.....	T. 1
Bradford, A. A........	T. 2, 3, 4	Clarkson, J. T........	S. 15
Bradford, Henry......	T. 1, 2	Colby, Leonard W.....	S. 14, 1887
Brown, Chas. H......	S. 14, 15, 1883	Collins, George F......	1891
Brown, David........	S. 8	Collyer, Thos. T.......	T. 6
Brown, Ezra..........	1883-5	Conger, W. H.........	1887
Brown, E. E........	S. 15, 1883	Conklin, A M.......	S. 8
Brown, J. Marion......	1891	Conner, A. H..........	1883-89
Brown, O. F..	1883	Coon, C. H...........	S. 16, 17
Brown, Richard......	T. 1, 2	Cornell, C. B.........	1889
Brown, R. G..........	1887	Correll, Erasmus M......	1893
Bryant, A. M.. ....S. 14		Coulter, John F.......	S. 15
Buckworth, A. D......	1885	Coulter, F. B........	1891

112   STATE AND TERRITORIAL GOVERNMENT.

NAMES.	SESSIONS.	NAMES.	SESSIONS.
Thayer, John M	T. 7	Wardell, W. W	T. 12
Thomas, E. W	S. 8		S. 2, 3, 4
Thomas, S. L	1891	Warner, C A	1891
Thomsen, John	1893	Welch, Frank	T. 9 8 1
Thummel, George H	S. 14	Wells, H. M	S. 16, 17
TiptonT. W	T. 7	Wetherald, F. W	1889
Tisdale, D. A	S. 1	Wigton, A. L	S. 15
Tzschuck, Bruno	1887	Wilber, M. C	S. 1
Tucker, Geo. P	S 8	Wilcox, M. W	S. 14
Turk, W. W	S. 16, 17	Williams, C. W	1891
Turner, M. K	S. 16, 17	Wilson, O.	S. 9, 10
Turner, Edward	1891	Wilson W. W	1891
Unthank, John A	T. 7, 8	Wherry, Robert A	S. 16, 17
Vandemark, J. K	1887	White C. C	S. 16, 17,
Van Housen, J. C	1891	Wolbach, J. N	1887-89
Van Wyck, Chas. H	S. 14, 15, 16	Woods, L. H	1891
	17	Wright, C. J	1887
Walker, P. H	1883	Young, Lewis W	1893
Walton, W. C	S. 14	Zehrung, Henry	S. 16, 17

MEMBERS OF THE HOUSE OF REPRESENTATIVES.

NAMES.	SESSIONS.	NAMES.	SESSIONS.
Abbe, Joshua G	T. 4	Baker, Alexander H	S. 11, 12, 13
Abbott, L. J	T. 12		14
Abbott, N. C	S. 16, 17	Baker, John B	T. 6, 7
Abel, Anton	1883	Baker, Sidney	S. 15
Abrahamson, Otto	1887-89	Baker, William	T. 12
Acton, A. M	T. 7		S. 2, 3, 4
Adams, John M	1885	Baker, B. S	1889
Adams, Thurman H	T 6	Baldwin, A. S	S. 16, 17
Agee, Alfred W	1887	Ballard, Jno. R	1887-89
Ahmanson, John	S. 8	Baltzley, O W	S. 3, 4, 9, 10
Atkin, Relzy M	1885-7	Barker, A. H	S. 1
Albert, Henry	1891	Barker, S	S. 14
Alden, J. M	1891	Barnard, E. H	T. 8 S. 5
Allen, Cyrus	S. 14	Barnard, Richard	T. 6
Allen, E. A	T. 8	Barnard, Samuel	S. 15
Alexander, Thos. J	1887	Barnes, J. B	S. 9, 10
Allgewahr, L	T. 8, 9	Barnes, John W	S. 11, 12, 13
Ames, George W	1893	Barney, Reuben E	1885
Ames, W. R	1891	Barnum, Guy C	T. 10, 11
Anderson, D. M	T. 12		S. 14
	S. 1, 2, 3, 4	Barnum, E. W	T. 7, 8
Anderson, Nils	S. 17	Barrett, James	T. 7
Andrews, Henry C	1887	Barrett, Jacob H	1887
Andres, Phillip	1887	Barrows, B. H	S. 11, 12, 13
Anyan, William	S. 14	Barry, Patrick H	1893
Armitage, H. G	1883	Bartholemew, H. C	1891
Armstrong Geo	T. 3, 4	Bartlett, E. M	S. 16, 17
Arnold, Anselm	T. 1	Bartlett, W. R	S. 9, 10
Arnold A, J	S. 9, 10	Barton, Lewis	1893
Arnold, Edward W	S. 1	Bassett, Samuel C	1885
Arnold Edward	1891	Bates, Barnabas	T. 6, 8
Arnold, Joseph	T. 11	Batty, R. A	S. 15
Ashburn, D. P	S. 9, 10	Baumer, John	S. 11, 12, 13
Ashby, Thomas F	1883	Beal, Charles W	1893
Austin Benjamin	T. 11	Beall, Enos	T. 8 S. 8
Ayer, Simon C	S. 16, 17	Beall, Seth W	S. 11, 12, 13
Babcock, A. H	S. 9, 10	Beardsley, J. M	S. 1
Babcock, C. F	1883	Beane, George	T. 14
Babcock, N. S	S. 16, 17	Bear, Alexander	S. 14
Babcock, Oscar	S. 15	Beck, William B	T. 2, 4
Babcock, Walter E	1887	Becker, John P	T. 9
Bain, Alexander	T. 6	Beckman, Henry	1889
Bailey, J. B	S. 16, 17	Beebe, Henry	S. 3, 4
Bailey, Stephen M	1885	Belden, David D	T. 6
Bailey, Orestus G		Belden, N. S	S. 14
Baird, Harlan	1887	Bell, T. R	S. 1

NAMES	SESSIONS	NAMES	SESSIONS
Grimes, H. M............S. 18		Herman, S. J..........S. 16, 17	
Grinnell, Edwin L....S. 8		Hicklin, Wm. M.....T. 12 S. 3, 4	
Grinstead, R. E... 1883		Hickman Wm..........S. 15	
Grout, A. P........ 1883		Hinds, L. B.......... 1893	
Gumær, Alfred W. 1885		Higgins, James M 1885	
Gunnett, I. M.......... 1891		Higgins, W. P 1893	
Gwyer, Wm. A........T. 5		Hinsdale, Geo A....T 6	
Hacker, Jonas.......T. 7		Hitchcock, H. M....T. 10	
Hagamon, Robert M..T. 8		Hill J. S.............. 1889	
Hagood, John McF...T. 2, 3, 4, 5, 6		Hill, W. C.............. 1889	
7		Hinkle, H. S............ 1891	
Hahn, Leopold....... S. 2 1889		Hoback, R. D...... . T. 9	
Hail, William B..... T. 1, 2, 3, 4		Hobbs, D............T. 9	
Haldeman, W. J.....S. 14		Hocknell, George,...... 1885	
Hall, Edward J.......... 1891		Hoebel, Louis.......... 1883	
Hall, G. A............T. 10		Hoile, Joseph T......T. 12	
Hall, George A........S. 4			S. 1, 2, 3, 4, 5
Hall, James...........S. 16, 17, 1883		Holcomb, H ....S. 9, 10	
Hall, Patrick J.......... 1885		Holladay, A. S.......T. 8	
Hall, Thomas F......S. 8		Holladay, C. T........T. 3, 4	
Hall, Wm. B..........T. 5		Hollman, Jos........S. 16, 17, 1889	
Hall, C. L.............. 1889		Holmes, Chas A ....S. 11, 12, 13	
Haller, William D...... 1893		Holmes, Edward P...... 1885	
Hamilton, W. R......S. 1		Holsworth, William.. .. 1885	
Hampton, I. B.......... 1889		Holt, Frank H......... .. 1885	
Hanna, J. R.......... 1889		Homer J. C............ 1883	
Hanscon, Andrew J..T. 1, 3 6		Hooper, Edward........ 1889	
Hanson, Robert.....S. 15		Hoover, Jerome......T. 2	
Hanson, Jas... 1889		Hoover, J. T. A.......T. 10	
Hardenberg, E. H...T. 12 S 2		Horst George............ 1887-93	
Harding, W. A......... 1889		Horne, O.............. 1889	
Hare, Thomas R......T. 2		Hostetter, Chris.....S. 16, 17	
Harlan, Nathan V...... 1885-87		Howard, Ezra E......... 1883	
Harmon, Frank P....... 1893		Howard, L. M........S. 9, 10	
Harrington, W........ 1883		Howe, Church........ S. 11, 12, 13-	
Harsh, Levi ....T. 2			16, 18, 1891-93
Harrison, Chas. J...... 1887		Hudson H J..........S. 8	
Harrison. Peter ......S. 14		Hullihen, T. G....... S. 14	
Harvey, A. E.. ......S. 14		Huff, Edward T..... ... 1885	
Harvey, Augustus F..T. 12		Humphrey, Geo. M..... 1883	
S. 2, 3. 4		Hunggate, J. H........ 1889	
Hastings, Alfred G .S. 11, 12, 13		Hunt, Jacob S........ S. 5, 6, 7	
Hastings George H...S. 11, 12, 13		Hunter, J. M.......... 1889	
Hatch. W. D 1883		Huse, Jessie B 1891	
Hathaway, H. D......S. 1		Hyde. Judson R......T. 7	
Haben, H. R.......... 1883		Imlay, Wm...........T. 10	
Hayden, Ben H........ 1887		Irwin, Wm. J.......... 1885-93	
Hayden C. M.........S. 11, 12, 13		Jackson, A. H........S. 16, 17	
Hays, C. W..........S. 17		Jackson, S. K........S. 16, 17	
Haywood C. F........T. 1, 2, 3, 4		James, P. H.......... 1893	
Hazen, Solon M........ 1885		Jeary, Edwin.......... 1887	
Heacock, P. S........S. 16, 17		Jenkins, D. C........S. 8	
Healey, Thomas A...S. 14		Jenkins, E. M.......... 1893	
Heath, E. L.......... 1891		Jenkins J. D.........S. 15	
Heath H.H...........T. 11		Jensen, John.......... 1893	
Heaton, Isaac E.......T. 9		Jensen, Thomas.. ....S. 16, 17, 1883	
Hedde, Frederick....T. 7		Jindra, Joseph.......... 1885	
Hedges, Rochester....T. 10		Johnson, Benj........S. 16, 17	
Heimrod, Geo........... 1887		Johnson, C. S.......... 1883	
Heinrich, John.......... 1885		Johnson, Erie.......... 1889	
Hefferman, John.....T. 10		Johnson, E. H........T. 10	
Hefferman, S. C......S. 14		Johnson, F. M........S. 14	
Helmer, Louis........S. 11, 12, 13		Johnson J. V.......... 1891	
Helms, John H......S. 16, 17,		Johnson, H...........T. 3	
Hendershot F J......S. 11, 12, 13		Johnson, Harrison....T. 6	
Hennick, C W.......... 1891		Johnson, T. B........S. 14	
Henry, David P..... ... 1887		Johnson Nathan 1893	
Henry, H. R............ 1891-93		Johnson, J. L.. 1893	
Herman, L. J.......... 1891		Johnston, B. J......... 1893	

NAMES	SESSIONS	NAMES	SESSIONS
Walling, Aug. M	S. 16, 17	Wiedensall, Jacob	S. 11, 12, 13
Walters, J. P	S. 14	Wilbur, Russell H	T. 11, S. 1
Walther, Charles F	T. 10	Wilbur, R. S	S. 9, 10
Wardlaw, John M	1887-93	Wilcox, Z. T	S. 14
Warner, J. F	S. 15	Wilcox, J. A	1889
Warrick, Amasa A	T. 12	Wihelmsen, Jens	1887
Warrington, T. L	S. 15	Wilson, John	1893
Watson, John C	1887-89-91	Wilson, John L	1887
	1893	Wilsey, Albert	S. 16, 1887
Wattles, Stephens H	T. 5, 8	Wiles, Isaac	T. 7, 12
Watts, Samuel F	S. 16, 17 1883		S. 2, 3, 4
Webster, J. L	S. 9, 10	Williams, Henry	1885
Weber B. R. B	1889	Williams, John W	1889-91
Weller, H. D	1889	Williams, T. J	1891
Wells, Joseph	1889	Wilson, C. J	1891
Wells, Henry C	S. 16, 17	Windam, R. B	S. 15, 16, 17
Wells, N. W	S. 14, 15	Winspear, James H	1885
Wescott, M. H	S. 17	Winter, Thaddeus	1889
Werhan, W. S.	1883	Wissenburgh, H	1883
Werner, Ernst	1891	Withnell C. H	1893
Wescott. M	1883	Wolbach, Samuel N	1885
West, Geo. P	T. 10	Wolcott, Frank M	S. 8
Westover, Herman	1889	Wolfe, Thomas	S. 14
Wetherald, F. M	1887	Wolenweber, Nicholas	1887
Whalen, John	T. 9	Wolpa, Henry C	T. 3, 1883
Whaley, Charles H	T. 7	Wood Joel M	T. 1
Whedon, Charles O	S. 16, 17, 1883	Woods, J. D	1893
Wheeler, Cyrus H	S. 9, 10	Woolworth, J. M	S. 3, 4
Whelpley, D. P	S. 14	Worl, J. W	1883
Whitcomb, E. W	S. 14	Wright, John B	1885
White, A. K	S. 9, 10	Wright, W. F	S. 11, 12, 13
White, Fred E	1885	Wright, Pierce G	1887
White, R. D	T. 3	Wyatt, C. C	S. 16, 17
White, Francis E	1887-89-91	York, W. R	S. 15
Whitehead, James	1889	Young Benjamin	1883
Whitford, A. D	1889	Young, Wm. J	T. 5
Whitemore, Wm. G	1885-87	Young Jas. R	1887
Whitted, Robert B	T. 1	Yutzy, Jos. C	1887-89
Whitzel, T. J	1883	Ziegler, J. A	S. 15, 16, 17
Whyman, F. E	1889	Zimmerman	S. 5, 6, 7
Wickham, James	S. 8		

PRESIDENTIAL ELECTORS.

Republican Electors for U. S. Grant—1868.

T. M. Marquet, Lewis Allgewahr, J. F. Warner.

Democratic Electors for H. Seymour—1868

James G. Megath, J. A. Hellmann, Vine Kummer.

Republican Electors for U. S. Grant—1872.

S. A. Strickland, Otto Funke, H. G. Heist.

Democratic Electors for Horace Greeley—1872.

John Creighton, O. P. Mason, ——Foster.

Republican Electors for R. B. Hayes—1876.

S. A. Strickland, Amasa Cobb, A. H. Connor.

Democratic Electors for S. J. Tilden, 1876.

S. H. Calhoun, St. John Goodrich, M. C. Keith.

Republican Electors for James A. Garfield—1880.

J. M. Thurston, G. W. Collins, James Laird.

Democratic Electors for W. S. Hancock—1880.

J. E. Boyd, Victor Vifquain, B. I. Hinman.

Greenback Electors for James B. Weaver—1880.

II. G. Cass, W. W. Connor, George Watkin.

Republican Electors for James G. Blaine—1884.

C. H. Dewey, Henry Sprick, R. B. Harrington, A. L. Burr, John Macken

Democratic (Fusion) Electors for Grover Cleveland—1884.

Patrick Hines, J. M. Patterson, W. H. Ashby, H. S. Alley, R. R. Shick.

Prohibition Electors for John P. St. John—1884,

A. L. Reinoehl, F. J. Sibley, J. G. Berdrow, L. B. Boggs, M. J. Garrett.

Republican Electors for Benjamin Harrison—1888.

II. C. Russell, G. H. Hastings, M. M. Butler, C. E. Iddings, James Mc-Neny.

Democratic Electors for Grover Cleveland—1888.

W. G. Sloan, Olof Hedstrom, A. F. Tibbets, S. C. Kesterson, C. W. Allen.

Prohibition Electors for Clinton B. Fisk—1888.

C. C. Crowell, R. A. Hawley, S. D. Fitch, E. S. Abbott, James R. Cary.

Union Labor Electors for A. J. Streeter—1888.

Allen Root, J. F. Black, C. W. Wheeler, L. H. Cahoon, Orin Colby.

Republican Electors for Benjamin Harrison—1892.

I. M. Raymond, W. J. Broatch, Cenek Duras, Chas. W. Johnson, H. A. Miller, Daniel M. Nettleton, E. P. Savage, Isaac Wiles.

People's Independent Electors for James B. Weaver—1892.

Elijah E. Link, Thomas H. Tibbles, Jetur R. Conklin, Peter Ebbeson, Thomas G. Ferguson, William A. Garrett, John I. Jones, Richard R. Shick

Democratic Electors for Grover Cleveland—1892.

—— Piasecki, John E. Shervin, H. E. Dunphy, T. V. Golden, Albert Gordon, J. Edgar Howard, George H. Thomas, Albert Watkins.

Prohibition Electors for Gen. John Bidwell—1892.

R. A. Hawley, Mary M. Lantry, E. T. Cassell, N. Christopherson, A. D. George, Isaiah Lightner, J. Phipps Roe, S. S. Stewart.

Peoples' Independent Electors for W. J. Bryan—1896.

Nels O. Alberts, Jacob N. Campbell, Fielden J. Hale, Michael F. Harrington, Stanley Louis Kostoryz, Fred Metz, Sr., Olof W. Palm, Xavier Piasecki.

Democratic Electors for W. J. Bryan—.896.

Joseph Bruenig, A. S. Godfrey, William Griffin, J. A. Kirk, Charles Nicolai, Fred Rennard, Alexander Scott, Charles Turner.

Republican Electors for William McKinley—'896.

Albert J. Burnham, George A. Derby, Solomon Draper, Albert C. Foster, Martin L. Fries, Jacob E. Houtz, John L. McPheely, Frank J. Sadilek.

National Electors—1896.

E. H. Agee, James K. Lane, A. Luth, Thomas W. Mathews, J. S. Miller, D. L. Pond, A. P. Seymour, Lem. J. Smith.

Prohibition Electors for Rev. —— Bentley—1896.

O. R. Beebe, C. L. Carpenter, S. M. Cozad, John F. Helin, D. W. C. Huntington, C. Lowenstein, N. Lowrie, Mary E. Rockwell.

Socialist Labor—1896.

II. S. Aley, Charles E. Baker, August Beermann, Thomas M. Conway, John C. Curtis, William H. Daniels, Fred Teickmeir, John W. Unangst.

ELECTION STATISTICS.

Popular and Electoral Vote of the United States for President and Vice-President, 1789—1892.

Year of Election.	POLITICAL PARTY.	Candidates.	VOTE. Popular.	Electoral.	Candidates.	Electoral vote.
			PRESIDENTS.*		VICE-PRESIDENTS.*	
1879		George Washington,		69		
		John Adams,.......				34
		John Jay, ...				9
		R. H. Harrison,.....				6
		John Rutledge,.....				6
		John Hancock, ...				4
		George Clinton,....				3
		Samuel Huntingdon				2
		ohn Milton,.......				2
		James Armstrong,..				1
		Benjamin Lincoln,.				1
		Edward Telfair,.....				1
		Vacancies,.......		4		4
1792	Federalist, .	George Washington,		132		
	Federalist, .	John Adams,......				77
	Republican,	George Clinton,.....				50
		Thomas Jefferson,..				4
		Aaron Burr,......				1
		Vacancies, ...		3		3
1796	Federalist, .	John Adams,.....		71		
	Republican,	Thomas Jefferson,..				68
	Federalist, .	Thomas Pinkney,...				59
	Republican,	Aaron Burr......				30
		Samuel Adams,....				15
		Oliver Ellsworth,...				11
		George Clinton,....				7
		John Jay,........				5
		James Iredell,......				3
		George Washington,				2
		John Henry....				2
		S. Johnson......				2
		Charles C. Pinckney				1
1800	Republican,.	Thomas Jefferson,..		†73		
	Republican,	Aaron Burr.......				†73
	Federalist, .	John Adams,......				65
	Federalist,...	Charles C. Pinckney				64
		John Jay,........				1

*Previous to the election of 1804, each elector voted for two candidates for President; the one receiving the highest number of votes, if a majority, was declared elected President, and the next highest Vice-President

†There having been a tie vote, the choice devolved upon the House of Representatives. A choice was made on the 36th ballot, which was us follows; Jefferson—Georgia, Kentucky Maryland, New Jersey, New York North Carolina, Pennsylvania, Tennessee, Vermont and Virginia—10 states; Burr—Connecticut, Massachusetts, New Hampshire and Road Island—4 states; Blank—Deleware and South Carolina—2 states.

POPULAR AND ELECTORAL VOTE—Continued.

Year of Election.	POLITICAL PARTIES.	PRESIDENTS.			VICE-PRESIDENTS.	
		CANDIDATES.	VOTE. Popular.	Electoral.	Candidates.	Electoral Vote.
1804	Republican.	Thomas Jefferson,.	....	162	George Clinton..	162
	Federalist. .	Charles C. Pinckney	....	14	Rufus King....	14
1808	Republican.	James Madison,....	....	122	George Clinton....	113
	Federalist.	Charles C. Pinckney	....	47	Rufus King.....	47
		George Clinton, ..	....	6	John Langdon..	9
					James Madison..	3
					James Monroe...	3
		Vacancy,.........		1	....	1
1812	Republican.	James Madison,....	....	128	Elbridge Gerry..	131
	Federalist. .	DeWit Clinton,....	....	89	Jared Ingersoll..	86
		Vacancy,.........	....	1	....	1
1816	Republican,	James Monroe,....	....	183	D. D. Tompkins.	183
	Federalist, .	Rufus King,.......	....	34	John E. Howard.	22
					James Ross.... ...	7
					John Marshall....	4
					Robert G. Harper	3
		Vacancy,.........		4	....	4
1820	Republican,	James Monroe,....	....	231	D. D. Tompkins..	218
	Opposit on, .	John Q. Adams,...	....	1	Richard Stockton	8
					Daniel Rodney..	4
					Robert G. Harper	1
					Richard Rush...	1
		Vacancy,.........		3	....	3
1824	Republican	Andrew Jackson,...	155,872	*99	John C. Calhoun.	182
	Coalition, .	John Q. Adams,....	105,321	84	Nathan Sanford..	30
	Republican,	Wm. H. Crawford,.	44,282	41	Nathan'l Macon..	24
	Republican,	Henry Clay,.......	46,587	37	Andrew Jackson.	13
					M. Van Buren....	9
					Henry Clay......	2
		Vacancy, ...			....	1
1828	Democrat, .	Andrew Jackson,...	647,231	178	John C. Calhoun	171
	Nat. Repub.	John Q. Adams.....	509,097	83	Richard Rush....	93
					Wm. Smith.......	7
1832	Democratic.	Andrew Jackson....	687,502	219	M. Van Buren....	189
	Nat. Repub.	Henry Clay, ...	530,189	47	John Sergeant....	49
		John Lloyd. }	} 33,168	{11	Henry Lee.......	11
		Wm. Wirt, }		{ 7	Amos Ellmaker..	7
					Wm. Wilkins....	30
		Vacancies		2	....	2
1836	Democratic,	Martin Van Buren,	761,549	170	R. M. Johnson..	147
	Whig, ...	Wm. H. Harrison, }		{73	Francis Granger.	77
	Whig, ...	Hugh L. White,	} 736,616	{ 26	John Tyler......	47
	Whig, ...	Daniel Webster,		{ 14	Wm. Smith.......	23
	Whig, ...	W. P. Mangum,		{11	....	...

*No choice having been made by the electoral college, the choice devolved upon the House of Representatives. A choice was made on the first ballot, which was as follows: Adams—Connecticut, Illinois, Kentucky, Louisiana, Maine, Maryland, Massachusetts, Missouri, New Hampshire, New York, Ohio, Rhode Island and Vermont.—13 states. Jackson—Alabama, Indiana, Mississippi, New Jersey, Pennsylvania, South Carolina and Tennessee.—7 states. Crawford—Delaware, Georgia, North Carolina and Virginia.—4 states.

†No candidate having received a majority of the votes of the electoral college, the senate elected R. M. Johnson, Vice President, who received 33 votes; Francis Granger received 16.

POPULAR AND ELECTORAL VOTE—Continued.

Year of Election	Political Party.	Candidates.	Popular.	Electoral	Candidates.	Electoral Vote
		PRESIDENTS.	**VOTE.**		**VICE-PRESIDENTS**	
1840	Whig........	Wm. H. Harrison...	1,275,017	234	John Tyler,.....	234
	Democratic..	Martin Van Buren..	1,128,702	60	R. M. Johnson,.	48
	Liberty......	James G. Birney..	7,059		FrancisLemoyne	
					James K. Polk,	1
					L. W. Tazwell..	11
1844	Democratic.	James K. Polk......	1,337,243	170	Geo. M. Dallas,.	170
	Whig	Henry Clay.........	1,299,068	105	T Frelinghuysen	105
	Liberty......	James G. Birney....	62,300		Thomas Morris,	
1848	Whig	Zachary Taylor....	1,360,101	163	Millard Filmore,	163
	Democratic.	Lewis Cass........	1,220,544	127	Wm. O. Butler,	127
	Free Soil....	Martin Van Buren..	291,263		Chas. F Adams,	
	Democratic..	Franklin Pierce....	1,601,474	254	Wm. R. King,..	254
1852	Whig.......	Winfield Scott......	1,386,578	42	Wm. A. Graham	42
	Free Dem...	John P. Hale.......	156,149		Geo. W. Julian,.	
1856	Democratic	James Buchanan...	1,838,169	174	J C Breckenridge	174
	Republican.	John C. Fremont...	1,341,264	114	Wm L. Dayton,	114
	Amer can....	Millard Filmore....	874,534	8	A. J. Donelson,..	8
1860	Republican	Abraham Lincoln..	1,866,352	180	H'nnibalHamlin	180
	Democratic.	J. C. Breckenridge.	845,763	72	Joseph Lane,....	72
	Cons. Union	John Bell..........	589,581	39	Edward, Everett	39
	Ind. Dem...	S. A. Douglas......	1,375,157	12	H. V. Johnson,..	12
1864	Republican.	Abraham Lincoln..	2,216,067	212	Andrew Johnson	212
	Democratic	Geo B. McClellan..	1,808,725	21	G. H. Pendleton	21
		*States not voting.		81		81
1868	Republican.	Ulyssess S. Grant...	3,015,071	214	Schyler Colfax,.	214
	Democratic	Horatio Seymour....	2,709,613	80	F. P. Blair, Jr..	80
		†States not voting..		23		23
1872	Republican.	Ulysses S. Grant....	3,597,070	286	Henry Wilson..	286
	Dem and Lib	Horace Greeley.....	2,834,079		B. Gratz Brown,	47
	Democratic.	Charles O'Conor....	29,408		Geo. W. Julian.	5
	Temperance.	James Black,..... ..	5,608		A. H. Colquitt..	5
		Thos. A. Hen ri ks			John M. Palmer	3
		B. Gratz Brown....		42	T. E. Bramlette.	1
		Chas. J. Jenkens...		18	W. S. Grossbeck	1
		David Davis.......		8	Willis B Machon	1
				1	N. P. Banks....	1
		Not Counted... ...:		17		17
1876	Republican.	R. B. Hayes........	4,033,950	185	Wm. A. Wheeler	185
	Democratic	Samuel J. Tilden...	4,284,885	184	TAHendricks,...	184
	Greenback ..	Peter Cooper........	81,780		Samuel Cary,..	
	Prohibition.	Green Clay Smith..	9,552		G. T. Stewart...	
		Scattering........	2,636			
1880	Republican ..	James A. Garfield..	4,449,053	215	ChesterA Arthur	214
	Democratic	Winfield S. Hancock	4,442,035	155	Wm. H. English	155
	Greenback ..	James B. Weaver...	307,306		B. J. Chambers,	
	Prohibition.	Neal Dow.....	10,305		H A. Thompson	
	American...	John W. Phelps ..	707		Sam. C Pomeroy	
		Scattering	989			

*Eleven states did not vote, viz: **Alabama,** Arkansas, Florida, Georgia, Louisiana, Mississippi, **North Carolina, South** Carolina, Tennessee, Texas and Virginia.

†Three states did not vote, viz: **Mississippi, Texas and** Virginia.

POPULAR AND ELECTORAL VOTE—Continued.

Year of Election	Political Party	PRESIDENTS.			VICE-PRESIDENTS	
		Candidates.	VOTE.		Candidates.	...rial Vote
			Popular.	Electoral.		
1884	Democratic	Grover Cleveland...	4,911,017	219	T. A. Hendrick-	219
	Republican	James G. Blaine.....	4,848,334	182	John A. Logan.	182
	Prohibition	John P. St. John....	151,809		Wm. Daniel...	
	Greenback	Benj. F. Butler.....	133,826		A. M. West.....	
		Scattering...........	11,362			
1888	Republican	Benj. Harrison.....	5,444,053	233	Levi. P. Morton	233
	Democratic	Grover Cleveland...	5,538,536	168	AllenGThurman	168
	Prohibition	Clinton B. Fisk.....	248,997		John A. Brooks.	
	Union Labor	A. J. Streeter	146,100		CE Cunningham	
	American ...	James L. Curtis....			J. R. Greer.....	
	UnitedLabor	R. H. Cowdery....			W H T Wakefield	
	Ind. Reform	Alfred E. Redstone.			John Colvin.....	
	Equal Rights	Belva Lockwood....			Chas. S. Wells...	
1892	Democratic	Grover Cleveland...	5,556,523	277	A. E. Stevenson	
	Republican	Benj. Harrison.....	5,175,517	145	Whitelaw Reed.	
	Peoples Ind.	James B. Weaver...	1,222,045	22	James G. Field..	
	Prohibition	John Bidwell.......	279,191		James B Cranfill	
	Social Labor	Simon Wing........	21,191		C. H. Matchet..	
1896	Democrat.. / Populist.... / Free Sil. R.	W. J. Bryan..........	6,502,600	176	Sewell .... Watson............	147 27
	Republican...	William McKinley..	7,126,542	271	Hobart.............	271
	Nat. Dem.....	John M. Palmer.....	134,731			
	Prohibition..	Levering...............	123,428			
	Prohibition..	Bentley...................	13,535			

ELECTION STATISTICS Continued.

VOTES CAST

For Presidential Candidates in Nebraska Since the Admission of the State.

1868.			1884.	
Grant, R	9,772		Blaine, R	76,912
Seymour, D	5,519		Cleveland and Fusion	54,391
			St. John, P	2,899
Majority	4,253			
1872.			Plurality	22,521
Grant, R	17,702		Majority	19,622
Greeley, L and D	7,548		1888.	
			Harrison, R	108,425
Majority	10,154		Cleveland, D	80,552
1876.			Fisk, P	9,429
Hayes, R	31,833		Streeter, U. L	4,226
Tilden, D	17,554			
			Plurality	27,873
Majority	14,279		Majority	14,218
1880.			1892.	
Garfield, R	54,979		Harrison, R	86,858
Hancock, D	28,523		Weaver, P. P	82,589
Weaver, G	3,950		Cleveland, D	24,740
			Bidwell, P	4,805
Plurality	26,476			
			Plurality	4,217
Majority	22,506			

POPULAR VOTE FOR MEMBERS OF CONGRESS SINCE 1855.

1855—Bird B. Chapman	380	
Hiram P. Bennett	292	
Scattering	18—	690
1857—Fenner Ferguson	1,642	
Bird B. Chapman	1,559	
Benjamin P. Rankin	1,241	
John M. Thayer	1,171	
Scattering	21—	5,634
1859—Experience Esterbrook	3,100	
Samuel G. Daily	2,800—	5,900
1860—J. Sterling Morton	2,957	
Samuel G. Daily	2,943—	5,900
1862—Samuel G. Daily	2,331	
John F. Kinney	2,180—	4,511
1864—Phineas W. Hitchcock	3,421	
George L. Miller	2,399	
Scattering	2—	5,822
1866—T. M. Marquett	4,821	
J. Sterling Morton	4,105—	8,926
John Taffe	4,820	
Algernon S. Paddock	4,072	
George Francis Train	30—	8,922
1868—John Taffe	8,724	
Andrew J. Poppleton	6,318—	15,042
1870—John Taffe	12,375	
George B. Blake	7,967—	20,342

1872—Lorenzo Crounse..17,124
      Jesse F. Warner.......................................10,412— 27,536

1874—**Lorenzo Crounse**..22,532
      James W. Savage... 8,386
      James G. Miller... 4,071
      James W. Davis................................... 972— 35,964

1876—Frank Welch (Rep)..30 900
      Joseph Holman (Dem.)..................................17,206
      M. Warren (Greenback)................................. 3,579
      Scattering .... 89—51,774

1878—E. K, **Valentine** (Rep).................................**28 341**
      J. W. Davis (Dem. and Greenback)................**21,752**
      Scattering... 21—50,247

      Thomas J. Majors (Rep) to fill vacancy..............**28,221**
      Alex, Bear (Dem.) **to** fill vacancy.................**21,124**
      Scattering .... 21—49,366

1880—E. K. Va'entine (Rep.)....................................52,647
      James E. North (Dem.)................................23,634
      Allen Root (Greenback)............................... 4 059
      Scattering .... 4,071—84,414

1882—A. J. Weaver, 1st **District**.............................**17,022**
      J. I. Redick **1st** '................................12,690
      G. S. Gilbert, **1st** "............................. 3,707
      Scattering... 12—33,421

      James Laird, 2nd District...........................12,983
      V. S. Moore, 2nd "..................................10,012
      F. A. Harman "...................................... 3 060
      Scattering... 56—26 **111**

      E. K. Valentine, 3rd District.......................11,284
      M. K. Turner, "..................................... 7 342
      W. H. **Munger,** "................................. 9,932
      Scattering .. .. 12—28,570

1884—A. J. Weaver, **1st District**...........................22,644
      Chas. H. **Brown** "................................21,669
      E. J. O'Neil "...................................... 1,024
      Scattering .... 2—45,339

      James Laird, 2nd District..........................2´,182
      J. H. Stickel "......................................17 650
      B. Crabb "...................................... 1,176
      Scattering "....................................... 49—40,057

      George W. **E.** Dorsey, 3d **District**..............25,985
      William **Neville,**.................................20,671
      Albert Fetch.. 572
      Scattering... 17—47,245

1886—John A. McShane 1st District..............................23,396
      Church Howe, "......................................17,373
      George Bigelow, "................................... 2,867
      Scattering... 43—42,679

      James Laird. 2d **District**........................18,373
      W. A. McKeighan '...................................16,315

C. S. Harrison, **2d District** 3 789

Scattering... **187—38,664**

George W. **E. Dorsey, 3d District**................. 28,717

W. H. Webster   `` 20,943

W. J. Olinger,   `` 2 383

Scattering.................................... ..... 112—52,155

1888—W. **J Connell, 1st District**...............................32,926

J. Sterling Morton `` 29 519

Edwin B. Graham **``**   2,962

J. W. Edgerton   ``   .... 650—66,057

James Laird, 2d District.. 30,969

W. G. Hastings,   `` 21,201

George Scott   ``   4,128

H. H. Rohr   **``**   .... 2,715—58,003

George W. **E.** Dorsey, 3d **District**.................**42,188**

E. B. Weatherby,   `` 32,118

A. M. **Walling,**   ``   2,995

F. O. **Jones,**   **``**   .... 4,487—77,788

1890—W. **J. Connell, 1st** District...........................25,663

W. J. Bryan,   `` 31,376

Allen Root   `` 13,066

E. H. Chapin,   **``**   .... 1,670—71,775

N. V. Harlan, 2d **District**...........................**21,776**

W. A. McKeighan `` 36,104

L. B. Palmer   ``   .... 1,200—59,080

George W. **E. Dorsey, 3d District**.................25,440

W. H. Thompson   **``** 22,353

O. M. Kem,   `` 31,831

W. L. Pierce,   **``**   .... 961—80,585

1892—W. J. Bryan. **1st** District 13,780

Allen W. Field,   `` 13,644

R. W. Maxwell   ``   863

Jerome Shamp   ``   .... 2,409—30,696

David Mercer, **2nd District** 11,488

Geo. W. Doane,   `` 10,388

R. H. Richardson **``**   362

Robert L. Wheeler **``**   .... 3,152—25,390

Geo. D. Meiklejohn, 3rd District 13 635

Geo, F. Keiper   `` 10,630

W. A. Poynter   **``**   9,636

F. P. Wigton.   **``**   .... 867—34,768

Eugene **J. Hainer, 4th** District 15,648

William H. Dech,   **``** 11,486

Victor Vifquain,   `   8,988

J. P. Kettlewell   **``**   .... 1,312—37,434

William A. McKeighan **5th District**........................17,490

William E. Andrews   `` 14,230

O. C. Hubbell,   ``   .... 838—32,558

Omer M. Kemm   **6th District** 16,328

James Whitehead,   `` 14 195

A. T. Gatewood,   **``**   4,202

Orlando R. Beebe,   **``**   .... 586—35,311

POPULAR VOTE FOR GOVERNOR SINCE FIRST ELECTION IN 1866.

1866—David Butler.. 4 093
    J. Sterling Morton.. 3 948— 8,041

1868—David Butler... 8,576
    J. R. Porter.. 6,349—14,925

1870—David Butler... 11,126
    John H. Croxton,............................... 8,648—19,774

1872—Robert W. Furnas.. 16,543
    Henry C. Lett............................... 11,227—27,770

1874—Silas Garber.. 21,568
    Albert Tuxbury....................... 8,045
    J. F. Gardner.......................... 4 159
    J. S. Church.......................... 1,346—36,019

1876—Silas Garber.. 31,947
    Paren England....................... 17,219
    J. F. Gardner......................... 3 022
    Scattering........................... 36— 52,234

1878—Albinus Nance.. 29,469
    W. H. Webster......................... 13 473
    Levi G. Todd.......................... 9,475—52,417

1880—Albinus Nance.. 55,237
    T. W. Tipton.......................... 28,167
    O. T. B. Williams.................... 3,898
    Scattering........................... 43— 87,345

1882—James W. Dawes.. 43,495
    J. Sterling Morton.................. 28,562
    E. P. Ingersoll....................... 16,991
    Scattering........................... 30—89,068

1884—James W. Dawes.. 72,835
    J. Sterling Morton.................. 57,634
    J. G. Miller.......................... 3,075
    Scattering........................... 11—133 555

1886—John M Thayer.. 75,956
    James E. North...................... 52,656
    H. W. Hardy.......................... 8 175
    J. Burrows........................... 1,422
    Scattering........................... 30—138,239

1888—John M. Thayer.. 103,983
    John A. McShane..................... 85,420
    George Bigelow....................... 9,511
    David Butler.......................... 3,941—202,855

1890—L. D. Richards... 68,878
    J. E. Boyd........................... 71 331
    J. H. Powers......................... 70,187
    B. L. Paine.......................... 3,676—214,072

1892—Lorenzo Crounse... **78,426**
    Chas. H. Van Wyck.................. 68,617
    J. Sterling Morton.................. 44,195
    C. E. Bentley.................... **6,235—197,473**

ABSTRACT OF VOTES CAST

In the First Congressional District for Member of Congress, at the General Election held in November, 1882, 1884, 1886, 1888 and 1890.

COUNTIES	1882 J. Weaver, R.	1882 John I. Redick, D.	1882 W. S. Gilbert, P.	1882 Scattering	1884 A. J. Weaver, R.	1884 Chas. H. Brown, D.	1884 E. J. O'Neill, P.	1884 Scattering	1886 Church Howe, R.	1886 Jno. A. McShane, D.	1886 Geo. Bigelow, P.	1886 Scattering	1888 W. J. Connell, R.	1888 J. Ster'g Morton, D.	1888 E. B. Graham, P.	1888 J. W. Edgerton, L.	1888 Scattering	1890 W. J. Connell, R.	1890 W. J. Bryan, D.	1890 Allen Root, I.	1890 E. H. Chapin, P.	1890 Scattering
Cass	1736	1609	207	2	2224	1850	24		1397	2158	178	3	3002	2962	129	115	8	1775	2354	862	46	3
Douglas	2099	2910	912		3110	6247	54		1909	7110	109	6	10508	10637	483	107	1	9594	15189	1042	256	8
Gage	1569	710	812	1	2755	2177	131		2268	2862	419	12	3897	2581	321		1	2990	2315	2095	204	
Johnson	938	672	221		1302	1032	21		937	1038	121	3	1245	957	114	75		941	731	807	22	
Lancaster	3819	1049	419		4003	2156	196	1	3424	2510	848	3	5355	3821	795			4419	3975	224	584	2
Nemaha	1236	930	60		1636	1226	27		1297	1101	182		1391	1146	119	107		1634	1057	933	47	
Otoe	1892	1396	231		1970	1969	112	1	1358	1600	347	4	1722	2467	334	11	17	1205	2225	1179	161	
Pawnee	999	361	156		1232	693	189		992	793	128	2	1297	647	147	136		1219	675	368	118	
Richardson	1956	1485		8	2194	1886	59		1296	2099	263		2048	1932	126	41	4	1459	1574	917	75	
Sarpy	496	633	4	1	580	651	21		365	796	59		632	874	72			601	970	231	45	
Saunders	1252	721	685		1618	1774	240		1190	1859	263	8	2319	1555	372	54	2	1097	1311	2357	106	8
Totals	17022	12996	3707	12	22641	21669	1024	2	16378	23396	2807	43	32925	29519	2962	630	22	25663	32376	13066	1670	8

ABSTRACT OF VOTES CAST

At the General Election held in the State of Nebraska on the Eighth day of November, A. D., 1892, for Governor, Lieutenant Governor, Secretary of State, Auditor of Public Accounts.

COUNTIES.	GOVERNOR.					LIEUTENANT GOVERNOR.				SECRETARY OF STATE.				AUDITOR OF PUBLIC ACCOUNTS.				
	C. E. BENTLEY, P.	LORENZO CROUNSE, R.	J. STERLING MORTON, D.	CHARLES H. VAN WYCK, P. I.	SCATTERING.	THOMAS J. MAJORS, R.	CHARLES D. SCHRADER, P. I.	JAMES STEPHEN, P.	SAMUEL N. WOLBACH, D.	JOHN C. ALLEN, R.	ISAAC BOOSTROM P.	FRANK M. CROW, D.	JAMES M. EASTERLING, P. I.	LOGAN McREYNOLDS, P. I.	EUGENE MOORE, R.	P. F. O'SULLIVAN, D.	J. C. THOMAS, P.	SCATTERING.
Adams	205	1507	638	1085		1539	1060	189	671	1482	167	784	1041	1061	1547	665	173	
Antelope	105	780	263	943		708	942	97	241	761	107	249	930	910	772	256	103	
Banner	18	182	31	176		186	175	16	32	188	21	35	167	177	176	32	16	
Blaine	8	58	38	48		57	55	8	34	60	10	31	50	53	58	35	8	
Boone	50	810	275	908		837	932	43	271	837	49	296	932	949	830	269	49	
Boyd	43	462	326	310		509	284	29	322	488	21	341	278	276	512	325	29	
Box Butte	25	349	234	519		358	514	18	232	367	19	240	508	510	361	222	25	
Brown	25	328	153	281		351	268	10	155	353	18	145	258	254	345	154	15	
Buffalo	93	1675	679	1752		1705	1747	95	685	1678	86	570	1916	1780	1713	643	86	
Butler	126	918	769	809		990	936	92	940	997	94	984	893	910	966	980	88	
Burt	91	1188	316	924		1242	771	88	296	1229	84	321	765	725	1217	328	84	
Cass	114	1909	1580			2045	690	106	1620	2057	119	1689	623	643	2064	1669	101	
Cedar	32	628	574	577		646	524	33	614	656	28	636	500	496	661	520	29	
Chase	29	296	169	394		857	397	12	120	368	18	114	388	397	324	135	21	
Cheyenne	34	433	327	316		453	310	27	299	467	27	294	311	313	454	287	83	

(Berry)
Clay
Colfax
Cuming
Custer
Dakota
Dawes
Dawson
Deuel
Dixon
Dodge
Douglas
Dundy
Fillmore
Franklin
Frontier
Furnas
Gage
Garfield
Gosper
Grant
Greeley
Hall
Hamilton
Harlan
Hayes
Hitchcock
Hooker
Holt
Howard
Jefferson
Johnson
Kearney
Keya Paha
Keith
Kimball
Knox
Lancaster
Lincoln
Logan

ABSTRACT OF VOTES CAST—Continue.

COUNTIES	GOVERNOR					LIEUTENANT GOVERNOR				SECRETARY OF STATE				AUDITOR OF PUBLIC ACCOUNTS				
	C. E. Bentley, P.	Lorenzo Crounse, R.	J. Sterling Morton, D.	Charles H. Van Wyck, P. I.	SCATTERING	Thomas J. Majors, R.	Charles D. Schrader, P. I.	James Stephies, P.	Samuel N. Wolbach, D.	John C. Allen, R.	Isaac Boostron, P.	Frank M. Crow, D.	James M. Easterling, P. I.	Logan McReynolds, P. I.	Eugene Moore, R.	P. F. O'Sullivan, D.	J. C. Thomas, P.	SCATTERING
Loup	5	102	21	108		106	118	3	24	110	3	20	107	105	163	28	2	
Madison	82	1100	880	776		1084	729	89	890	1000	93	922	677	633	1248	845	83	
Merrick	121	745	329	664		716	607	127	388	755	109	390	644	686	748	339	115	
McPherson	3	27	14	26		29	28	1	13	32	1	11	27	25	30	14	2	
Nance	87	354	88	742		565	717	43	115	569	37	109	724	720	567	109	38	
Nemaha	73	1063	578	1075		1315	924	51	490	1124	69	611	962	953	1106	514	71	
Nuckolls	53	911	377	1116		955	1100	43	368	942	43	364	1112	1116	924	368	44	
Otoe	109	1052	1411	1733		1491	1114	144	1405	1443	140	1549	1086	983	1424	1558	163	
Pawnee	154	1146	354	604		1199	497	142	401	1199	143	405	501	478	1210	427	125	
Perkins	17	205	128	424		307	437	16	134	301	20	147	425	429	307	136	17	
Pierce	25	235	422	888		231	329	24	446	298	25	455	317	394	384	438	25	
Phelps	152	662	182	1029		664	1009	136	158	628	178	164	1073	391	647	151	135	
Platte	55	700	960	1044		750	824	58	1094	721	60	1100	923	1078	777	1136	63	
Polk	110	606	191	1140		673	1086	109	188	677	146	159	1099	853	689	169	111	
Red Willow	43	714	322	763		787	710	34	272	800	45	263	678	1103	769	287	38	
Richardson	119	1754	737	1348		1876	936	91	1645	1866	108	1143	512	690	1851	1136	102	
Rock	14	308	100	191		329	167	12	109	882	13	108	161	164	390	106	11	

ABSTRACT OF VOTES CAST—Continued.

COUNTIES.	GOVERNOR					LIEUTENANT GOVERNOR.				SECRETARY OF STATE.				AUDITOR OF PUBLIC ACCOUNTS.				
	C. E. BENTLEY, P.	LORENZO CROUNSE R.	J. STERLING MORTON, D	CHARLES H. VAN WYCK, P. I.	SCATTERING.	THOMAS J. MAJORS, R.	CHARLES D. SCHRADER, P. I.	JAMES STEPHENS, P.	SAMUEL N. WOLBACH, D.	JOHN C. ALLEN, R.	ISAAC BOOSTROM, P.	FRANK M. CROW D.	JAMES M. EASTERLING, P. I.	LOGAN McREYNOLDS, P. I.	EUGENE MOORE, R.	P. F. O'SULLIVAN, D.	J. C. THOMAS, P.	SCATTERING.
Saline	126	1464	885	1021		1682	768	175	1009	1550	185	958	776	760	1550	1047	177	
Sarpy	37	501	567	362		522	303	32	558	523	36	601	262	265	531	608	31	
Saunders	193	1252	830	1791	1	1249	1722	190	863	1212	240	843	1753	1720	1284	862	201	
Scott's Bluff		199	71	161		606	140	10	71	297	11	78	140	187	208	75		
Seward	70	1237	965	1655		1268	1093	61	990	1288	60	990	972	989	1272	994	62	
Sheridan	45	523	229	954		553	909	53	223	572	43	226	914	990	573	230	47	
Sherman	40	405	155	640		399	622	25	201	429	27	163	642	644	406	169	28	
Sioux	4	121	86	81		180	178	3	81	129		87	177	177	125	88	1	
Stanton	26	324	404	257		387	229	21	421	338	17	424	224	208	352	435	18	
Thayer	87	1168	618	880		1219	792	76	646	1228	77	682	778	754	1210	681	80	
Thomas		33	38	18		34	19		34	36	2	97	15	21	36	38	1	
Thurston	10	423	97	191		408	192	16	159	440	18	140	96	92	444	166	12	
Valley	31	52	175	750		543	749	34	190	546	33	180	760	738	534	178	37	
Washington	66	983	729	605		968	587	46	781	976	49	787	512	513	996	778	49	
Wayne	33	606	336	560		565	444	35	404	603	41	406	440	427	631	427	41	
Webster	67	883	842	964		948	964	50	890	913	67	812	961	916	916	204	56	
Wheeler	5	104	32	152		106	155	7	33	108	6	34	157	151	111	35	5	
York	139	1684	431	1351		1750	1390	112	468	1776	126	455	1329	1320	1768	455	111	
Totals	6235	78426	44195	68617	1	81500	62501	5594	46421	82053	6979	46867	60822	60991	82557	46572	5750	

ABSTRACT OF VOTES CAST

At the General Election held in the State of Nebraska on the Eighth day of November A. D., 1892, for Treasurer, Attorney General, Commissioner of Public Lands and Buildings, Superintendent of Public Instruction.

COUNTIES	TREASURER			ATTORNEY GENERAL					COMMISSIONER PUBLIC LANDS AND BUILDINGS				SUPERINTENDENT PUBLIC INSTRUCTION			
	Joseph S. Bartley, R.	Andrew Beckman, D.	Jerry Denslow P.	Jacob V. Wolfe, P. I.	Martin I. Brower, P.	Matthew Gering, D.	George H. Hastings, R.	Virgil O. Strickler, P. I.	Jacob M. Gunnett, P. I.	A. R. Humphrey, R.	Charles E. Smith, P.	Jacob Wiggins, D.	Belle G. Bigelow, P.	A. K. Goudy, R.	Harman H. Hiatt, P. I.	J. A. Hornberger, D.
Adams	1550	678	188	1025	186	672	1504	1046	1092	1568	172	648	202	1489	1071	655
Antelope	753	259	109	933	115	258	741	932	916	737	103	250	102	743	918	267
Banner	181	40	12	174	21	37	178	164	167	187	13	34	20	182	171	35
Blaine	55	41	4	54	8	34	56	52	54	56	8	81	11	50	51	31
Boone	826	297	47	926	74	277	806	944	938	814	51	270	54	880	942	228
Boyd	653	187	21	286	34	366	458	282	296	463	27	342	41	431	804	354
Box Butte	364	226	19	524	26	241	346	510	514	365	18	225	26	359	512	226
Brown	346	143	15	255	19	161	339	232	244	340	15	158	15	344	251	149
Buffalo	1714	671	79	1784	92	639	1720	1772	1759	1751	80	616	95	1722	1767	631
Butler	973	993	94	901	102	1067	984	884	967	970	88	971	107	966	915	1004
Burt	1067	609	65	689	87	347	1110	726	743	1380	82	826	93	1316	763	320
Cass	2030	1737	99	662	185	1804	1974	632	645	2023	111	1687	122	2035	627	1660
Cedar	643	660	32	502	43	633	624	507	491	633	41	536	84	644	494	636
Chase	336	133	16	408	21	187	326	394	392	325	14	140	20	322	393	128

County																				
Cheyenne																				
Cherry																				
Clay																				
Colfax																				
Cuming																				
Custer																				
Dakota																				
Dawes																				
Dawson																				
Deuel																				
Dixon																				
Dodge																				
Douglas																				
Dundy																				
Fillmore																				
Franklin																				
Frontier																				
Furnas																				
Gage																				
Garfield																				
Gosper																				
Grant																				
Greeley																				
Hall																				
Hamilton																				
Harlan																				
Hayes																				
Hitchcock																				
Hooker																				
Holt																				
Howard																				
Jefferson																				
Johnson																				
Kearney																				
Keya Paha																				
Keith																				
Kimball																				
Knox																				
Lancaster																				

ABSTRACT OF VOTES CAST—Continued.

COUNTIES.	SUPERINTENDENT PUBLIC INSTRUCTION J. A. Hornberger, D.	Harman H. Hiatt, P. I.	A. K. Goudy, R.	Belle G. Bigelow, P.	COMMISSIONER PUBLIC LANDS AND BUILDINGS Jacob Wiggins, D.	Charles E. Smith, P.	A. R. Humphrey, R.	Jacob M. Gensert, P. I.	ATTORNEY GENERAL Virgil O. Strickler, P. I.	George H. Hastings, R.	Mathew Gering, D.	Martin I. Brower, P.	TREASURER Jacob V. Wolfe, P. I.	Jerry Denslow, P.	Andrew Beckman, D.	Joseph S. Bartley, R.
Lincoln	236	1074	885	68	325	61	786	1091	1160	784	249	73	1078	64	325	784
Logan	42	114	120	3	39	4	120	109	118	118	43	4	114	2	45	121
Loup	18	112	106		18	2	104	109	109	108	21		112	19	19	108
Madison	1181	621	927	87	940	85	1064	648	670	1064	969	94	669	98	901	1140
Merrick	349	651	740	119	351	112	738	642	661	727	339	121	646	106	356	745
McPherson	14	26	30	1	25	1	31	25	25	25	12	2	27	11	11	31
Nance	111	717	655	42	100	39	538	714	717	546	106	85	712	42	118	569
Nemaha	570	916	1139	82	589	92	1091	1025	960	1082	606	86	955	68	611	944
Nuckolls	360	1116	927	55	363	50	918	1005	1164	925	369	56	1185	85	367	1124
Otoe	1551	991	1410	145	1550	163	1430	1005	996	1897	1625	169	1046	142	1545	1435
Pawnee	421	487	1219	148	424	152	1191	498	491	1188	429	154	528	146	384	1210
Perkins	137	435	297	24	140	19	289	484	482	299	141	24	435	14	115	303
Pierce	468	309	337	21	466	25	347	314	313	360	471	19	321	18	468	364
Phelps	143	1006	641	139	135	134	635	1085	1069	632	161	141	1096	121	320	635
Platte	1142	880	716	65	1099	62	722	894	884	719	1128	70	918	58	1133	715
Polk	172	1107	675	112	165	105	964	1093	1099	674	174	118	1100	105	205	675
Red Willow	282	693	767	65	286	44	730	693	701	753	288	68	705	44	293	768

Richardson	1858	1189	99	824	194	1220	1812	797	764	1886	125	1193	164	1866	785	107
Rock	384	98	7	170	14	111	322	185	159	326		100	13	325	162	1154
Saline	1551	946	182	808	208	982	1654	731	777	1548	192	1031	210	1548	788	1041
Sarpy	527	619	32	259	48	647	507	228	246	520	46	621	44	523	241	608
Saunders	1175	1052	175	1680	203	884	1217	1733	1730	1226	397	864	202	1245	1718	856
Scotts Bluff	208	78	10	189	12	78	201	189	141	206	73	11	11	209	138	72
Seward	1281	1005	54	978	68	1011	1229	972	966	1283	57	1010	70	1226	981	987
Sheridan	578	231	41	902	47	297	574	923	918	396	47	224	48	591	914	226
Sherman	416	178	22	646	44	168	393	642	683	405	27	162	80	409	649	160
Sioux	180	95	7	176	6	90	185	181	177	126	9	99	11	126	173	89
Stanton	526	451	24	225	21	446	328	219	222	337	21	432	23	309	199	478
Thayer	1222	686	81	779	87	686	1210	766	745	1201	78	691	79	1216	788	684
Thomas	35	35		26	2	30	34	21	18	36	14	36	2	32	20	57
Thurston	432	179	15	90	14	163	433	94	99	488	38	159	14	434	95	165
Valley	544	177	28	778	40	188	623	760	732	528	57	170	56	529	774	180
Washington	984	632	61	478	65	813	978	489	494	997	30	780	67	966	487	785
Wayne	608	456	82	411	82	452	616	417	219	617	85	416	84	604	398	439
Webster	942	314	58	955	81	289	920	964	936	927	6	301	71	989	960	291
Wheeler	107	37	4	146	4	31	109	155	153	109	85	84	9	110	153	34
York	1174	474	115	1306	124	471	1765	1808	1823	1745	106	446	145	1766	1802	444
Totals	80421	49826	5537	61887	6756	48460	78919	62142	60721	79868	5999	48179	6513	81051	60623	47295

ABSTRACT OF VOTES CAST.

At the General Election held November 8, 1892, for Members of Congress, in the Fourth, Fifth and Sixth Congressional Districts, and For and Against the proposed amendments to the constitution, "adding to the number of executive officers" and "permitting investment of public school money in school district bonds."

COUNTIES.	Congressman Fourth District.				Congressman Fifth District.			Congressman Sixth District.				Amendments.				Total Vote.
	William H. Dech. (P.I.)	Eugene J. Hainer. (R.)	J. P. Kettlewell. (P.)	Victor Vifquain. (D.)	William E. Andrews. (R.)	O. C. Hubbell. (P.)	William A. McKeighan. (P.I. & D.)	Orlando K. Beebe. (P.)	A. T. Gatewood. (D.)	Omer M. Kem. (P.I.)	James Whitehead. (R.)	Executive Officers. For	Executive Officers. Ag'nst	Permanent School Fund. For	Permanent School Fund. Ag'nst	
Adams					1685	103	1591					1294	275	1892	184	2518
Antelope												875	254	1078	116	2095
Banner								16	28	178	189	196	12	164	14	411
Blaine								7	23	61	61	51	17	62	10	154
Boone												919	182	1004	125	2200
Boyd								17	299	324	583	422	35	484	33	1207
Box Butte								18	174	536	413	534	129	545	85	1158
Brown								14	100	308	344	305	44	346	40	801
Buffalo								79	503	1866	1794	1118	1001	1953	207	4516
Butler	928	963	90	1022								851	7	911	185	3291
Burt												1237	115	1259	96	2555
Cass												1648	340	1769	148	4901
Cedar												445	14	552	107	1843

Chase
Cheyenne
Cherry
Clay
Colfax
Cuming
Custer
Dakota
Dawes
Dawson
Deuel
Dixon
Dodge
Douglas
Dundy
Fillmore
Franklin
Frontier
Furnas
Gage
Garfield
Gosper
Grant
Greeley
Hall
Hamilton
Harlan
Hayes
Hitchcock
Hooker
Holt
Howard
Jefferson
Johnson
Kearney
Keya Paha
Keith
Kimball
Knox
Lancaster

ABSTRACT OF VOTES CAST.

At the General Election held November 8, 1892, for Members of Congress, in the Fourth, Fifth and Sixth Congressional Districts, and For and Against the proposed amendments to the constitution, "adding to the number of executive officers" and "permitting investment of public school money in school district bonds."

COUNTIES	CONGRESSMAN FOURTH DISTRICT — William H. Dech (P.I.)	Eugene J. Hainer (R.)	J.P. Kettlewell (P.)	Victor Vifquain (D.)	CONGRESSMAN FIFTH DISTRICT — William E. Andrews (R.)	O.C. Hubbell (P.)	William A. McKeighan (P.I. & D.)	CONGRESSMAN SIXTH DISTRICT — Orlando R. Beebe (P.)	A.T. Gatewood (D.)	Omer M. Kem (P.I.)	James Whitehead (R.)	AMENDMENTS — Executive Officers For	Executive Officers Ag'nst	Permanent School Fund For	Permanent School Fund Ag'nst	Total Vote
Lincoln								59	191	1137	876	770	290	938	144	2459
Logan								3	34	117	123	124	25	135	12	295
Loup								1	17	120	107	92	18	98	11	255
Madison												1119	397	1136	176	2853
Merrick												878	119	919	93	2005
McPherson								1	12	26	82	34	5	30	7	74
Nance												356	60	478	60	1557
Nemaha												1607	222	1684	159	2947
Nuckolls					995	47	1346					1139	303	1041	115	2607
Otoe												1230	445	1287	402	4518
Pawnee					353	17	504					706	224	810	149	2423
Perkins												433	55	457	52	899
Pierce												451	99	427	61	1203

County																	
Phelps	2043	173	925	225	785											682	1121
Platte	3041	76	781	247	1054				107	740		101					
Polk	2212	164	832	303	705												
Red Willow	1810	68	846	122	784				40	822	175					
Richardson	4191	133	1882		1896												
Rock	617	117	263	124	243	828	210	72			1130	186	1507	690
Saline	3932	120	1179	26	1098							172	1253	
Sarpy	1594	40	587	47	619						904	63	1278	1744
Saunders	445	201	1924	278	1847	216	159	58	7		980			990
Scotts Bluff	464	28	175	32	159									
Seward	3418	299	1472	344	1422	603	961	177	45				1216	608
Sheridan	1883	58	632	52	587	413	659	143	25					
Sherman	1308	125	398	160	360	188	188	79	1					
Sioux	450	23	153	39	121									
Stanton	1011	117	494	154	458				2		884	72		
Thayer	2934	156	1056	218	1020			29						
Thomas	108	10	31	15	29	41								
Thurston	806	49	295		316									
Valley	1596	101	536		807	528	729	150	27					
Washington	2375	101	672		542									
Wayne	1455	76	581	27	621					1006				
Webster	2494	189	1026	219	990	105	163	93	7	1133				
Wheeler	807	18	126	41	100									
York	2852	140	1919	209	1884				54		519	111	1763	1227
Totals	20259	11258	84426	14185	80032	14190	16328	8292	586	17480	838	14290	8988	1312	15645	11496

ABSTRACT OF VOTES CAST
November 8, 1892, for Members of Congress, in the following **Districts** recently demarcated:

FIRST CONGRESSIONAL DISTRICT.

COUNTIES.	WILLIAM J. BRYAN.	ALLEN W. FIELD.	R. W. MAXWELL.	JEROME SHAMP.
Cass	2201	1994	84	226
Johnson	914	1112	64	254
Lancaster	4700	5010	355	650
Nemaha	1355	1089	46	315
Otoe	1808	1493	114	693
Pawnee	904	1135	121	117
Richardson	1902	1811	79	154
Totals	13784	13644	863	2409

SECOND CONGRESSIONAL DISTRICT.

COUNTIES.	GEO. W. DOANE.	DAVID H. MERCER.	R. W. RICH- ARDSON.	ROBT. L. WHEELER.
Douglas......................	8892	9953	283	2440
Sarpy........................	647	533	28	240
Washington...................	849	1002	51	472
Totals	10388	11488	362	3152

THIRD CONGRESSIONAL DISTRICT.

COUNTIES.	GEO. F. KEIPER.	GEO. D. MEIKLE- JOHN.	W. A. POYNTER.	F. P. WIGTON.
Antelope	248	787	922	95
Boone..............................	255	837	978	25
Burt...............................	833	1219	770	72
Cedar	655	649	474	35
Colfax.............................	757	572	542	29
Cuming	1197	890	329	43
Dakota	500	444	183	12
Dixon	496	604	458	73
Dodge..............................	1721	1453	523	82
Knox...............................	510	859	598	79
Madison	983	1090	634	95
Merrick....	407	779	618	87
Nance..............................	83	652	716	21
Pierce.............................	508	371	293	15
Platte.............................	942	982	896	46
Stanton	435	345	213	14
Thurston...........................	133	494	86	7
Wayne	467	603	403	27
Totals................	10630	13635	9636	867

ABSTRACT OF VOTES CAST

At the General Election held in the State of Nebraska, on the 3d day of November, A. D., 1891, for Judge of the Supreme Court, and Regents of the University.

COUNTIES.	ALFRED M. POST, R	JOSEPH W. EDGERTON, I.	A. M. BITTENBENDER, P.	SCATTERING	CHARLES MARPLE, R.	H. P. SHUMWAY, R.	A. d'ALLEMAND I.	E. A. HADLEY I.	WILLIAM GOBST, P.	C. M. WOODWARD, P.	SCATTERING
Adams	1258	1240	137		1204	1104	1158	1187	149	181	
Antelope	953	659	73		588	589	891	885	191	92	
Banner	146	173	22		129	132	177	171	17	23	
Blaine	78	90	17		71	68	74	84	21	16	
Boone	729	862	77		697	678	865	894	68	71	
Boyd	521	223	89		263	359	291	237	122	73	
Box Bute	439	489	41		388	363	463	461	63	54	
Brown	297	329	30		299	293	271	283	40	45	
Buffalo	1499	1638	134		1329	1213	1583	1555	141	208	
Butler	1150	1123	106	1	934	910	934	1042	136	141	
Burt	830	894	121	2	799	817	807	802	128	104	5
Cass	1956	1307	156		1802	1678	1147	1119	131	185	
Cedar	453	694	40		375	443	627	657	58	44	
Chase	277	368	27		256	253	358	358	37	40	
Cheyenne	403	379	47		362	356	325	349	47	45	
Cherry	429	512	43		382	362	418	414	40	48	197
Clay	1097	1360	113		1012	1007	1293	1291	132	141	
Colfax	866	675	41		646	625	592	594	68	71	
Cuming	963	567	67		842	822	536	443	123	76	
Custer	1465	1869	160		1408	1318	1619	1961	145	154	
Dakota	408	540	45		552	394	457	470	45	33	
Dawes	778	637	76		688	702	595	593	109	123	
Dawson	890	968	49		824	794	904	946	60	62	
Deuel	237	239	33		214	190	195	248	43	48	
Dixon	569	637	119		474	572	534	508	103	79	
Dodge	1638	1023	161	4	1436	1350	914	971	179	165	
Douglas	12517	5739	364		11564	10049	3766	4015	580	799	
Dundy	325	333	36		309	299	358	350	37	38	
Filmore	1064	1386	121		992	961	1342	1356	143	173	
Franklin	549	661	49		539	510	608	655	45	58	
Frontier	449	754	33		435	418	821	764	24	33	
Furnas	524	847	46		489	464	927	845	57	60	
Gage	2640	1833	328		2394	2301	1798	1842	302	425	
Garfield	144	168	8		131	127	163	171	7	8	
Gosper	143	369	22		126	115	375	363	15	25	
Grant	40	61	6		29	37	58	48	4	10	
Greeley	344	549	30		226	193	627	728	19	34	
Hall	1379	1135	94	1	1224	1178	1082	1197	104	184	
Hamilton	1015	1076	118		913	860	1048	1061	127	137	2
Harlan	431	757	76		391	383	758	729	99	111	
Hayes	316	319	24		322	390	298	289	29	25	
Hitchcock	378	569	25		320	310	526	538	37	27	
Hooker	13	34	8		16	15	47	43	4	4	
Holt	1155	1167	166		1017	991	1156	1198	159	142	
Howard	528	980	54		491	458	900	975	58	68	

ABSTRACT OF VOTES CAST—*Concluded.*

COUNTIES.	JUDGE SUPREME COURT.				REGENTS STATE UNIVERSITY						
	ALFRED M. POST.	JOSEPH W. EDGERTON,	A. M. BUTTENBENDER, P.	SCATTERING.	CHARLES MARPLE, R	H. P. SHUMWAY, R	A. d'ALLEMAND.	E. A. HADLEY, I.	WILLIAM GORST, P	C. M. WOODWARD, P.	SCATTERING.
Jefferson...............	1002	1012	145		885	821	912	975	131	150	
Johnson	892	733	140		772	782	752	753	121	159	11
Kearney..............	715	843	110		643	611	785	814	105	117	
Keya Paha...	255	377	20		265	256	653	371	25	21	
Keith.............	138	228			168	147	247	257			
Kimball............	106	63	16		93	91	54	52	22	19	3
Knox...	657	781	96		625	633	735	735	104	97	
Lancaster	4269	3158	514		3882	3940	3044	3016	578	705	
Lincoln	802	879	62		773	758	932	921	87	94	
Logan.	116	133	4		108	105	120	122	6	6	
Loup	103	108	11		90	89	106	119	12	12	
Madison	1107	1006	123		991	942	897	910	163	113	
Merrick............	707	747	86		587	514	634	639	97	107	366
McPherson.........	25	43			23	22	41	36	4	2	8
Nance	489	621	39		435	439	629	637	61	56	
Nemaha	949	904	126		883	868	951	863	141	148	
Nuckolls...	577	914	63		599	578	988	999	79	78	
Otoe......	1361	1399	188		1258	1135	1271	1235	185	172	
Pawnee............	1004	696	133		1029	991	658	133	645	147	1
Perkins............	263	444	21		206	211	408	428	39	38	2
Pierce	346	531	33		212	228	319	308	42	36	
Phelps.............	396	813	108		384	361	853	842	159	140	555
Platte	1148	1154	68		911	878	1220	1259	107	134	
Polk	507	111	92		415	382	997	1029	85	96	
Red Willow	756	705	62		632	599	688	680	65	68	
Richards..........	1468	1249	150		1430	1408	1109	1172	130	133	
Rock	291	206	32		301	5	221	216	75	74	
Saline.............	1466	1417	221		1191	1105	1365	1388	219	234	
Sarpy.............	528	520	65		493	438	445	452	82	57	
Saunders	1500	2006	183		1458	1396	1767	1762	209	209	
Scott's Bluff......	213	153	18		194	191	144	133	21	24	
Seward............	1196	1223	88		1148	1089	1127	1165	97	184	
Sheridan...........	618	968	112		555	562	910	945	107	112	
Sherman	314	593	24		280	244	584	583	33	51	
Sioux...	152	222	24		147	143	190	187	26	24	
Stanton	437	322	46		408	379	204	318	8	8	
Thayer	935	1027	90		972	910	962	965	79	108	
Thomas	60	39	8		45	44	41	38	10	13	
Thurston...	282	162	25		280	275	132	135	27	27	
Valley	463	676	52		493	453	665	690	48	68	
Washington.......	925	710	118		814	816	682	704	156	138	
Wayne	442	407	62		352	446	394	389	163	61	
Webster	790	981	89		704	702	903	918	75	105	
Wheeler...........	138	157	6		128	129	146	148	8	2	52
York	1517	1422	113		1490	1450	1423	1422	110	143	
Totals	79,447	72311	7322	8	69607	65932	66924	67690	8997	9177	1203

ABSTRACT OF VOTES CAST.

At the General **election in** the State of Nebraska on November **4th, 1890,** for and against **the amendment** to prohibit **the sale of malt, spirituous, and vinous liquors;** for and against an amendment increasing the number of Judges **of the** Supreme Court; and for and against an amendment increasing **the salaries of** Judges of the Supreme and District Courts, with the **total** vote cast in the state.

COUNTIES	FOR PROHIBITION	AGAINST PROHIBITION	FOR LICENSE	AGAINST LICENSE	FOR JUDGES	AGAINST JUDGES	FOR SALARY	AGAINST SALARY	TOTAL VOTE
Adams	1708	1777	622	1821	1100	919	1009	922	3790
Antelope	1930	876	617	1082	272	975	125	1044	2187
Banner	167	157	132	153	93	116	80	118	419
Blaine	95	118	54	82	70	20	57	27	246
Boone	990	758	542	945	432	956	335	964	1923
Box Butte	486	677	574	500	594	290	516	843	1471
Brown	517	389	117	43.	283	366	257	383	964
Buffalo	2209	1885	1475	2433	1564	1743	1320	1928	4572
Butler	1377	1781	904	1367	979	1634	320	1995	3591
Burt	1464	857	465	1527	1122	360	655	649	2638
Cass	1741	2800	1545	2886	2114	640	1108	1019	5145
Cedar	463	798	203	418	395	380	312	420	1469
Chase	427	265	181	320	276	215	181	246	868
Cheyenne	300	628	228	280	497	64	436	56	1029
Cherry	434	666	240	390	614	145	496	151	1246
Clay	1947	1206	861	1965	843	480	301	938	3569
Colfax	574	1491	239	1640	1240	207	811	302	2214
Cuming	467	2174	324	438	1379	693	1278	740	2785
Custer	2193	2048	1790	2117	1125	1728	766	2101	4460
Dakota	365	784	205	312	731	87	641	88	1284
Dawes	822	558	795	844	9 6	297	658	571	1893
Dawson	1206	846	627	1321	669	967	665	967	2371
Deuel	178	217	171	206	260	96	165	109	552
Dixon	872	645	544	848	719	286	564	380	1693
Dodge	1401	2610	1412	1515	2755	468	2308	539	4394
Douglas	1555	23918	22786	1946	23499	97	2259	117	26263
Dundy	443	198	156	300	135	100	223	....	828
Filmore	1683	1554	978	1386	1566	398	1151	414	3589
Franklin	903	586	457	853	144	644	78	649	1640
Frontier	928	701	619	826	287	705	146	690	1713
Furnas	963	718	503	999	466	643	213	697	1860
Gage	3883	3102	1556	3459	2296	1424	2016	1497	7004
Garfield	180	162	103	198	60	231	40	239	397
Gosper	371	404	224	532	254	446	116	528	957
Grant	54	78	62	25	65	46	32	50	161
Greeley	285	701	186	540	254	445	173	455	1075
Hall	889	2950	340	3499	715	3124	674	3165	3839
Hamilton	1239	1381	773	1465	574	1247	344	1317	2955
Harlan	965	478	306	908	205	512	133	471	1580
Hayes	337	367	233	431	83	600	58	662	873
Hitchcock	570	465	309	554	410	184	211	208	1129
Hooker	20	40	33	25	41	18	12	44	73
Holt	1361	1093	888	1475	898	601	783	668	2969
Howard	779	1038	422	1013	309	667	165	701	1991
Jefferson	1367	1501	1077	1462	885	762	605	968	3097
Johnson	1372	1047	855	1424	213	806	158	1853	2528
Kearney	1079	868	590	1289	297	1407	158	1533	2092
Keya Paha	409	361	247	455	160	422	137	433	85u

ABSTRACT OF VOTES CAST—Concluded.

COUNTIES	For Prohibition	Against Prohibition	For License	Against License	For Judges	Against Judges	For Salary	Against Salary	Total Vote
Keith	173	210	114	253	240	96	192	89	478
Kimball	95	65	36	87	136	28	124	31	204
Knox	815	997	767	877	1156	298	876	365	2138
Lancaster	4561	5215	4306	4851	6537	1148	6069	1226	11448
Lincoln	901	956	402	1362	1242	498	842	669	2234
Logan	178	94	80	181	167	78	111	121	298
Loup	117	133	70	165	37	162	22	182	310
Madison	1039	1762	853	891	1075	881	953	899	3006
Merrick	987	740	508	1012	552	619	454	639	2010
McPherson	15	20	24	12	28	......	20	......	49
Nance	614	630	556	612	549	241	298	303	1878
Nemaha	1397	1389	900	1550	208	1851	150	1913	3098
Nuckolls	1478	792	367	1593	579	836	432	975	2471
Otoe	1402	2083	2511	1493	1709	1402	1489	1523	4798
Pawnee	1482	731	611	1350	382	1085	164	1288	2410
Perkins	516	305	255	466	320	138	174	157	895
Pierce	333	713	337	564	364	277	300	307	1160
Phelps	1610	426	389	1533	365	1169	314	1204	2180
Platte	792	2300	111	272	1593	614	1102	759	3304
Polk	1311	672	540	1307	370	270	282	227	2250
Red Willow	693	893	668	738	828	209	321	320	1748
Richardson	1596	2049	1619	1526	600	1178	455	1159	4071
Rock	348	274	138	308	215	297	128	338	666
Saline	2051	2119	1840	2305	1690	911	774	1359	4557
Sarpy	366	1220	615	451	819	182	725	215	1752
Saunders	1955	2556	2021	2062	1449	1120	944	1766	4896
Scotts Bluff	171	130	118	161	237	55	147	96	413
Seward	1571	723	836	1840	898	1218	418	1416	3700
Sheridan	1029	774	612	1030	482	692	284	791	2019
Sherman	508	704	469	637	211	733	112	760	1300
Sioux	142	256	137	145	164	143	106	171	455
Stanton	249	398	172	886	560	115	462	139	1044
Thayer	1197	1340	653	1247	1024	354	620	360	2795
Thomas	73	47	46	68	60	35	45	40	131
Thurston	291	331	373	181	616	7	596	13	687
Valley	768	626	571	772	627	582	358	720	1515
Washington	1026	1378	686	1284	1271	180	1102	185	2794
Wayne	512	669	222	544	533	412	431	479	1359
Webster	1252	757	470	1413	296	1469	190	1540	2370
Wheeler	161	178	137	149	96	142	56	150	396
York	1954	1510	1213	2100	1263	1637	593	2251	8829
Totals	82292	111728	75462	91084	86418	53022	69192	61519	214861

POPULAR VOTE FOR GOVERNOR.

1894—Silas A. Holcomb.. 97,815
      T. J. Majors... 94,613
      E. A. Gerrard 4,439
      P. D. Sturdevant... 6,985—203,852
1896—Silas A. Holcomb..116,415
      John H. McColl.. 94,723
      Robert S. Bibb.. 3,577
      Joel Warner... 1,560
      Chas. Sadilek... 578—217,853

POPULAR VOTE FOR MEMBERS OF CONGRESS.

1894—Jesse B. Strode, 1st District.............. 18,185
      A. H. Weir,   " 12,730
      R. A. Hawley,   "   .... 1,078— 31,993
      David H. Mercer, 2d District 12,946
      D. Clem. Deaver,   "   3,962
      James E. Boyd,   "   8,165
      Geo. D. Woodbey,   "   ....   393— 25,466
      Geo. D. Meiklejohn, 3d District.......................16,513
      J. M. Devine,   " 11,738
      W. A. Hensley,   "   8,019
      J. C. Thomas,   "   ....   861— 37,131
      Eugene J. Hainer, 4th District....................19,493
      W. L. Stark,   " 15,542
      S. S. Alley,   "   2,703
      Mrs. C. M. Woodward, "   ....   905— 38,703
      William E. Andrews, 5th District 16,310
      W. A. McKelgan   " 15,450
      Thomas F. Ashby,   "   875
      O. C. Hubbell,   "   ....   651— 33,286
      Omer M. Kem, 6th District 17,077
      Matt. Dougherty,   " 14,676
      William Bone,   "   ....   891— 32,644

1896—Jefferson H. Broady, 1st District............... 17,137
      Jesse B. Strode   "   - 17,356
      George E. Hampton,   "   218
      Charles E. Smith,   "   ....   429— 35,140
      David H. Mercer, 2d District....................... 14,861
      Edward R. Daffie,   "   13,286
      Charles Watts,   "   202
      George W. Woodbey,   "   ....   59— 28,408
      Samuel Maxwell, 3d District 23,487
      Ross L. Hammond,   "   18,633
      C. M. Griffith,   "   254
      David Brown,   "   ....   521— 42,895
      Wm. L. Stark, 4th District.................. 26,515
      Eugene J. Hainer   "   18,844
      B. Spurlock,   "   425
      R. E. Dunphy,   "   697
      W. H. Dech,   "   ....   114— 40,595
      R. D. Sutherland, 5th District................ 18,332
      W. E. Andrews,   "   15,621
      R. S. Proudfet,   "   453
      C. W. Preston,   "   266
      J. S. Miller,   "   ....   153— 34,805
      W. L. Green, 6th District... 19,378
      A. E. Cody,   "   14,841
      A. D. George,   "   436
      A. C. Sloan,   "   ....   119— 34,674

ABSTRACT OF VOTES CAST

At the General Election held in the State of Nebraska, on the Seventh day of November, A. D. 1893, for Judges of the Supreme Court, and Regents of the University.

COUNTIES.	Ada M. Bittenbender, P.	Thos. O. C. Harrison, R.	Silas A. Holcomb, P. I.	Frank Irvine, D.	Scattering.	Milton H. Doolittle, D.	Henry D. Estabrook, R.	E. L. Heath, P. I.	A. A. Monroe, P. I.	James M. Pile, D.	A. E. Ricker, P.	Mrs. C. H. Walker, P.	Charles Weston, R.	C. L. Brainard, P. I.	John P. Heald, P.	Chas. W. Kaley, R.	Charles Klosan, D.
Adams	129	1316	1074	525		589	1386	982	1015	652	122	127	1234	971	145	1348	567
Antelope	93	615	925	177		217	689	878	809	192	91	92	625	785	95	637	195
Banner	18	139	156	59		73	179	141	137	65	13	12	162	131	17	167	73
Blaine	2	108	20	19		60	60	28	28	34	9	6	56	17	9	56	41
Boone	58	776	963	203		242	829	928	916	218	71	62	788	851	78	810	225
Box Butte	25	298	533	134		212	315	538	601	164	34	28	286	499	82	232	215
Boyd	41	410	366	223		316	398	328	523	232	19	22	279	325	52	383	261
Brown	17	301	344	130		144	324	313	304	115	15		303	296	16	297	122
Buffalo	86	1622	1573	309		456	1721	1672	1647	869	91	93	1614	1666	87	1650	427
Burt	86	853	807	292		272	963	603	688	254	56	71	867	600	84	698	239
Butler	98	927	1194	835		1105	1015	608	719	976	83	124	1609	806	119	942	1020
Cass	109	1874	951	816		1330	1978	581	692	1298	107	97	940	412	122	1870	1270
Cedar	40	603	523	657		732	661	393	395	725	57	62	578	383	40	617	676
Chase	29	309	365	120		140	309	351	348	126	21	23	296	369	22	288	131
Cherry	24	315	505	160		171	348	461	461	165	17	17	338	560	27	333	170

Cheyenne
Clay
Colfax
Cuming
Custer
Dakota
Dawes
Dawson
Deuel
Dixon
Dodge
Douglas
Dundy
Fillmore
Franklin
Frontier
Furnas
Gage
Garfield
Gosper
Grant
Greeley
Hall
Hamilton
Harlan
Hayes
Hitchcock
Holt
Hooker
Howard
Jefferson
Johnson
Kearney
Keith
Keya Paha
Kimball
Knox
Lancaster
Lincoln

ABSTRACT OF VOTES CAST—*Continued.*

COUNTIES.	JUDGE SUPREME COURT					REGENTS STATE UNIVERSITY								REGENTS STATE UNIVERSITY, TO FILL VACANCY			
	ADA M. BITTENBENDER, P	THOS. O. C. HARRISON, R	SILAS A. HOLCOMB, P.I.	FRANK IRVINE, D	SCATTERING.	MILTON H. DOOLITTLE, D	HENRY D. ESTABROOK, R	E. L. HEATH, P.I.	A. A. MONROE, P.I.	JAMES M. PILE, D	A. E. RICKER, P	MRS. C. H. WALKER, P	CHARLES WESTON, R	C. L. BRAINARD, P.I.	JOHN P. HEALD, P	CHAS. W. KALEY, R	CHARLES KLOMAN, D
Logan	3	88	125	26		37	97	99	97	36	2	1	95	87	5	95	38
Loup	8	108	118	10		18	97	116	114	11	3	4	89	112	3	96	15
Madison	83	1124	881	824		1069	1190	530	508	1043	78	95	1094	528	96	1055	924
McPherson	1	31	51	12		13	32	44	42	14	1	2	32	49	2	33	14
Merrick	91	543	569	234		291	525	477	442	268	104	96	586	447	110	586	286
Nance	32	583	660	129		123	623	647	627	119	34	85	546	667	40	603	127
Nemaha	92	852	977	415		497	923	857	900	464	65	72	810	842	72	944	553
Nuckolls	67	940	995	242		302	967	972	940	319	43	52	925	977	61	1082	523
Otoe	142	1357	1078	1222		1292	1374	874	863	1211	130	153	1290	892	154	1354	1323
Pawnee	114	1130	552	288		356	1121	466	387	259	202	93	1049	409	138	1014	267
Perkins	28	212	495	113		129	239	453	444	118	25	23	217	461	33	229	117
Phelps	138	608	1053	94		125	629	923	971	93	145	119	560	988	146	697	105
Pierce	17	353	392	360		410	361	339	327	387	15	15	313	337	28	314	361
Platte	89	690	869	1030		1200	678	773	733	1150	74	81	663	703	90	697	1144
Polk	116	612	1117	161		190	658	1028	1025	170	103	107	626	1002	541	618	177
Red Willow	51	676	712	168		185	720	681	672	173	66	50	688	658	67	702	184
Richardson	106	1440	670	796		1056	1664	484	456	996	84	85	1502	631	95	1501	1015
Rock	17	224	212	108	1	133	261	158	148	114	15	17	243	145	14	247	86

Saline	128	1352	945	646		877	1475	675	354	778	145	140	1340	609	151	1369	783
Sarpy	63	282	601	438		538	494	214	236	519	57	60	409	242	71	456	664
Saunders	171	1178	1744	639	1	764	1325	1610	1507	660	160	142	1169	1388	229	1048	698
Scott's Bluff	21	152	152	77		82	194	115	108	69	14	13	184	96	13	192	77
Seward	65	1200	960	744	2	635	1341	739	764	824	46	50	1154	773	40	1236	689
Sheridan	64	429	931	193		208	471	857	789	169	51	77	583	823	30	369	157
Sherman	27	298	767	62		91	366	655	637	73	23	24	829	625	36	351	75
Sioux	14	116	203	89		101	120	196	180	84	9	14	113	190	10	112	92
Stanton	28	406	253	425		438	431	172	167	456	23	39	380	178	17	431	471
Thayer	84	1131	646	683		830	1209	480	480	798	69	73	1150	445	78	1192	797
Thomas	2	66	33			46	48	16	14	49	2		41	11	3	43	66
Thurston	16	315	120	259		283	322	78	119	278	13	11	294	77	29	807	275
Valley	36	598	684	114		137	547	725	690	129	32	27	484	696	42	539	154
Washington	83	688	464	562		616	841	537	362	607	68	80	740	306	82	782	578
Wayne	39	511	341	365		379	558	246	214	653	28	28	65	281	41	483	40
Webster	77	668	952	247		274	902	884	846	261	63	68	819	831	62	1061	228
Wheeler	4	111	137	22		27	98	147	149	25	7	6	94	147	6	95	23
York	106	1626	1455	284		364	1739	1220	1167	353	83	89	1621	1228	101	1718	359
Totals	6357	75082	65666	375545	6	43069	78079	55016	54547	40855	6078	6306	68787	53821	6927	73119	41279

A BSTRACT OF VOTES CAST

At the General Election held in the State of Nebraska, on the Sixth day of November, A. D. 1894, for Governor, Lieutenant Governor, Secretary of State, and Auditor of Public Accounts.

COUNTIES	GOVERNOR				LIEUT. GOVERNOR				SECRETARY OF STATE					AUDITOR OF PUBLIC ACCOUNTS			
	E. A. Gerrard, P.	Silas A. Holcomb, D. P. I.	Thomas J. Majors, R.	Phelps D. Sturdevant, S. D.	Belle G. Bigelow, P.	Rodney R. Dunphy, S. D.	James N. Gaffin, D. P. I.	Robert E. Moore, R.	Francis I. Ellick, D.	L. Hoepes, P.	H. W. McFadden, P. I.	Joel A. Piper, R.	D. Forrest P. Rolfe, S. D.	Otto Baumann, S. D.	Eugene Moore, R.	Levi J. Smith, P.	John W. Wilson, P. I.
Adams	91	1656	1836	67	128	190	1639	1664	162	120	1440	1818	88	143	1847	131	1445
Antelope	61	1154	872	51	79	80	1039	906	75	71	1007	889	62	168	916	72	989
Banner	5	161	175	18	5	25	141	189	15	4	134	173	21	29	173	9	138
Blaine	6	82	65	9	6	16	56	65	10	5	55	65	11	15	68	8	52
Boone	68	1126	974	65	61	116	1065	988	89	61	1013	909	78	140	1010	67	1608
Box Butte	11	621	541	48	20	93	539	545	62	20	507	523	90	126	634	26	507
Boyd	56	616	443	49	31	69	556	471	59	31	541	463	30	83	479	31	529
Brown	14	357	404	27	15	48	325	404	36	12	299	400	42	73	400	13	304
Buffalo	45	2065	1798	59	66	98	1940	1833	155	54	1782	1825	114	198	1841	53	1874
Burt	60	1064	1146	23	61	69	979	1249	111	68	757	1275	55	164	1253	72	794
Butler	92	1903	1852	87	101	187	1744	1279	454	99	1826	1278	122	358	1306	130	1480
Cass	105	1884	2373	140	130	387	1656	2472	416	110	1373	2526	235	411	2555	152	1588

County																						
Cedar																						
Chase																						
Cherry																						
Cheyenne																						
Clay																						
Colfax																						
Cuming																						
Custer																						
Dakota																						
Dawes																						
Dawson																						
Dixon																						
Deuel																						
Dodge																						
Douglas																						
Dundy																						
Fillmore																						
Franklin																						
Frontier																						
Furnas																						
Gage																						
Garfield																						
Gosper																						
Grant																						
Greeley																						
Hall																						
Hamilton																						
Harlan																						
Hayes																						
Hitchcock																						
Holt																						
Hooker																						
Howard																						
Jefferson																						
Johnson																						
Kearney																						
Keith																						
Keya Paha																						
Kimball																						

ABSTRACT OF VOTES CAST—*Continued.*

COUNTIES	GOVERNOR — E. A. GERRARD, P.	GOVERNOR — SILAS A. HOLCOMB, D.P.	GOVERNOR — THOMAS J. MAJORS, R.	GOVERNOR — PHELPS D. STURDEVANT, S.D.	LIEUT. GOVERNOR — BELLE G. BIGELOW, P.	LIEUT. GOVERNOR — RODNEY E. DURPHY, S.D.	LIEUT. GOVERNOR — JAMES N. GAFFIN, D.P.	LIEUT. GOVERNOR — ROBERT E. MOORE, R.	SEC. OF STATE — FRANCIS I. ELLICK, D.	SEC. OF STATE — L. HOMPES, P.	SEC. OF STATE — H. W. McFADDEN, P.	SEC. OF STATE — JOEL A. PIPER, R.	SEC. OF STATE — D. FORREST P. ROLFE, S.D.	AUDITOR — OTTO BAUMAN, S.D.	AUDITOR — EUGENE MOORE, R.	AUDITOR — LEM J. SMITH, P.	AUDITOR — JOHN W. WILSON, P.
Knox	100	1205	912	86	87	154	1065	870	153	91	896	976	131	263	1040	107	870
Lancaster	336	4275	6997	221	496	431	3672	7189	541	468	3151	6986	422	740	7165	523	3122
Lincoln	46	1688	990	37	50	60	972	1079	68	42	914	1083	44	73	1046	83	953
Logan	4	110	105	9	3	18		105	13	3	94	104	10	25	102	4	92
Loup	3	122	112	1		4	113	114	2	1	102	114	3	5	112	5	111
Madison	66	1509	1404	167	75	311	1250	1492	380	63	818	1472	174	396	1713	51	920
McPherson	1	47	43			4	41	44		1	41	37	3	5	39	4	38
Merrick	73	887	840	60	88	109	773	876	111	83	692	877	73	142	880	95	719
Nance	29	801	652	25	41	36	763	660	59	34	702	665	32	51	676	39	726
Nemaha	49	1362	1528	61	52	107	1341	1465	179	69	1162	1434	103	144	1431	80	1257
Nuckolls	52	1339	1197	58	47	84	1283	1210	133	57	1170	1187	76	130	1222	61	1218
Otoe	106	1568	2080	409	130	696	1552	1928	352	145	1257	1174	848	854	1934	157	1307
Pawnee		920	1361	73	105	120	825	1398	187	114	654	1389	86	268	1396	123	749
Perkins	10	291	241	26	104	47	286	247	24	8	269	240	30	49	234	16	268
Phelps	53	1136	840	34	81	57	992	931	25	72	975	842	89	61	935	92	963

County																	
Pierce	22	700	574	60	30	122	606	588	306	28	355	566	69	188	654	31	458
Platte	76	1734	992	166	80	359	1508	1001	888	61	934	991	205	623	1061	74	1233
Polk	88	1293	792	89	87	66	1186	855	52	84	1166	841	50	78	831	100	1172
Red Willow	41	876	1001	39	35	62	845	997	37	41	640	970	47	75	973	46	815
Richardson	121	1784	2107	218	116	352	1611	2105	671	116	1003	2108	213	415	2107	142	1461
Rock	12	252	323	70	7	15	363	340	55	7	207	388	10	33	542	9	339
Saline	124	1615	2063	207	144	463	1259	2068	456	150	971	2098	234	518	2068	191	1124
Sarpy	36	973	570	54	60	172	783	565	346	37	418	629	122	333	688	54	636
Saunders	91	2582	1708	93	94	181	2441	1744	336	116	1969	1813	199	377	1821	143	2062
Scotts Bluff	16	135	200	30	14	42	133	202	33	12	133	200	82	47	201	14	131
Seward	53	1605	1436	140	47	325	1389	1318	416	54	1083	1530	170	343	1576	63	1284
Sheridan	48	1075	350	45	50	84	1017	583	90	50	1008	588	82	92	565	40	1017
Sherman	13	719	389	15	17	39	666	436	27	17	685	440	81	41	565	25	639
Sioux	8	185	144	57	6	48	167	102	38	6	189	162	37	61	130	8	157
Stanton	12	668	494	96	20	145	561	533	273	21	331	527	77	223	584	22	414
Thayer	67	1150	1387	154	82	238	1082	1566	163	112	977	1537	162	273	1557	85	1021
Thomas	4	86	55	9	8	22	37	49	13	10	31	59	10	26	59	4	29
Thurston	11	572	313	40	13	59	522	322	306	16	206	322	53	160	319	21	239
Valley	17	793	594	25	22	39	740	613	28	23	719	612	27	45	614	27	715
Washington	49	1291	1111	60	70	197	985	1266	441	57	878	1245	134	396	1308	69	738
Wayne	31	890	780	88	30	176	643	828	235	86	468	833	98	286	874	45	507
Webster	45	1188	1150	57	53	125	1091	1149	77	46	1043	1148	97	355	1163	54	1043
Wheeler	4	180	95	8	5	16	167	96		3	163	98	10	16	98	6	185
York	87	1608	1824	66	96	129	1396	1983	80	85	1555	1980	60	144	1990	92	1506
Totals	4439	97548	94613	6965	5189	13785	85393	97298	19464	56052	69883	96579	9602	19536	98728	5619	75669

ABSTRACT OF VOTES CAST

At the General Election held in the State of Nebraska, on the Sixth day of November, A. D. 1894, for Treasurer, Attorney General, Commissioner of Public Lands and Buildings, and Superintendent of Public Instruction.

COUNTIES	TREASURER					SUPERINTENDENT PUBLIC INSTRUCTION				ATTORNEY GENERAL				COMMISSIONER PUBLIC LANDS AND BUILDINGS			
	Joseph S. Bartley, R.	Lake Bridenthal, S.D.	Gottlieb A. Luikart, D.	D.L. Pond, P.	John H. Powers, P.L.	Henry R. Corbett, R.	Milton Doolittle, S.D.	William A. Jones, D.P.L.	F. Bernice Kearney, P.	John H. Ames, S.D.	Daniel B. Carey, D.P.L.	Arthur S. Churchill, R.	J.L. Mack, P.	Jacob Bigler, S.D.	Henry M. Hill, P.	Sidney J. Kent, D.P.L.	Henry C. Russell, R.
Adams	1814	126	134	104	1447	1603	165	1612	93	131	1464	1859	118	137	126	1533	1814
Antelope	889	64	120	74	996	891	94	1040	74	86	1047	887	75	78	77	1058	882
Banner	190	24	8		143	184	34	125	7	25	132	180	12	24	10	133	198
Blaine	66	15	4	4	53	65	17	55	4	18	53	66	3	17	5	53	66
Boone	972	109	65	71	1025	954	125	1006	70	118	1006	1009	61	129	65	1031	989
Box Butte	536	98	32	19	511	540	116	502	15	100	548	529	14	102	20	544	519
Boyd	461	70	27	82	516	497	90	538	24	70	554	461	29	63	29	566	485
Brown	402	35	42	19	206	404	51	321	12	48	321	405	14	15	15	319	402
Buffalo	1804	133	137	63	1412	1792	145	1901	48	137	1998	1890	53	128	50	1927	1826
Burt	1560	84	67	65	750	1253	67	825	53	63	869	1227	38	73	67	825	1254
Butler	1290	225	382	94	1263	1816	186	1671	87	174	1732	1276	97	177	106	1700	1297
Cass	2509	304	422	127	1301	2604	358	1542	146	344	1631	2573	125	338	130	1646	2558

Cedar.........
Chase.........
Cherry........
Cheyenne......
Clay..........
Colfax........
Cuming........
Custer........
Dakota........
Dawes.........
Dawson........
Deuel.........
Dixon.........
Dodge.........
Douglas.......
Dundy.........
Fillmore......
Franklin......
Frontier......
Furnas........
Gage..........
Garfield......
Gosper........
Grant.........
Greeley.......
Hall..........
Hamilton......
Harlan........
Hayes.........
Hitchcock.....
Holt..........
Hooker........
Howard........
Jefferson.....
Johnson.......
Kearney.......
Keith.........
Keya Paha.....
Kimball.......

ABSTRACT OF VOTES CAST—Continued.

COUNTIES	COMMISSIONER PUBLIC LANDS AND BUILDINGS				ATTORNEY GENERAL				SUPERINTENDENT PUBLIC INSTRUCTION				TREASURER				
	Henry C. Russell, R.	Sidney J. Kent, D.P.I.	Henry M. Hill, P.	Jacob Bigler, S.D.	J.L. Mack, P.	Arthur S. Churchill, R.	Daniel B. Carey, D.P.I.	John H. Ames, S.D.	F. Berwick Kearney, P.	William A. Jones, D.P.I.	Milton Doolittle, S.D.	Henry R. Corbett, R.	John H. Powers, P.I.	D.L. Pond, P.	Gottlieb A. Luikart, D.	Lars Brudenthal, S.D.	Joseph S. Bartley, R.
Knox	986	1042	96	151	93	990	1062	139	89	1010	173	1000	893	96	162	149	984
Lancaster	6981	3810	484	547	512	6851	3402	831	448	3428	566	7036	3173	448	404	528	7017
Lincoln	1056	953	58	56	54	1063	936	53	44	932	66	1070	935	43	47	63	1042
Logan	100	95	4	19	3	101	94	19	5	93	18	114	111	3	8	16	101
Loup	111	115		4		113	114	3		112	3	114	614				114
Madison	1494	1228	79	310	77	1467	1214	316	68	1227	320	1461		61	845	175	1428
McPherson	41	38		6	1	43	42	4	1	43	4	41	42				41
Madison													692	81	104	91	865
Merrick	863	760	92	105	85	873	736	109	84	738	109	886	709	52	45	45	864
Nance	668	732	88	41	37	639	752	43	27	736	43	675	1182	53	162	115	1431
Nemaha	1349	1367	58	101	57	1144	1341	105	59	1331	105	1905	1167	165	100	107	1199
Nuckolls	1307	1287	48	85	56	1292	1261	85	52	1262	75	1239	1309	110	417	554	1364
Otoe	1870	1466	101	783	145	1935	1446	784	153	1488	737	1879	652	13	188	120	1396
Pawnee	1390	795	122	127	109	1899	788	132	100	737	129	1430	286		12	41	230
Perkins	236	207	13	50	12	236	272	39	9	270	43	230		64	21	53	
Phelps	924	988	76	53	716	932	985	49	72	965	55	935	1060				909

County																
Pierce	563	112	268	30	257	578	129	583	24	124	592	502	24	129	22	596	675
Platte	999	347	639	60	913	1002	390	1532	65	539	1607	1008	64	383	64	1559	1012
Polk	825	68	83	89	1168	861	68	1128	92	63	1184	689	208	60	103	1163	840
Red Willow	970	46	42	44	828	959	68	831	45	69	817	891	89	75	50	831	970
Richardson	2103	310	667	115	934	2160	358	1513	103	342	1546	2113	114	341	118	1555	2113
Rock	333	23	61	16	201	339	28	250	5	25	257	337	5	19	14	237	533
Saline	2056	428	251	152	1010	2114	440	1174	146	477	1194	2067	138	483	160	1171	2069
Sarpy	613	179	323	53	408	648	183	631	53	177	659	633	67	193	64	677	604
Saunders	1799	260	197	119	2002	1861	202	2178	120	214	2262	1799	134	207	127	2217	1824
Scotts Bluff	196	39	15	16	128	200	47	131	12	47	127	205	14	43	12	133	194
Seward	1533	206	391	60	1073	1537	239	1381	46	242	1388	1536	56	249	60	1405	1535
Sheridan	550	66	58	48	1019	570	90	1009	51	57	1006	668	53	89	53	1013	568
Sherman	440	34	16	20	634	450	45	631	14	58	648	446	17	82	18	654	437
Sioux	145	44	35	5	146	151	64	158	4	56	154	165	17	55	7	158	149
Stanton	517	130	218	29	844	533	157	508	14	146	598	532	28	165	19	529	517
Thayer	1562	217	136	78	938	1592	231	1044	71	230	1039	1589	67	236	78	1064	1562
Thomas	58	19	6	4	31	62	19	32	3	24	85	58	2	21	3	31	58
Thurston	324	88	274	15	206	332	76	470	14	60	491	329	15	68	11	483	313
Valley	606	41	15	26	714	617	43	723	22	49	740	616	23	40	23	740	611
Washington	1260	227	335	64	590	1318	248	789	54	214	932	1262	45	292	85	873	1290
Wayne	827	164	191	44	459	874	178	595	26	159	640	848	25	165	82	622	832
Webster	1127	120	74	55	1034	1173	117	1053	49	132	1068	1151	49	133	54	1076	1129
Wheeler	103	15	4	1	162	101	16	150	3	16	164	100	2	16	6	161	102
York	1979	135	69	82	1338	2094	119	1395	71	130	1367	1967	101	143	93	1374	1943
Totals	96514	13172	16684	5114	69402	98326	15051	80978	4794	14585	82823	97411	5044	14653	5500	88298	965312

ABSTRACT OF VOTES CAST

November 6, 1894, for Members of Congress, in the various Congressional Districts.

FIRST CONGRESSIONAL DISTRICT.

COUNTIES	R. A. HAWLEY, P.	JESSE B. STRODE, R.	AUSTIN H. WEIR, D. P. I.
Cass	128	2617	1817
Johnson	67	1428	978
Lancaster	412	7037	4015
Nemaha	64	1456	1413
Otoe	148	2107	1929
Pawnee	103	1388	906
Richardson	156	2152	1672
Totals	1078	18185	12730

SECOND CONGRESSIONAL DISTRICT.

COUNTIES	JAMES E. BOYD, D.	D. CLEM. DEAVER, P. I.	DAVID MERCER, R.	GEORGE D. WOODBY, P.
Douglas	6946	3092	11019	294
Sarpy	581	394	642	51
Washington	638	521	1285	48
Totals	8165	3962	12946	393

THIRD CONGRESSIONAL DISTRICT.

COUNTIES	JOHN M DEVINE, P. I.	W. A. HENSLEY, D.	GEO. D. MEIKLEJOHN, R.	J. C. THOMAS, P.
Antelope	993	142	908	55
Boone	982	180	1005	52
Burt	740	167	1241	54
Cedar	673	430	802	33
Colfax	744	566	737	34
Cuming	438	933	1143	82
Dakota	258	355	602	23
Dixon	718	370	778	47
Dodge	787	1279	1887	90
Knox	861	258	1012	141
Madison	819	708	1526	58
Merrick	730	163	876	71
Nance	672	103	723	19
Pierce	410	291	602	19
Platte	188	1223	1009	55
Stanton	434	281	511	18
Thurston	241	227	342	15
Wayne	450	342	827	35
Totals	**11738**	**8019**	**16513**	**851**

FOURTH CONGRESSIONAL DISTRICT.

COUNTIES	SHANNON S. ALLEY, D.	EUGENE J. HAINER, R.	WM. L. STARK, S. D. P. I.	MRS. C. M. WOODWARD, P.
Butler	204	1310	1586	81
Fillmore	158	1719	1496	50
Gage	704	6574	1758	172
Hamilton	40	1270	1406	33
Jefferson	283	1729	968	58
Polk	66	832	1160	93
Saline	457	2128	1137	134
Saunders	208	1850	2190	100
Seward	298	1561	1346	46
Thayer	237	1548	1073	70
York	108	1972	1422	68
Totals	2763	49493	15542	905

FIFTH CONGRESSIONAL DISTRICT.

COUNTIES	WM. E. ANDREWS, R.	THOS. F. ASHBY, S.D.	O.C. HUBBELL, P.	W.A. MC-KEIGHAN, D.P.L.
Adams	1915	51	89	1604
Chase	299	24	4	244
Clay	1752	78	86	1543
Dundy	288	14	7	262
Franklin	837	54	21	870
Frontier	783	47	14	803
Furnas	1190	41	28	1071
Gosper	365	26	13	589
Hall	1687	61	61	1256
Harlan	759	27	66	882
Hayes	316	31	7	246
Hitchcock	448	23	16	526
Kearney	1019	67	51	941
Nuckolls	1214	65	44	1320
Perkins	259	28	14	270
Phelps	1014	34	52	957
Red Willow	997	40	40	865
Webster	1128	48	38	1201
Total	16310	875	651	15450

SIXTH CONGRESSIONAL DISTRICT.

COUNTIES	WM. BONE, R.	MATT. A. DAUGHERTY, R.	O.M. KEM, D.P.L.
Banner	7	295	133
Blaine	5	83	54
Box Butte	21	616	544
Boyd	44	519	518
Brown	15	408	358
Buffalo	67	1847	1980
Cherry	38	502	678
Cheyenne	29	435	380
Custer	86	1503	1756
Dawes	50	682	882
Dawson	81	832	1060
Deuel	20	310	276
Garfield	8	160	154
Grant	10	63	89
Greeley	11	359	598
Holt	127	963	1277
Hooker	2	33	20
Howard	40	710	1077
Keith	13	225	265
Keya Paha	14	224	375
Kimball	4	160	80
Lincoln	49	1050	978
Logan	3	113	101
Loup	2	113	124
McPherson	2	42	43
Rock	9	349	261
Scott's Bluff	12	237	151
Sheridan	64	555	1067
Sherman	14	480	839
Sioux	9	176	170
Thomas	1	60	65
Valley	19	630	764
Wheeler	5	101	174
Totals	891	14676	17077

Abstract of votes cast **at** the general election, held on the fifth day of November, A. D. 1895.

| COUNTIES | JUDGE SUPREME COURT | | | | | |
	Timothy J. Mahoney, D.	Samuel Maxwell, P. I.	T. L. Norval, R.	Charles J. Phelps, D.	A. G. Wolfenbarger, P.	Scattering.
Adams	243	1317	1451	112	105	..
Antelope	81	978	723	30	51	..
Banner	15	102	167	12	5	..
Blaine	26	46	57	4	3	..
Boone	91	1171	762	34	42	..
Box Butte	108	433	437	33	16	..
Boyd	73	521	328	26	16	..
Brown	65	213	308	30	5	..
Buffalo	129	1814	1471	117	46	..
Burt	107	786	1202	64	62	..
Butler	350	1344	928	303	103	..
Cass	351	1252	2020	584	100	..
Cedar	255	773	800	173	22	..
Chase	30	202	258	42	7	..
Cherry	128	488	448	41	20	..
Cheyenne	83	309	449	51	28	..
Clay	135	1312	1380	84	70	..
Colfax	190	797	525	332	35	1
Cuming	468	626	911	417	30	..
Custer	146	1705	1224	38	78	..
Dakota	290	357	443	130	27	..
Dawes	108	820	613	43	22	..
Dawson	75	1275	901	88	44	..
Deuel	55	176	241	25	6	..
Dixon	249	849	675	90	62	..
Dodge	464	1709	1172	232	62	..
Douglas	4364	4802	9512	994	240	..
Dundy	20	332	283	8	10	..
Fillmore	125	1321	1172	58	64	..
Franklin	107	823	697	59	66	..
Frontier	42	825	622	99	21	..
Furnas	123	1024	1010	81	63	..
Gage	900	1290	2503	178	186	..
Garfield	12	186	129	3	5	..
Gosper	35	510	345	13	12	..
Grant	13	67	79	11	4	..
Greeley	113	546	291	47	11	..
Hall	258	1253	1328	167	48	..
Hamilton	98	1165	1185	63	69	..
Harlan	98	851	740	34	104	..
Hayes	78	194	297	34	7	..
Hitchcock	40	521	408	10	12	..
Holt	165	1170	781	64	73	..
Hooker	2	29	11	1	2	1
Howard	130	838	624	77	33	..
Jefferson	209	722	1161	88	67	..
Johnson	163	615	1165	162	114	..
Kearney	98	1029	779	16	41	..

ABSTRACT OF VOTES CAST—*Continued*

COUNTIES	JUDGE SUPREME COURT					
	Timothy J. Mahoney, D.	Samuel Maxwell, P. I	T. L. Norval, R.	Charles J. Phelps, D.	A. G. Wolfenbarger, P.	Scattering.
Keith	32	215	186	18	6	
Keya Paha	40	247	155	20	10	
Kimball	3	64	66	12	3	
Knox	139	1100	999	81	75	
Lancaster	529	2557	5420	611	451	
Lincoln	88	992	963	35	41	
Logan	12	92	80	9	1	
Loup	4	103	96	5	2	
Madison	445	989	1234	205	68	
McPherson	8	39	35	1		
Merrick	106	837	652	67	48	
Nance	54	765	644	27	24	
Nemaha	128	1209	1187	117	72	
Nuckolls	109	1054	877	41	25	
Otoe	723	1106	1532	271	112	
Pawnee	93	457	1162	158	92	
Perkins	24	231	163	8	7	
Phelps	43	1073	777	18	56	
Pierce	219	490	459	92	25	
Platte	620	1128	748	403	55	
Polk	42	1206	693	34	70	
Red Willow	58	811	905	65	35	
Richardson	433	580	1222	796	108	
Rock	40	186	312	23	5	
Saline	435	905	1401	244	121	
Sarpy	360	542	422	128	96	
Saunders	267	1986	1446	135	80	
Scott's Bluff	36	142	215	22	10	
Seward	199	932	1435	202	34	
Sheridan	102	796	467	38	35	
Sherman	46	629	394	8	10	
Sioux	47	133	152	27	7	
Stanton	205	334	538	137	14	
Thayer	248	671	1096	290	57	
Thomas	25	27	45	7	2	
Thurston	262	248	387	37	12	
Valley	47	716	614	20	21	
Washington	327	674	972	159	42	
Wayne	246	401	721	126	20	
Webster	162	942	976	56	55	
Wheeler	15	160	83	5	3	
York	107	1312	1574	59	75	
Totals	18636	70566	**79291**	10079	4314	2

Abstract of votes cast at the general election held on the fifth day of November, 1895, for

COUNTIES	John H. Ames, D.	Woodson S. Ashby, D.	James H. Bayston, P. I.	Alfred T. Blackburn, D.	Josiah J. Bryant, P.	H. L. Goold, R.	Robert Kittle, D.	C. H. Morrill, R.	Ella W. Peattie, P. I.	Anna R. Woodbey, P	Scattering	Total Vote.
Adams......	296	233	1119	109	124	1462	166	1449	1081	127	..	3410
Antelope....	85	64	847	37	72	780	41	743	808	69	2	1975
Bacner......	13	12	89	6	16	163	12	157	80	14	..	321
Blaine........	24	17	38	7	..	59	5	53	39	3	..	147
Boone........	97	79	1075	35	60	848	65	830	1067	60	..	2298
Box Butte..	124	76	379	36	21	457	60	448	348	29	..	1168
Boyd	70	58	444	78	35	350	32	348	413	23	..	1069
Brown.......	78	68	170	35	23	303	31	298	168	10	.	672
Buffalo	216	176	1842	53	90	1529	98	1486	1596	94	..	3843
Burt	151	122	613	67	102	1265	89	1243	553	74	..	2424
Butler........	550	490	837	316	149	1098	442	1060	730	120	..	3294
Cass...........	695	555	496	529	167	2141	762	2058	523	153	..	4729
Cedar........	352	279	467	243	70	803	255	764	449	44	..	2246
Chase........	52	38	174	24	28	287	32	249	153	12	..	547
Cherry	137	101	426	53	34	451	55	423	407	23	..	1260
Cheyenne ...	110	98	235	37	54	440	47	386	212	35	..	1050
Clay	181	139	1116	102	117	1423	117	1435	1072	80	..	3090
Colfax........	370	253	522	237	66	646	359	610	498	50	..	2267
Cuming......	611	458	247	434	72	978	635	952	235	64	..	2787
Custer........	140	98	1603	43	115	1293	47	1244	1539	98	..	3377
Dakota......	286	218	274	128	39	444	149	415	205	36	..	1566
Dawes........	132	100	683	61	46	672	79	638	600	43	..	1774
Dawson	94	69	1095	32	62	985	56	969	1082	57	..	2533
Deuel	68	66	90	17	31	328	41	259	105	9	..	588
Dixon........	374	219	609	113	84	702	157	659	578	79	..	2108
Dodge........	777	486	488	560	149	1471	1142	1457	635	130	..	3639
Douglas.....	4473	3199	1813	1670	609	9562	2118	9670	4164	810	..	21166
Dundy........	28	16	291	5	11	294	14	292	286	16	..	681
Fillmore	224	195	1055	52	105	1231	81	1254	1018	78	..	2868
Franklin.....	148	214	713	50	61	686	69	696	713	61	..	1860
Frontier	71	68	789	66	36	637	39	624	734	36	..	1676
Furnas	142	118	958	83	78	1019	63	999	886	72	..	2375
Gage..........	736	601	996	214	271	2643	257	2655	953	251	..	5450
Garfield.....	12	4	144	7	12	149	5	141	137	9	..	354
Gosper.......	51	31	481	13	15	339	18	234	435	9	..	933
Grant........	20	19	43	11	4	86	19	88	33	5	..	174
Greeley......	139	114	438	65	24	303	69	283	424	24	..	1064
Hall..........	400	289	853	155	111	1420	271	1394	875	85	..	3326
Hamilton...	132	112	1108	46	99	1237	87	1182	1046	87	2	2753
Harlan......	128	118	763	24	99	742	42	724	719	103	..	1911
Hayes........	83	67	184	23	12	301	33	285	164	10	..	639
Hitchcock..	47	40	459	14	29	417	15	427	444	18	..	1060
Holt	184	101	1043	255	101	766	96	766	1008	90	..	2445
Hooker......	4	1	19	2	3	13	1	18	20	1	..	54
Howard......	170	138	749	61	45	656	119	657	699	50	..	1702
Jefferson....	227	207	574	101	103	1126	107	1161	530	87	..	2469
Johnson	211	184	549	118	124	1137	154	1127	516	157	..	2373
Kearney ...	109	109	926	26	70	799	30	757	885	64	..	2085

ABSTRACT OF VOTES CAST—*Continued.*

COUNTIES	John H. Ames, D.	Woodson S. Asbby, D.	James H. Bayston, P. I.	Alfred T. Blackburn, D.	Josiah J. Bryant, P.	H. L. Goold, R.	Robert Kittle, D.	C. H. Morrill, R.	Ella W. Peattie, P. I.	Anna R. Woolbey, P.	Scattering	Total Vote.
Keith	35	21	152	11	11	301	14	175	141	14	..	492
Keya Paha	45	38	208	28	12	164	19	160	212	12	..	472
Kimball	6	6	56	6	5	71	14	71	55	3	..	166
Knox	234	86	921	90	107	952	158	918	846	107	..	2678
Lancaster	1382	567	1833	372	479	5167	477	5685	1789	412	..	10020
Lincoln	97	76	888	33	69	971	59	939	852	70	..	2289
Logan	21	16	85	7	3	74	9	69	86	6	..	205
Loup	8	3	88	4	5	98	7	95	83	6	..	221
Madison	600	443	528	253	102	1261	374	1232	514	97	..	3331
McPherson	8	5	32	3	....	42	2	32	23	1	..	90
Merrick	141	111	574	73	94	772	90	754	655	95	..	1847
Nance	69	50	692	14	40	689	46	677	689	35	..	1584
Nemaha	210	176	1035	116	108	1191	144	1182	960	85	..	2982
Nuckolls	125	94	962	32	52	919	54	885	926	41	..	2230
Otoe	975	715	787	303	131	1562	330	1531	720	149	..	4262
Pawnee	153	136	354	133	123	1172	152	1175	334	110	..	2092
Perkins	25	30	192	10	10	193	13	166	181	14	..	464
Phelps	54	50	949	13	106	805	18	789	917	78	..	2078
Pierce	275	187	368	86	37	467	153	445	328	30	..	1473
Platte	925	597	708	250	90	868	612	830	622	89	..	3388
Polk	59	40	1031	24	178	714	28	761	1000	93	..	2134
Red Willow	64	56	843	26	51	849	39	827	726	59	..	1954
Richardson	638	583	407	655	146	1989	820	1979	376	116	..	4326
Rock	64	58	105	33	16	327	37	322	109	11	..	612
Saline	600	440	546	246	146	1508	336	1544	468	129	..	3398
Sarpy	387	275	270	173	70	495	256	492	323	68	..	1716
Saunders	474	403	1536	163	169	1517	285	1506	1407	127	..	4377
Scott's Bluff	54	45	94	12	23	227	27	222	99	14	..	457
Seward	379	281	694	205	109	1310	287	1318	674	55	..	2968
Sheridan	120	89	682	62	44	504	86	488	638	55	..	1529
Sherman	47	30	600	7	28	416	23	407	580	15	..	1175
Sioux	60	43	123	27	9	132	26	129	106	13	..	404
Stanton	329	250	181	89	34	545	171	526	174	19	..	1436
Thayer	329	270	474	175	78	1127	260	1097	446	81	..	2436
Thomas	27	26	18	10	5	39	13	35	12	6	..	122
Thurston	281	220	157	38	32	378	51	343	153	14	..	1181
Valley	51	38	689	14	32	626	32	608	671	28	..	1492
Washington	319	289	391	205	78	1659	333	1020	418	65	..	2523
Wayne	282	208	265	110	34	731	180	660	293	40	..	1793
Webster	172	153	847	48	87	940	80	960	823	72	..	3326
Wheeler	9	12	141	5	9	90	8	86	138	8	..	266
York	156	109	1084	61	138	1664	88	1645	1019	96	..	3233
Totals	24124	17842	53268	10682	6947	81847	14895	80962	53351	6207	4	197811

Abstract of votes cast at the general election held on the third **day of** November, A. D. 1896 for

COUNTIES	GOVERNOR						LIEUTENANT GOVERNOR					
	ROBERT S. BIBB	RICHARD A. HAWLEY	SILAS A. HOLCOMB	JOHN H. MACCOLL	CHARLES SADILEK	JOEL WARNER	O. F. BIGLIF	JAMES E. HARRIS	FRED HERMAN	L. O. JONES	OSCAR KENT	ORLANDO TEFFT
	D	N	D P-I	R	SL	P	D	D P-I	SL	P	N	R
Adams	49	19	2054	1626	8	38	52	2033	12	32	35	1660
Antelope	26	2	1243	905	1	32	34	1225	5	35	12	920
Banner	6	...	124	161	1	3	5	115		5	1	166
Blaine	4	...	66	77	...		3	64		1	...	77
Boone	27	8	1283	1012	3	28	31	1298	10	36	8	1035
Box Butte	24	3	554	407	7	4	29	531	3	9	2	401
Boyd	28	5	633	471	11	15	38	610	12	18	4	464
Brown	4	2	327	347	2	1	10	312	1	6	2	351
Buffalo	48	16	2495	1697	6	25	55	2442	15	37	7	1742
Burt	33	16	1323	1432	4	20	27	1213	11	28	6	1495
Butler	40	29	2277	1158	7	17	52	2180	8	30	26	1202
Cass	115	41	2417	2411	17	35	121	2325	19	55	23	2495
Cedar	50	11	1470	985	4	12	63	1416	9	15	9	998
Chase	9	2	258	235	...	7	14	254		8	...	229
Cherry	35	1	700	571	3	7	42	668	7	13	1	570
Cheyenne	14	1	511	407	2	11	33	482	1	11	2	419
Clay	33	18	1770	1536	...	25	30	1743	9	34	13	1564
Colfax	91	18	1363	770	12	12	93	1334	14	9	8	775
Cuming	81	14	1760	1151	8	6	77	1705	9	21	7	1212
Custer	31	17	2462	1406	3	30	42	2393	14	41	13	1414
Dakota	65	1	863	573	4	16	59	821	7	13	2	564
Dawes	25	3	944	724	5	8	37	889	6	10	4	741
Dawson	22	3	1418	1063	3	28	36	1362	10	35	2	1068
Deuel	16	2	291	263	1	4	18	261	4	9	3	265
Dixon	62	9	1279	836	4	26	80	1216	6	38	7	866
Dodge	168	23	2203	2098	14	38	216	1994	27	49	17	2120
Douglas	312	46	12071	11474	206	116	485	11261	210	256	53	11454
Dundy	9	...	286	266	...	4	8	281		5	1	268
Fillmore	39	20	1801	1536	8	19	45	1738	8	39	16	1550
Franklin	27	15	1048	802	4	16	23	1056	3	25	16	808
Frontier	20	4	1010	749	2	14	20	997	3	21	7	744
Furnas	25	9	1439	1104	3	22	29	1431	1	30	9	1089
Gage	232	26	2683	3250	10	55	170	2592	21	111	241	3307
Garfield	1	4	221	140	...		4	211		3	1	145
Gosper	14	3	683	375	2	5	26	681	3	6	3	384
Grant	3	2	101	87	...		11	82	1	1	...	86
Greeley	27	3	755	353	2	5	39	743	3	4	1	366
Hall	52	7	1874	1820	6	15	72	1807	16	27	7	1801
Hamilton	22	9	1548	1307	6	19	25	1537	7	29	15	1297
Harlan	18	26	1142	797	1	19	18	1156	2	38	26	781
Hayes	15	1	286	237	2	2	15	278	3	3	...	301
Hitchcock	9	2	491	400	3	2	6	482	1	1	2	402
Holt	55	27	1354	872	4	34	119	1291	14	39	26	830
Hooker	1	...	39	9	...		2	39		...	...	10
Howard	35	7	1231	641	8	12	28	1227	9	11	5	671
Jefferson	52	9	1534	1337	4	16	60	1458	11	32	6	1556

ABSTRACT OF VOTES CAST—Continued.

COUNTIES	GOVERNOR						LIEUTENANT GOVERNOR					
	ROBERT S. BIBB	RICHARD A. HAWLEY	SILAS A. HOLCOMB	JOHN H. MACCOLL	CHARLES SADILEK	JOEL WARNER	O. F. BIGLIN	JAMES E. HARRIS	FRED HERMAN	L. O. JONES	OSCAR KENT	ORLANDO TEFFT
	D	N	D P-I	R	SL	P	D	D P-I	SL	P	N	R
Johnson	37	30	1223	1346	1	23	44	1191	12	31	27	1348
Kearney	22	7	1165	911	2	22	21	1130	4	25	10	917
Keith	5	1	233	180	3	1	12	210	4	4	2	174
Keya Paha	13	3	293	174		6	16	279	3	10	2	172
Kimball	5		65	92		1	4	62		3		87
Knox	51	5	1591	953	12	46	58	1562	9	42	7	961
Lancaster	101	73	5741	6115	20	96	120	5389	55	212	72	6170
Lincoln	24	1	1362	1044	2	19	44	1326	4	25	6	1049
Logan	4		128	67			4	122		1		64
Loup	1	1	145	108		2		136				116
Madison	67	9	1736	1655	7	29	104	1642	11	39	11	1674
McPherson			43	37			1	43				35
Merrick	16	9	1064	895	1	28	22	984	6	53	13	905
Nance	17	2	937	690	1	5	27	910	2	10	3	711
Nemaha	44	22	1934	1390	4	29	50	1884	14	53	9	1395
Nuckolls	40	8	1368	1056	2	18	43	1366	5	18	3	1071
Otoe	99	34	2703	2068	8	30	160	2479	22	53	26	2126
Pawnee	23	12	1170	1408	4	37	26	1139	1	56	16	1400
Perkins	8	3	247	147			15	233	1	2	1	156
Phelps	11	8	1268	864		18	9	1191	3	31	8	884
Pierce	29	5	964	552	6	15	49	915	3	20	3	556
Platte	90	19	2206	1186	5	14	146	2066	20	23	12	1197
Polk	11	21	1510	754	3	13	17	1492	4	22	21	758
Red Willow	25	6	1003	915	1	11	30	958	4	19	7	928
Richardson	98	14	2451	2162	8	35	87	2445	11	54	5	2172
Rock	15		212	339	3	2	18	206	3	6		338
Saline	74	42	2012	1932	22	33	85	1906	47	54	31	1920
Sarpy	39	8	1188	555	6	15	34	1133	5	24	4	587
Saunders	81	23	2789	1650	8	32	96	2690	13	56	19	1896
Scott's Bluff	4	4	231	223		5	4	225	2	4	4	225
Seward	49	6	1951	1530	3	14	61	1878	5	22	2	1563
Sheridan	23	6	856	479	4	14	37	829	8	26	2	482
Sherman	8	3	876	391	10	7	7	847	10	11	2	407
Sioux	15	2	275	152			16	268		2	2	151
Stanton	49	6	849	564	5	10	60	772	8	14	3	591
Thayer	54	11	1404	1403	10	27	61	1351	5	29	8	1445
Thomas	4		73	32			7	69				31
Thurston	20	6	678	486		9	15	665	5	11	3	482
Valley	15	2	917	641	5	5	23	809	3	12		650
Washington	64	6	1494	1384		13	94	1369	10	21	2	1406
Wayne	48	6	1055	931		3	64	1004	5	15	4	925
Webster	36	8	1376	1027	5	20	38	1312	5	31	13	1060
Wheeler	5		164	88		2	7	163	2	2	1	92
York	14	15	1779	1809		28	24	1765	6	33	14	1817
Totals	3557	930	116415	94723	578	1560	4431	111729	875	2458	810	95757

Abstract of votes cast at the general election held on the 3d day of November, A. D. 1896, for

COUNTIES	SECRETARY OF STATE						AUDITOR OF PUBLIC ACCOUNTS					
	Bernhard Bruning	James M. Dilworth	Albert Fitch, Jr	John Mattes, Jr	Joel A. Piper	William E. Porter	John F. Cornell	C. C. Crowell	Edward A. Gerrard	Peter Olof Hedlund	Emil Heller	Gustave Teickmeir
	SL	N	P	D	R	D P-I	D P-I	P	N	R	D	SL
Adams	8	25	30	55	1674	2009	1915	33	27	1691	60	8
Antelope	4	11	35	38	900	1215	1155	44	7	938	34	4
Banner	1		4	13	144	122	105	7	3	160	7	
Blaine			1	6	78	56	56		1	78	7	
Boone	6	4	32	44	1033	1298	1255	35	13	1041	46	5
Box Butte	9	1	7	26	400	534	509	9	3	399	29	5
Boyd	11	5	20	45	462	601	575	23	4	457	50	13
Brown		2	2	8	356	305	294	3	2	364	11	1
Buffalo	11	12	35	70	1733	2384	2300	50	13	1763	58	10
Burt	6	9	28	31	1485	1196	1116	41	9	1514	40	7
Butler		33	21	61	1198	2175	2124	26	39	1220	49	7
Cass	21	27	51	166	2435	2280	2194	62	27	2497	123	17
Cedar	10	6	14	73	977	1387	1316	13	10	1011	65	3
Chase	2	1	10	13	245	234	242	9		248	11	
Cherry	7	3	12	40	556	662	623	10	3	557	42	2
Cheyenne	6	3	14	36	421	440	427	13	5	428	38	1
Clay	4	13	28	37	1577	1735	1701	43	9	1590	36	2
Colfax	12	7	12	120	798	1259	1302	19	9	814	139	6
Cuming	8	9	21	136	1194	1614	1557	21	8	1191	180	2
Custer	9	14	50	68	1449	2312	2244	57	12	1462	34	6
Dakota	8	3	13	75	562	799	755	15	18	565	60	8
Dawes	7	1	10	40	746	872	838	17	2	752	46	7
Dawson	8	8	23	37	1080	1355	1305	35	4	1100	40	5
Deuel	2	4	5	30	257	261	226	7	2	289	26	3
Dixon	5	7	37	75	837	1183	1136	43	9	877	73	2
Dodge	28	19	45	249	2108	2002	1826	56	20	2133	281	21
Douglas	318	37	175	672	11105	11168	10035	296	55	11565	780	174
Dundy	1		7	10	266	271	270	8		274	7	
Filmore	12	8	24	52	1570	1707	1632	30	10	1610	51	6
Franklin	3	12	36	42	782	1013	997	18	16	825	29	2
Frontier	6	5	16	24	747	978	937	19	3	756	20	4
Furnas	1	11	21	39	1078	1404	1288	32	11	1096	41	1
Gage	10	32	82	188	3322	2506	2418	91	34	3380	178	5
Garfield	4	1	1	2	144	207	202	2	1	148	2	1
Gosper	3	2	6	28	393	666	659	8	5	391	23	1
Grant	1		1	8	85	82	82	1	1	90	7	
Greeley	4	5	4	40	372	708	691	8	2	373	37	3
Hall	18	14	26	87	1778	1761	1701	33	8	1843	70	15
Hamilton	4	10	36	33	1312	1511	1459	35	11	1339	34	4
Harlan	1	25	30	27	842	1065	1061	28	32	819	24	4
Hayes	3	1	3	17	301	276	270	3		303	18	5
Hitchcock	3		2	8	409	475	459	4		407	6	
Holt	5	25	43	73	846	1323	1288	43	25	858	56	8
Hooker				3	10	38	38			10	2	
Howard	9	4	21	51	662	1158	1187	16	7	691	26	10
Jefferson	9	11	30	73	1530	1446	1312	35	13	1577	68	12

ABSTRACT OF VOTES CAST—*Continued.*

COUNTIES	SECRETARY OF STATE						AUDITOR OF PUBLIC ACCOUNTS					
	BERNHARD BRUNING	JAMES M. DILWORTH	ALBERT FITCH, JR	JOHN MATTES, JR	JOEL A. PIPER	WILLIAM F. PORTER	JOHN F. CORNELL	C. C. CROWELL	EDWARD A. GERRARD	PETER OLOF HEDLUND	EMIL HELLER	GUSTAVE TEICKMEIER
	S L	N	P	D	R	D P-I	D P-I	P	N	R	D	S L
Johnson	4	40	24	53	1325	1181	1103	37	30	1343	46	4
Kearney	1	5	31	32	937	1119	1079	35	6	965	23	3
Keith	4	1	3	14	176	238	232	6	......	176	11	3
Keya Paha	1	1	9	19	171	269	269	11	2	175	16	1
Kimball	......	1	1	1	85	60	58	3	......	96	4	......
Knox	12	6	49	49	946	1531	1406	45	8	977	66	4
Lancaster	32	74	123	160	6155	5319	5021	149	87	6380	148	33
Lincoln	8	2	29	54	1041	1294	1267	33	4	1062	46	4
Logan	......	......	1	5	63	124	124	......	......	61	2	......
Loup	......	1	3	1	107	133	132	1	1	111	3	2
Madison	12	7	36	120	1650	1613	1506	46	11	1693	107	8
McPherson	......	......	......	2	31	44	43	......	......	35	1	......
Merrick	......	7	59	30	844	1036	930	52	12	914	30	1
Nance	2	1	12	31	716	912	863	18	8	728	22	1
Nemaha	15	11	40	95	1404	1798	1752	54	13	1420	63	6
Nuckolls	6	5	23	60	1043	1354	1290	26	5	1073	49	3
Otoe	8	34	46	377	2026	2313	2220	65	40	2174	203	15
Pawnee	3	13	57	27	1394	1117	1035	54	16	1415	24	4
Perkins	2	1	3	12	155	221	218	4	1	157	11	......
Phelps	5	9	30	11	891	1190	1075	29	9	1010	12	......
Pierce	13	1	16	63	551	895	854	23	1	570	52	4
Platte	26	14	31	173	1192	2000	1958	82	19	1229	167	10
Polk	1	25	20	15	751	1181	1406	25	30	780	16	......
Red Willow	4	5	16	34	927	965	903	21	7	948	32	2
Richardson	4	11	41	104	2138	2432	2326	42	8	2173	76	9
Rock	3	......	4	20	330	201	190	3	......	340	18	4
Saline	22	37	38	120	1923	1866	1803	50	35	1942	102	16
Sarpy	12	5	30	75	585	1073	1061	31	9	600	45	6
Saunders	11	14	49	122	1894	2636	2521	54	17	1988	107	13
Scott's Bluff	2	4	10	6	215	230	215	9	6	230	3	......
Seward	2	3	13	63	1573	1839	1749	23	4	1592	68	......
Sheridan	6	1	18	39	491	823	799	26	5	488	34	2
Sherman	11	4	11	14	410	841	814	9	3	414	11	11
Sioux	1	1	1	14	146	205	262	2	4	146	13	1
Stanton	13	2	15	66	562	755	709	19	3	589	65	5
Thayer	6	10	19	69	1452	1819	1261	24	6	1456	71	6
Thomas	......	......	......	5	33	68	70	......	......	83	5	......
Thurston	4	6	10	30	470	664	615	8	7	477	24	5
Valley	6	......	13	30	642	879	847	13	2	653	32	6
Washington	13	3	22	98	1412	1328	1245	68	4	1400	98	9
Wayne	5	2	12	71	908	907	918	17	6	922	74	2
Webster	1	10	24	40	1082	1306	1228	33	12	1064	45	3
Wheeler	......	......	1	8	92	162	156	......	1	93	6	......
York	2	16	32	27	1825	1733	1707	42	18	1851	23	2
Totals	891	820	2149	5523	95023	109587	104314	2643	953	97468	5148	608

Abstract of votes cast at the general election held on the 3d day of November, A. D. 1896, for

| COUNTIES | TREASURER | | | | | | SUPT. PUB. INSTRUCTION | | | | |
| | CHARLES E. CASEY | S. T. DAVIES | STEPHEN J. HERMAN | THOMAS McCULLOCH | FRANK McGIVERIN | JOHN B. MESERVE | HENRY R. CORBETT | MARTHA E. DONOVAN | SAMUEL G. GLOVER | WILLIAM R. JACKSON | E. A. WHITWAM |
	R	P	SL	N	D	D P-I	R	SL	D	D P-I	P-N
Adams	1688	41	3	23	59	2022	1733	11	56	1913	54
Antelope	939	36	3	10	34	1198	930	6	28	1190	33
Banner	166	7	.....	1	5	110	150	3	14	119	3
Blaine	75	1	.....	1	9	56	74	1	9	57	.....
Boone	1062	37	5	7	47	1308	1051	4	46	1280	38
Box Butte	409	10	8	5	39	529	402	14	30	542	16
Boyd	472	25	9	6	44	593	470	17	41	570	27
Brown	375	2	1	2	10	308	360	3	15	306	5
Buffalo	1760	49	9	7	62	2397	1784	20	63	2307	42
Burt	1521	45	7	6	44	1204	1464	17	54	1193	47
Butler	1254	29	2	33	49	2172	1229	9	53	2115	52
Cass	2449	75	18	31	151	2342	2467	28	165	2120	88
Cedar	1014	16	8	7	68	1403	1032	10	55	1298	22
Chase	256	10	2	1	11	236	245	2	12	243	8
Cherry	575	18	3	4	43	665	571	9	63	643	14
Cheyenne	429	17	2	4	35	441	418	6	33	441	13
Clay	1610	34	5	6	38	1749	1635	20	45	1715	37
Colfax	816	18	10	9	145	1296	806	10	137	1291	23
Cuming	1225	26	8	7	124	1622	1243	12	121	1521	19
Custer	1475	51	10	15	45	2356	1506	12	50	2288	62
Dakota	584	20	8	7	63	810	582	9	60	776	12
Dawes	773	15	5	3	44	876	723	17	58	873	23
Dawson	1112	29	5	......	42	1367	1111	13	41	1318	24
Deuel	264	15	......	1	16	229	271	5	30	244	6
Dixon	884	50	6	6	71	1215	881	9	71	1148	36
Dodge	2120	59	17	18	387	1922	2061	33	324	1937	60
Douglas	11764	251	190	81	657	10896	10043	344	1336	11082	366
Dundy	267	6	1	2	8	281	265	5	5	267	8
Fillmore	1608	37	14	10	46	1716	1638	18	46	1620	41
Franklin	817	27	1	13	31	1082	802	8	23	981	25
Frontier	763	15	3	4	19	981	771	6	23	822	19
Furnas	1154	25	3	8	39	1372	1120	5	88	1247	40
Gage	3438	86	26	25	181	2511	3447	19	189	2431	101
Garfield	150	3	......	3	3	206	150	1	4	198	5
Gosper	390	6	3	5	23	678	405	7	27	669	5
Grant	86	2	1	1	11	85	84	2	9	84	1
Greeley	380	6	3	2	38	700	374	9	36	714	7
Hall	1825	41	11	10	92	1768	1831	15	91	1686	31
Hamilton	1339	31	5	10	35	1526	1318	8	51	1514	41
Harlan	896	35	6	29	26	1111	827	11	24	1038	46
Hayes	303	4	3	......	20	273	302	1	19	281	4
Hitchcock	423	3	......	......	5	461	416	2	7	450	6
Holt	804	46	4	20	70	1328	805	15	53	1372	47
Hooker	10	......	......	......	3	37	......	......	......	......	......
Howard	684	16	7	5	43	1197	678	17	34	1194	16
Jefferson	1594	42	3	10	66	1436	1588	8	63	1341	36

ABSTRACT OF VOTES CAST—*Continued.*

COUNTIES	TREASURER						SUPT. PUB. INSTRUCTION				
	CHARLES E. CASEY	S. T. DAVIES	STEPHEN J. HERNAN	THOMAS McCULLOCH	FRANK McGIVERIN	JOHN B. MESERVE	HENRY R. CORBETT	MARTHA E. DONOVAN	SAMUEL G. GLOVER	WILLIAM R. JACKSON	E. A. WHITWAM
	R	P	SL	N	D	D P-I	R	SL	D	D P-I	P-N
Johnson	1381	33	5	26	50	1156	1395	2	49	1168	*53
Kearney	961	31	3	4	24	1072	945	2	37	1143	34
Keith	178	4	4	2	13	239	178	6	10	238	3
Keya Paha	180	7		1	16	281	180	3	18	286	9
Kimball	93	2			4	59	79	1	5	65	5
Knox	983	51	6	9	63	1515	965	7	65	1436	51
Lancaster	6882	161	49	81	142	5270	6854	49	165	5103	173
Lincoln	1078	37	1	3	43	1307	1060	9	37	1289	37
Logan	69	1			4	125	68	1	4	121	1
Loup	115	1		1	2	132	112		4	129	3
Madison	1711	51	8	5	118	1616	1693	17	131	1508	46
McPherson	34				1	43	34			40	
Merrick	923	48	8	12	29	979	915	7	36	974	58
Nance	755	12	1	4	25	901	716	7	29	872	20
Nemaha	1462	44	10	17	70	1794	1409	18	70	1779	43
Nuckolls	1092	29	6	5	50	1349	1122	7	40	1288	25
Otoe	2156	105	9	110	186	2313	2213	33	177	2384	77
Pawnee	1491	37	1	11	26	1100	1444	4	28	1069	36
Perkins	157	3		2	11	228	152		12	226	6
Phelps	914	39	4	11	10	1176	919	4	12	1155	44
Pierce	578	19	5	1	62	890	572	8	47	860	19
Platte	1232	27	14	20	164	2010	1180	34	174	2096	36
Polk	786	22	4	26	21	1484	770	7	23	1474	58
Red Willow	879	16	2	5	25	1055	958	8	22	925	25
Richardson	2247	49	6	6	93	2414	2244	22	103	2328	40
Rock	343	4	3	1	20	201	341	4	16	195	3
Saline	1976	45	86	35	100	1849	1972	23	103	1749	78
Sarpy	608	30	4	5	60	1091	596	23	50	1070	29
Saunders	1963	59	11	17	132	2640	1972	16	120	2536	58
Scott's Bluff	230	7	1	5	2	224	227	1	4	223	10
Seward	1600	13	4	3	64	1837	1601	9	59	1783	16
Sheridan	507	22	6	5	37	820	512	10	34	843	22
Sherman	406	14	10	3	11	843	410	10	15	808	12
Sioux	151	2		1	12	207	146	4	16	273	2
Stanton	606	11	7	2	75	744	595	12	64	711	23
Thayer	1486	34	3	12	66	1320	1461	19	70	1276	43
Thomas	34			1	5	68	31		6	74	
Thurston	486	6	6	7	30	611	477	7	19	617	16
Valley	672	11	7	1	23	876	671	7	23	845	17
Washington	1456	27	7	3	106	1335	1389	24	168	1295	25
Wayne	940	17	1	13	57	988	951	7	66	910	12
Webster	1090	32	3	10	32	1307	1107	8	43	1229	37
Wheeler	95	3	1		7	167	91	2	5	159	3
York	1869	45	1	17	30	1738	1856	11	35	1740	46
Totals	98314	2628	746	961	5222	109489	96143	1249	5966	106737	2969

Abstract of **votes cast at** the general election held **on the 3d day of No-**
vember, A. D. 1896, for

COUNTIES	ATTORNEY-GENERAL						COMMISSIONER PUBLIC LANDS AND BUILDINGS					
	ARTHUR S. CRUBCHILL	FRED NYGAARD	FRANK G. ODELL	ROBERT W. PATRICK	CONSTANTINE J. SMYTH	D. M. STRONG	GEORGE N. BAER	JOHN E. HOPPER	J. PHIPPS ROE	HENRY C. RUSSELL	PETER P. SCHMIDT	JACOB V. WOLFE
	R	S L	N	D	D P-I	P	D	P	N	R	S L	D P-I
Adams	1747	2	22	58	1996	28	62	45	26	1706	7	1993
Antelope	967	5	7	30	1208	28	35	36	12	939	3	1212
Banner	164	3	1	4	116	6	5	5	2	165		113
Blaine	77			9	55		7			78		56
Boone	1681	5	10	50	1313	34	46	35	12	1051	8	1309
Box Butte	415	7	1	29	545	6	32	9	2	409	10	539
Boyd	478	9	3	50	584	23	45	16	5	471	14	602
Brown	385		2	9	310	1	9	3	2	375		310
Buffalo	1805	12	10	66	2376	33	56	38	9	1781	14	2375
Burt	1535	11	6	47	1166	26	34	32	14	1527	6	1192
Butler	1251	1	36	32	2146	21	50	30	38	1235	6	2187
Cass	2525	20	26	155	2250	51	134	63	28	2515	33	2222
Cedar	1043	6	6	46	1388	14	47	13	11	1032	10	1382
Chase	245			15	242	10	11	10	1	246	1	248
Cherry	599	4	6	42	652	16	40	15	3	570	7	645
Cheyenne	426	3	3	34	448	18	31	20	5	423	3	440
Clay	1645	7	12	37	1715	26	46	50	11	1616	2	1724
Colfax	815	5	6	127	1323	19	112	20	5	846	13	1307
Cuming	1246	8	7	114	1623	14	97	30	15	1231	9	1618
Custer	1502	12	14	52	2357	39	55	61	22	1478	5	2356
Dakota	589	8	10	58	803	13	57	14	8	584	11	814
Dawes	781	9	4	41	884	11	47	22	9	746	8	876
Dawson	1117	5	3	41	1339	30	36	34	6	1105	5	1344
Deuel	280	1	4	30	239	3	22	7	3	278	3	244
Dixon	896	4	9	74	1203	37	71	41	10	899	5	1217
Dodge	2198	21	12	282	1979	65	241	49	18	2201	32	1949
Douglas	11580	205	54	773	11047	166	620	236	165	11537	208	10795
Dundy	273	1	1	6	280	6	6	6	2	271		273
Fillmore	1628	8	11	49	1732	20	49	36	12	1594	12	1711
Franklin	831	2	18	28	1025	15	25	23	17	801	1	1027
Frontier	765	3	3	22	982	17	20	15	6	766	2	996
Furnas	1128	2	8	36	1380	19	33	22	16	1119	11	1383
Gage	3455	10	37	179	2528	82	159	89	33	3415	13	2491
Garfield	151		1	2	205	1	3	2	1	153	1	205
Gosper	401	1	4	20	675	7	21	9	4	390	1	675
Grant	85			11	85	1	12	2	1	85		80
Greeley	373	5	2	41	721	4	33	3	8	376	5	711
Hall	1867	15	3	82	1787	22	84	37	12	1813	7	1811
Hamilton	1355	4	13	28	1526	31	28	36	12	1842	10	1521
Harlan	824	4	29	23	1114	22	20	34	32	806	7	1101
Hayes	308	2	1	16	281	3	14	7	1	316	2	266
Hitchcock	416	1	2	13	463	3	9	4		415	5	471
Holt	858	8	23	72	1346	33	62	39	23	871	10	1313
Hooker	10			2	38		3			10		37
Howard	699	16	8	42	1210	15	57	17	8	695	13	1149
Jefferson	1573	5	9	72	1437	30	75	36	10	1574	6	1408

ABSTRACT OF VOTES CAST—*Continued.*

COUNTIES	ATTORNEY-GENERAL						COMMISSIONER PUBLIC LANDS AND BUILDINGS					
	Arthur S. Churchill	Fred Nygaard	Frank G. Odell	Robert W. Patrick	Constantine J. Smyth	D. M. Strong	George N. Baer	John E. Hopper	J. Phipps Roe	Henry C. Russell	Peter P. Schmidt	Jacob V. Wolfe
	R	S L	N	D	D P-I	P	D	P	N	R	S L	D P-I
Johnson	1370	6	26	58	1174	26	42	27	32	1376	9	1167
Kearney	868	6	7	28	1125	29	27	28	9	975	3	1103
Keith	178	3	......	14	246	5	8	3	......	178	4	249
Keya Paha	185	1	1	15	205	9	18	11	2	184	1	279
Kimball	91	......		4	62	1	3	2	1	91	......	60
Knox	978	4	7	52	1509	52	58	46	8	274	10	1504
Lancaster	6341	35	110	174	5274	156	159	139	106	6263	36	5439
Lincoln	1090	4	1	48	1301	31	38	33	6	1065	5	1292
Logan	69	......	......	4	126	......	4	......	......	67	......	125
Loup	118	1	1	3	134	......	2	4	......	113	2	133
Madison	1729	10	12	122	1584	41	103	34	7	1724	15	1589
McPherson	36	......	......	1	43	......	......	......	......	35	1	43
Merrick	939	3	13	36	970	46	31	49	15	925	6	969
Nance	747	2	6	29	899	8	148	12	3	648	1	871
Nemaha	1461	11	9	76	1781	39	73	45	13	1445	9	1797
Nuckolls	1090	6	3	40	1362	18	37	31	9	1088	4	1357
Otoe	2281	13	29	169	2443	43	183	61	40	2214	16	2400
Pawnee	1445	1	13	26	1108	53	24	61	21	1440	......	1112
Perkins	138	1	1	7	228	5	10	7	1	153	......	228
Phelps	916	2	16	13	1188	28	12	38	11	929	5	1171
Pierce	597	5	1	55	880	14	45	22	1	584	4	897
Platte	1244	10	14	143	2078	21	176	38	16	1226	16	2024
Polk	801	3	27	18	1456	27	16	25	29	790	2	1461
Red Willow	989	......	6	27	917	21	26	16	8	973	6	946
Richardson	2295	13	22	89	2413	39	103	64	10	2210	9	2384
Rock	349	3	......	29	203	4	18	6	2	341	4	203
Saline	1944	22	39	100	1901	41	77	51	42	1854	24	1898
Sarpy	623	11	4	52	1085	26	53	34	7	606	10	1087
Saunders	2018	12	22	119	2617	41	108	55	18	1970	12	2609
Scott's Bluff	259	......	7	1	223	9	3	5	6	233	......	217
Seward	1611	6	3	59	1842	16	62	21	10	1594	3	1860
Sheridan	515	5	1	34	848	16	31	18	5	495	4	843
Sherman	414	10	3	11	838	11	18	10	4	413	12	834
Sioux	156	......	1	14	276	......	18	1	7	152	......	270
Stanton	612	8	4	66	736	11	53	17	3	606	11	749
Thayer	1488	6	7	67	1336	27	71	31	10	1474	9	1333
Thomas	53	1	......	5	70	......	5	......	......	33	......	69
Thurston	486	1	6	26	642	15	26	7	8	483	8	637
Valley	666	1	1	30	876	8	31	12	7	651	9	868
Washington	1468	13	5	93	1311	16	81	28	10	1443	17	1315
Wayne	971	15	3	61	976	8	64	11	8	964	3	962
Webster	1112	3	9	41	1302	24	47	31	11	1082	3	1306
Wheeler	96	1	1	6	162	3	6	2	1	93	......	160
York	1852	7	19	25	1756	29	28	36	19	1843	3	1752
Totals	99067	730	907	5115	109774	2067	4904	2523	1155	97856	917	109268

Abstract of votes cast at the general election held on the 3d day of November A. D. 1896, for

COUNTIES	REGENT OF THE UNIVERSITY						Amendment to the Constitution relating to the number of Judges of the Supreme Court and their term of office.	
	JENS C JACOBSEN	THEODORE JOHNSON	CHARLES R LAWSON	J. L. LEAS	THOMAS RAWLINS	WILLIAM G. WHITMORE		
	S L	N	P	D	D P-I	R	Yes	No
Adams	6	28	36	62	1945	1695	1388	662
Antelope	2	11	34	39	1161	946	971	438
Banner		1	7	5	113	165	147	19
Blaine				7	55	78	87	17
Boone	6	9	39	35	1312	1069	1129	426
Box Butte	8	2	5	31	528	411	552	138
Boyd	11	4	26	39	584	473	621	133
Brown	1	2	3	8	302	377	331	98
Buffalo	10	8	45	67	2346	1791	1910	732
Burt	11	7	34	26	1180	1541	1039	491
Butler	2	40	26	45	2186	1258	1159	561
Cass	21	28	69	139	2241	2458	1704	558
Cedar	10	6	10	52	1363	1027	875	479
Chase			12	14	241	239	174	55
Cherry	5	4	13	42	634	570	562	310
Cheyenne	2	4	16	35	445	431	511	138
Clay	3	21	27	44	1688	1631	1304	513
Colfax	8	2	22	119	1299	800	809	373
Cuming	10	10	21	112	1598	1219	1133	727
Custer	7	16	45	41	2363	1522	1764	693
Dakota	10	5	16	54	797	580	507	291
Dawes	4	3	11	89	809	757	862	264
Dawson	5	5	28	45	1314	1118	1269	397
Deuel	5	2	6	27	236	276	265	75
Dixon	3	8	36	67	1255	820	846	453
Dodge	23	13	54	259	1843	2190	1693	667
Douglas	289	43	207	607	10549	11787	13405	3135
Dundy	1	1	6	5	275	275	308	104
Fillmore	6	12	28	39	1675	1625	1520	319
Franklin	3	17	22	26	1009	812	830	306
Frontier	2	3	18	21	984	764	739	423
Furnas	3	10	22	31	1342	1137	650	913
Gage	16	33	79	164	2464	3408	1732	1446
Garfield		1		2	205	156	148	136
Gosper	2	4	7	20	654	396	623	154
Grant	1		2	14	78	85	38	83
Greeley	3	3		35	703	374	724	90
Hall	16	6	33	76	1748	1826	1589	552
Hamilton	2	9	32	28	1492	1336	700	736
Harlan	2	28	32	14	1089	811	876	315
Hayes	1		6	19	274	299	367	132
Hitchcock	1		3	8	470	418	379	270
Holt	3	24	42	70	1283	871	1238	463
Hooker				3	37	9	38	1
Howard	14	7	19	39	1312	693	756	559

ABSTRACT OF VOTES CAST—*Continued.*

COUNTIES	REGENT OF THE UNIVERSITY						Amendment to the Constitution relating to the number of Judges of the Supreme Court and their term of office.	
	JENS C. JACOBSEN	THEODORE JOHNSON	CHARLES R. LAWSON	J. L. LEAS	THOMAS RAWLINS	WILLIAM G. WHITMORE		
	S L	N	P	D	D P-I	R	Yes	No
Jefferson	10	12	28	69	1388	1579	836	512
Johnson	2	27	31	43	1143	1370	559	965
Kearney	5	8	33	29	1071	958	584	636
Keith	3	1	4	10	245	176	287	65
Keya Paba		2	9	17	285	181	160	107
Kimball			3	3	64	89	114	9
Knox	7	8	66	54	1481	982	1031	395
Lancaster	39	84	149	164	5142	6407	4525	2563
Lincoln	6	6	36	35	1257	1065	1340	294
Logan			1	3	125	68	109	27
Loup		2	2	2	133	112	98	52
Madison	10	7	88	113	1560	1729	1014	361
McPherson					43	36	35	17
Merrick	4	10	51	23	942	919	752	230
Nance	3	2	16	29	871	755	829	274
Nemaha	8	12	43	64	1745	1438	351	739
Nuckolls	2	4	31	39	1333	1096	982	418
Otoe	14	29	49	176	2301	2248	1300	945
Pawnee	1	15	61	22	1100	1436	649	549
Perkins		2	5	11	228	156	252	70
Phelps	5	17	37	13	1163	916	618	481
Pierce	4	4	19	48	850	579	471	109
Platte	8	11	26	154	1992	1230	1026	511
Polk	3	29	21	16	1421	808	840	482
Red Willow	1	9	24	29	**913**	966	1086	328
Richardson	5	11	52	95	**2357**	2229	1158	854
Rock	5		6	17	198	346	420	46
Saline	14	33	55	79	1811	1987	1150	662
Sarpy	10	7	28	46	1041	804	596	279
Saunders	11	17	51	110	2331	1979	1507	683
Scott's Bluff		6	8	5	217	233	162	65
Seward	1	1	19	65	1835	1622	1117	809
Sheridan	3	1	19	45	829	494	534	343
Sherman	11	2	12	11	840	410	640	291
Sioux		1	1	18	267	154	236	102
Stanton	7	2	14	58	722	617	476	318
Thayer	4	6	27	62	1301	1492	1367	474
Thomas			1	5	70	31	80	13
Thurston	1	6	8	21	647	479	236	107
Valley	3	2	13	28	857	671	747	232
Washington	8	4	22	85	1280	1453	999	539
Wayne	4	2	12	57	960	952	570	240
Webster		9	24	50	1256	1108	953	379
Wheeler	1	1	2	6	158	96	161	22
York	2	14	28	28	1713	1867	1282	583
Totals	763	866	2391	4781	106967	98651	84579	37896

Abstract of Votes Cast.

November 3, 1896, for Members of Congress, in the Six Congressiona Districts.

COUNTIES	CONGRESSMAN— First Dist.				COUNTIES	CONGRESSMAN— Second Dist.			
	JEFFERSON H. BROADY	HAMPTON E. GEORGE	CHARLES E. SMITH	JESSE B. STRODE		EDWARD R. DUFFIE	DAVID H. MERCER	CHARLES WATTS	GEORGE W. WOODBEY
	D P-I	N	P	R		D P-I	R	P	N
Cass	2371	36	57	2568	Douglas	10796	12703	153	51
Johnson	1237	27	18	1368	Sarpy	1127	657	22	6
Lancaster	5418	75	128	6141	Washington	1363	1501	27	2
Nemaha	1885	17	53	1444					
Otoe	2547	34	59	2202	Totals	13286	14861	202	59
Pawnee	1165	14	54	1407					
Richardson	2514	15	60	2226					
Totals	17137	218	429	17356					

Abstract of Votes Cast—*Continued.*

COUNTIES	CONGRESSMAN—Third Dist.				COUNTIES	CONGRESSMAN—Fourth Dist.				
	DAVID BROWN	CHARLES M. GRIFFITH	ROSS L. HAMMOND	SAMUEL MAXWELL		WILLIAM H. DECH	R. E. DUNPHY	EUGENE J. HAINER	B. SPURLOCK	WILLIAM L. STARK
	P	N	R	D P-I		*	D	R	P-N	D P-I
Antelope	30	7	943	1208	Butler	8	45	1246	38	2188
Boone	29	18	1053	1309	Fillmore	8	37	1627	27	1732
Burt	35	16	1501	1184	Gage	15	170	3413	91	2535
Cedar	18	11	1029	1455	Hamilton	2	19	1308	18	1602
Colfax	26	7	829	1394	Jefferson	12	63	1605	22	1462
Cuming	22	31	1240	1752	Polk	4	12	781	45	1472
Dakota	19	14	592	857	Saline	5	72	1973	51	1917
Dixon	37	10	901	1272	Saunders	45	103	2001	42	2635
Dodge	57	28	2171	2304	Seward	8	81	1594	14	1841
Knox	61	18	1000	1543	Thayer	3	64	1465	25	1358
Madison	58	15	1758	1712	York	4	31	1831	52	1773
Merrick	46	10	921	1008	Totals	114	697	18844	425	20515
Nance	10	9	741	940						
Pierce	18	3	598	929	*By Petition.					
Platte	37	15	1273	2098						
Stanton	14	7	627	810						
Thurston	6	26	474	677						
Wayne	18	9	982	1035						
Totals	521	254	18633	23487						

Abstract of Votes Cast—*Continued.*

COUNTIES	CONGRESSMAN— Fifth Dist.					COUNTIES	CONGRESSMAN— Sixth Dist.				TOTAL VOTE
	WILLIAM E. ANDREWS	J. S. MILLER	CHARLES W. PRESTON	RANSOM S. PROUDFIT	R. D. SUTHERLAND		ADDISON E. CADY	A. D. GEORGE	WILLIAM L. GREENE	A. C. SLOAN	
	R	N	P	D	D P-I		R	P	D P-I	N	
Adams	1757	16	21	43	2050	Banner	169	5	113	1	318
Chase	247	...	8	7	255	Blaine	92	1	56	....	149
Clay	1638	9	23	35	1759	Box Butte	432	9	650	6	1086
Dundy	280	...	3	4	287	Boyd	515	24	605	8	1265
Franklin	816	18	29	31	1043	Brown	382	4	312	1	734
Frontier	766	3	15	17	996	Buffalo	1805	53	2433	7	4480
Furnas	1151	13	16	31	1423	Cherry	603	11	681	4	1410
Gosper	298	8	10	17	676	Cheyenne	460	19	459	6	1008
Hall	1851	6	27	66	1773	Custer	1515	56	2354	12	4267
Harlan	820	35	24	20	1127	Dawes	773	21	894	5	1873
Hayes	304	1	..	17	280	Dawson	1152	34	1396	3	2705
Hitchcock	426	...	..	5	478	Deuel	313	9	236	1	612
Kearney	959	6	21	21	1115	Garfield	156	5	199	3	381
Nuckolls	10 6	4	17	35	1409	Grant	83	....	99	....	206
Perkins	161	1	4	9	238	Greeley	410	4	727	2	1214
Phelps	917	15	21	9	1198	Holt	847	38	1289	22	2448
Red Willow	958	9	9	22	937	Hooker	10	....	39	....	52
Webster	1095	9	24	44	1318	Howard	821	22	1138	2	2108
						Keith	187	6	248	1	469
Totals	15621	153	266	473	18332	Keya Paha	187	9	297	3	512
						Kimball	94	5	58	....	169
						Lincoln	1098	34	1311	5	2600
						Logan	72	....	126	....	208
						Loup	113	1	142	1	267
						McPherson	36	2	43	....	87
						Rock	350	4	226	2	605
						Scott's Bluff	235	9	223	4	495
						Sheridan	486	23	867	8	1515
						Sherman	432	9	862	5	1345
						Sioux	155	1	279	4	480
						Thomas	31	1	75	....	119
						Valley	705	14	884	3	1609
						Wheeler	94	3	163	....	276
						Totals	14841	436	19378	119	230795

We, the Joint Committee appointed by the Senate and House of Representatives of the State of Nebraska, under authority of an act to provide for the recount of the ballots cast on November 8th 1896 on the Constitutional Amendment relating to judges ... approved March 25th 1897, have completed the work assigned us and herewith return our findings:

Counties	For Amendment	Against Amendment	Total Vote
Adams	1996	790	2786
Antelope	1500	1157	2652
Baxter	1818	591	2692
Buck	1157	886	2011
Blaine	107	13	181
Buffalo	2012	737	4189
Banner	183	17	318
Boyd	765	185	1344
Brown	689	120	734
Box Butte	508	123	1136
Boone	1188	663	2603
Cedar	1249	485	2465
Cheyenne	553	147	1128
Cuming	1386	766	2223
Colfax	865	481	2585
Cherry	1165	38	1212
Chase	791	20	829
Clay	1454	1424	3602
Custer	1389	767	3113
Crow	2014	675	5836
Dakota	876	288	1242
Dodge	2167	261	4826
Dundy	381	120	457
Dawson	982	687	2270
Dixon	385	63	613
Dawes	1088	592	2052

REPORT OF JOINT COMMITTEE—*Continued.*

Counties	For Amendment	Against Amendment	Total Vote
Dawson			
Douglas			
Frontier			
Fillmore			
Franklin			
Furnas			
Gosper			
Gage			
Hayes			
Hitchcock			
Harlan			
Holt			
Howard			
Hamilton			
Johnson			
Keya Paha			
Kearney			
Keith			
Kimball			
Hall			
Jefferson			
Keith			
Loup			
Logan			
Lincoln			
Lancaster			
Merrick			
Madison			
McPherson			
Nuckolls			
Nance			
Nemaha			
Otoe			
Pierce			
Polk			
Pawnee			

REPORT OF JOINT COMMITTEE—*Continued.*

Counties	For Amendment	Against Amendment	Last Vote
Perkins	262	31	536
Phelps	648	573	2226
Platte	1163	854	3788
Red Willow	1163	867	2126
Richardson	1360	672	5052
Rock	427	86	448
Saunders	1584	602	4704
Lyon	258	105	462
Seward	1200	815	7491
Saline	466	326	1885
Salene	1782	667	4885
Sarpy	629	392	1912
Scotts Bluff	842	18	495
Sheridan	577	324	1517
Sherman	990	288	1248
Sumter	485	7	1820
Thomas	52	7	110
Thayer	1214	283	3058
Valley	782	202	1748
Webster	1182	402	2265
Wheeler	429	30	227
Wayne	902	144	2039
Washington	1203	582	2185
York	2842	162	3841
Total	9-644	37030	70076

Stuart, J. Loomis, J. P. Lyden, J. S. Saunday, H. Funke, M. C. Thomas, Richard Graham, J. H. Phelps,

OFFICERS OF THE SENATE—TWENTY-THIRD SESSION—1893.

HON. THOMAS J. MAJORS, LIEUTENANT GOVERNOR, PRESIDENT

NAME	OCCUPATION	POSTOFFICE	COUNTY	NATIVITY	MARRIED OR SINGLE	AGE	POLITICS
E. M. Correll, President pro tem	Editor	Hebron	Thayer	Canada	Married	46	Republican.
H. A. Edwards, Secretary	Lawyer	Grand Island	Hall	Ohio	Married	38	Independent.
G. R. Doughty, 1st Assistant Secretary	Lawyer	Schuyler	Colfax	New York	Married	34	Democrat.
B. S. Littlefield, 2d Assistant Secretary	Editor	Grant	Perkins	Massachusetts	Single	30	Independent.
J. G. P. Hildebrand, cl'k com.of whole	Journalist	Lincoln	Lancaster	Virginia	Married	39	Democrat.
J. M. Snyder, Chaplain	Clergyman	Venlurette	Sherman	West Virginia	Married	67	Independent.
Timothy T. Kelliher, Bookkeeper	Machinist	North Platte	Lincoln	Pennsylvania	Single	26	Independent.
J. H. Dundas, Engrossing Clerk	Editor	Auburn	Nemaha	Illinois	Married	47	Independent.
Frank R. Morrissey, Enrolling Clerk	Newspaper Man	Omaha	Douglas	New York	Married	37	Democrat.
T. D. Worrall, Supply Clerk	Commercial Traveler	Lincoln	Lancaster	Illinois	Married	53	Democrat.
S. S. Alley, Sergeant-at-Arms	Lawyer	Wilber	Saline	Indiana	Married	47	Democrat.
Keen Ladden, 1st Ass't Serg't-at-Arms	Farmer	Wayland	Polk	Wisconsin	Married	49	Democrat.
R. L. Rossiter, 2d Ass't Serg't-at-Arms	Surveyor	Columbus	Platte	Ireland	Married	49	Independent.
W. A. J. Raum, Postmaster	Farmer	Crawford	Dawes	Pennsylvania	Married	46	Democrat.
John Steinhart, Assistant Postmaster	Insurance	Nebraska City	Otoe	Germany	Married	60	Democrat.
A. Wagner, Doorkeeper	Farmer	Atlanta	Phelps	New York	Married	43	Democrat.
W. S. Conrad, 1st Assistant Doorkeeper	Editor	Fremont	Dodge	New York	Married	32	Independent.
L. Shrader, Stenographer	Stenographer	Logan	Logan	Wisconsin	Single	23	Independent.
John F. Sherman, Bill Clerk	Editor	Waboo	Saunders	New York	Married	40	Democrat.
Henry Kessler, Janitor	Laborer	Nebraska City	Otoe	Germany	Married	50	Democrat.
John C. Gorin, Custodian of Senate	Farmer	Palisade	Hitchcock	Kentucky	Married	47	Independent.

MEMBERS OF THE SENATE—TWENTY-THIRD SESSION—1893.

NAME	OCCUPATION	P. O. ADDRESS	COUNTY	NATIVITY	MARRIED OR SINGLE	AGE	POLITICS
Babcock, Wm. N.	Manager Stock Yards	Omaha	Douglas	New York	Married	45	Democrat.
Campbell, Jacob N.	Farmer & Stock Raiser	Fullerton	Nance	Missouri	Married	27	Independent.
Clarke, Chas. H.	Hardware Merchant	Omaha	Douglas	Nebraska	Single	23	Republican.
Correll, Erasmus M.	Editor	Hebron	Thayer	Canada	Married	46	Republican.
Dale, Walter F.	Farmer	Atlanta	Phelps	Wisconsin	Married	36	Independent.
Darner, J. H.	Merchant and Minister	Cozad	Dawson	Ohio	Married	51	Independent.
Dysart, William	Farmer	Superior	Nuckolls	Ohio	Married	51	Independent.
Eagleston, G. W.	Grain Dealer	Bennett	Lancaster	England	Married	43	Republican.
Everett, Fremont	Lawyer	Lyons	Burt	Iowa	Married	37	Republican.
Graham, Alexander	Real Estate	Beatrice	Gage	Ohio	Married	47	Republican.
Gray, W. M.	Farmer	North Loup	Valley	Pennsylvania	Married	46	Independent.
Hahn, Leopold	Carpenter	Hastings	Adams	Germany	Married	46	Re-, oblican.
Hale, F. J.	Farmer and Merchant	Battle Creek	Madison	Virginia	Married	50	Democrat.
Harris, James E.	Minister	Talmage	Otoe	Ohio	Married	52	Independent.
Johnson, L. L.	Farmer & Sorghum M'f'r.	Inland	Clay	Ohio	Married	42	Independent.
Lobeck, C. O.	Hardware Merchant	Omaha	Douglas	Illinois	Married	41	Republican.
G. W. Lowley	Lawyer	Seward	Seward	England	Married	50	Republican.
Mattes, John Jr.	Manager Brewing Co.	Nebraska City	Otoe	Germany	Married	33	Democrat.
Miller, James P.	Farmer	York	York	Ohio	Married	58	Republican.
Moore, R. E.	Banker	Lincoln	Lancaster	Illinois	Married	43	Republican.
McCarty, T. F.	Farmer	St. Paul	Howard	New York	Married	50	Ind. Democrat.
McDonald, R. F.	Farmer	Pender	Thurston	Ohio	Married	42	Republican.
Mullen, J. P.	Farmer	Emmett	Holt	Pennsylvania	Married	37	Independent.
North, James E.	Real Estate	Columbus	Platte	Ohio	Married	54	Democrat.
Packwood, Samuel	Farmer	Creighton	Knox	Indiana	Married	64	Independent.
Pope, John Dudley	Lawyer	Friend	Saline	Illinois	Married	36	Republican.
Sanders, W. A.	Farmer	Ashland	Saunders	Pennsylvania	Married	66	Independent.
Scott, A. R.	Lawyer	Falls City	Richardson	Pennsylvania	Married	51	Republican.
Smith, G. N.	Farmer	Kearney	Buffalo	New Hampshire.	Married	49	Independent.
Stewart, H. G.	Farmer	Crawford	Dawes	Wisconsin	Married	39	Independent.
Tefft, Orlando	Banker	Avoca	Cass	Illinois	Married	50	Republican.
Thomsen, John	Real Estate, Insurance.	Fremont	Dodge	Germany	Single	39	Democrat.
Young, Lewis W	Farmer	Wilsonville	Furnas	New York	Married	56	Independent.

OFFICERS OF THE HOUSE—TWENTY-THIRD SESSION—1893.

NAME	OCCUPATION	POSTOFFICE	COUNTY	NATIVITY	MARRIED OR SINGLE	AGE	POLITICS
J. N. Gaffin, Speaker	Farmer	Colon	Saunders	Illinois	Married	37	Independent.
Eric Johnson, Chief Clerk	Editor	Hastings	Adams	Sweden	Married	34	Independent.
Ed. J. Hall, 1st Assistant Clerk	Editor	Grand Island	Hall	Iowa	Married	46	Democrat.
J. H. Edmisten, 2d Assistant Clerk	Farmer	Eddyville	Dawson	Texas	Married	37	Independent.
D. R. Carpenter, 3d Assistant Clerk	Editor	Indianola	Red Willow	Indiana	Married	39	Independent.
Wm. G. Dungan, Sergeant-at-Arms	Farmer	Newark	Kearney	Indiana	Married	53	Independent.
L. A. Beltzer, 1st Ass't Serg't-at-Arms	Nurseryman	Osceola	Polk	Maryland	Married	53	Independent.
E. H. Higgins, 2d Ass't Serg't-at-Arms	Farmer	Cambridge	Furnas	Nebraska	Single	24	Independent.
W. B. Hall, Chaplain	Clergyman	Sargent	Custer	Vermont	Married	48	Independent.
Chas. Dockhorn, Doorkeeper	General Merchandise	Falls City	Richardson	Germany	Married	59	Democrat.
E. L. Simon, Assistant Doorkeeper	Brick Layer	Lincoln	Lancaster	Illinois	Married	30	Democrat.
O. N. Sullivan, Custodian Cloak Room	Clerk	Lincoln	Lancaster	Illinois	Single	26	Democrat.
A. Stedwell, Ass't "	Bee Keeper	Kearney	Buffalo	New York	Married	68	Independent.
Norman Ross, Postmaster	Real Estate	Schuyler	Colfax	Prince Ed's I'd	Single	32	Democrat.
Mrs. N. J. Boulware, Ass't Postmaster	Dressmaker	Nebraska City	Otoe	Nebraska	Single	30	Democrat.
G. P. Porter, Mail Carrier	Farmer	Clarks	Merrick	Ohio	Married	29	Independent.
W. F. Wright, Bookkeeper	Farmer	Lincoln	Lancaster	Michigan	Married	54	Independent.
Geo. L. Butler, Bill Clerk	Farmer	Ewing	Holt	Pennsylvania	Married	35	Independent.
Otis H. Clark, Assistant Bill Clerk	Farmer	Woodville	Platte	New York	Single	45	Independent.
S. Keene, Time-keeper	Editor	Gandy	Logan	Illinois	Married	32	Independent.
W. H. Talcott, Cus. Chief Clerk's office	Farmer	Tecumseh	Johnson	Illinois	Married	45	Independent.

MEMBERS OF THE HOUSE—TWENTY-THIRD SESSION—1893.

NAME	OCCUPATION	P.O. ADDRESS	COUNTY	NATIVITY	MARRIED OR SINGLE	AGE	POLITICS
Ames, George W	Real Estate	Omaha	Douglas	New York	Married	35	Democrat
Barry, Patrick H	Farmer	Greeley Center	Greeley	Ireland	Married	48	Independent
Beal, Charles W	Editor	Broken Bow	Custer	Missouri	Single	32	Independent
Brockman, John M	Farmer & Stock Raiser	Stella	Richardson	Illinois	Married	51	Republican
Burns, Joseph	Contractor	Lincoln	Lancaster	Ireland	Married	44	Republican
Brown, David J	Farmers & Cattle Feeder	Seward	Seward	Tennessee	Married	48	Republican
Cain, J. B	Farmer	Aurora	Hamilton	Ohio	Married	37	Republican
Carpenter, G. J	Nurseryman, fr't grower	Fairbury	Jefferson	New York	Married	39	Republican
Casper, C. D	Editor	David City	Butler	Delaware	Married	47	Democrat
Colton, Geo. R	Banker	David City	Butler	Illinois	Married	58	Republican
Cooley, Alfred S	Farmer	Eagle	Cass	Ohio	Married	46	Republican
Cornish, A. J	Lawyer	Lincoln	Lancaster	Iowa	Married	36	Republican
Crane, Thomas D	Lawyer	Omaha	Douglas	Massachusetts	Single	37	Republican
Cross, George	Editor	Fairbury	Jefferson	Wisconsin	Married	51	Republican
Davies, John A	Lawyer	Plattsmouth	Cass	Iowa	Single	34	Republican
Dew, J. S	Farmer	Tecumseh	Johnson	Illinois	Married	31	Republican
Dickerson, Albert	Farmer	Litchfield	Sherman	Kentucky	Married	57	Independent
Dimmick, J. M	Farmer	Franklin	Franklin	Illinois	Married	50	Independent
Dobson, Richard	Farmer	Grafton	Fillmore	England	Married	48	Independent
Eickhoff, Arnold	Farmer	Aten	Cedar	Germany	Married	55	Democrat
Elder, Samuel M	Farmer	Clay Center	Clay	Kentucky	Married	43	Independent
Fitts, Enos E	Farmer	Allen	Dixon	Iowa	Married	41	Republican
Farrell, John *	Farmer	North Bend	Dodge	Ireland	Married	60	Democrat
Farnsworth, J. B	Farmer	Springview	Keya Paha	Maine	Married	62	Independent
Felton, G. A	Farmer	Angus	Nuckolls	Vermont	Married	42	Independent
Ford, Philo	Farmer	Bertrand	Phelps	New York	Married	55	Independent
Fulton, S	Farmer	Alma	Harlan	Pennsylvania	Married	45	Independent
Gaffin, J. N	Farmer & Stock Raiser	Colon	Saunders	Illinois	Married	37	Democrat
Gerdes, H	Farmer	Borada	Richardson	Illinois	Married	37	Republican
Gifford, W. M	Farmer & Stock Raiser	Lewiston	Pawnee	Indiana	Married	47	Republican
Goldsmith, Bennett	Merchant	West Point	Cuming	Germany	Married	48	Republican
Goss, Chas A	Lawyer	Omaha	Douglas	Ohio	Married	29	Republican

* Deceased

Name	Occupation	Post Office	County	State/Country		Age	Party
Goss, T. S.	Farmer	Wayne	Wayne	Massachusetts	Married	41	Republican
Grammer, Chas.	Farmer	St. Paul	Howard	Illinois	Married	43	Independent
Griffith, Peter	Farmer	Juniata	Adams	New York	Married	66	Republican
Haller, William D.	Druggist	Blair	Washington	Wisconsin	Married	46	Republican
Harmon, Frank P.	Farmer	Pauline	Adams	Iowa	Married	35	Independent
Henry, H. P.	Farmer	Mineola	Holt	Ohio	Married	43	Independent
Hinds, L. B.	Merchant	Odell	Gage	Vermont	Married	30	Republican
Higgins, W. P.	Farmer & Stock Raiser	Wescott	Custer	Missouri	Married	28	Independent
Howe, Church	Farmer & Stock Breeder	Howe	Nemaha	Massachusetts	Married	53	Republican
Horst, George	Farmer	Osceola	Polk	Wisconsin	Single	38	Independent
Irwin, W. J.	Farmer	West Hill	Platte	New York	Married	46	Independent
James, P. H.	Farmer & Stock Raiser	Cortland	Gage	Ohio	Married	50	Republican
Jenkins, E. M.	Druggist, Stock Raiser	Alexandria	Thayer	Illinois	Married	44	Republican
Jensen, John	Attorney and Banker	Geneva	Fillmore	North Germany	Married	49	Republican
Johnston, B. J.	Farmer and Preacher	Howe	Nemaha	Missouri	Married	63	Independent
Johnson, Nathan	Farmer & Stock Raiser	York	York	Rhode Island	Married	52	Republican
Johnson, J. L.	Real Estate	Abbott	Hall	Sweden	Married	44	Independent
Kaup, William	Farming, Stock Raising	Western	Saline	Germany	Married	43	Republican
Kessler, John F.	Farmer	Oakland	Burt	Pennsylvania	Married	39	Republican
Keckley, Chas. R.	Farmer, Stock Raiser	York	York	Ohio	Married	43	Republican
Keyes, Clarence F.	Farmer, Stock Raiser	Springfield	Sarpy	Massachusetts	Married	33	Republican
Kloke, Robert F.	Banker	West Point	Cuming	Wisconsin	Married	46	Republican
Kyner, James H.	Contractor	Omaha	Douglas	Ohio	Married	29	Independent
Kruse, J. G.	Farmer	Creighton	Knox	Iowa	Married	49	Independent
Krick, Edward	Farmer	Minden	Kearney	Pennsylvania	Married	39	Independent
Lingenfelter, Geo. C.	School Teacher	Sidney	Cheyenne	Ohio	Married	40	Democrat
Laikart, G. A.	Banker	Tilden	Madison	Germany	Married	45	Republican
Lockner, Augustus	Merchant and Farmer	Omaha	Douglas	New York	Married	43	Democrat
Leidigh, J. W.	Commission, Ice Dealer	Nebraska City	Otoe	Pennsylvania	Married	54	Independent
Lynch, J. O.	Farmer	Lexington	Dawson	New York	Married	48	Republican
Merrick, H. J.	Farmer	Adams	Gage	Pennsylvania	Married	51	Independent
McCutcheon, Wm. A.	Farmer	St. Edwards	Boone	Ohio	Married	35	Republican
McKesson, J. C. F.	Farmer	Emerald	Lancaster	Illinois	Married	49	Independent
McVey, E. A.	Farmer	Sutton	Clay	Indiana	Married	39	Republican
Nason, W. N.	Sec. Board of Trade	Douglas	Douglas	Pennsylvania	Married	39	Republican
Nelson, N. P.	Farmer	Hooper	Dodge	Sweden	Married	40	Democrat
Newberry, Fred	Farmer	Aurora	Hamilton	Minnesota	Married	34	Independent
Oakley, R. H.	Coal Merchant	Lincoln	Lancaster	New York	Married	46	Republican
Olson, P. B.	Farmer	Malmo	Saunders	Sweden	Married	39	Independent

MEMBERS OF THE HOUSE—TWENTY-THIRD SESSION—1893.

NAME	OCCUPATION	P. O. ADDRESS	COUNTY	NATIVITY	MARRIED OR SINGLE	AGE	POLITICS
Porter, W. F.	Farmer	Clarks	Merrick	Illinois	Married	22	Independent.
Rhea, Robert C.	Farmer	Milford	Seward	Ohio	Married	44	Republican.
Rhodes, H. F.	Farmer	Ord	Valley	New York	Married	36	Independent.
Ricketts, M. O.	Physician and Surgeon	Omaha	Douglas	Kentucky	Married	64	Republican.
Riley, Austin	Farmer	Rosemont	Webster	Iowa	Married	39	Independent.
Robinson, Chas. S.	Farmer	Midvale	Brown	New York	Married	61	Republican.
Ruggles, L. G.	Farmer & Stock Raiser	Hiawatha	Dundy	Kentucky	Married	57	Republican.
Schappel, Chas. A.	Farmer	Pawnee City	Pawnee	New York	Married	39	Independent.
Schel, Wm.	Farmer	Platte Center	Platte	Germany	Married	44	Independent.
Schotfeld, Henry	Brick Manufacturer	Grand Island	Hall	Illinois	Married	35	Democrat.
Scott, Andrew J	Farmer	Kearney	Buffalo	West Virginia	Married	43	Independent.
Sheridan, I. A.	Hardware	Indianola	Red Willow	Ohio	Married	43	Independent.
Sinclair, John	Grain Dealer	Burr	Otoe	Wisconsin	Married	38	Democrat.
Sisson, Edwin F	Farmer	Arizona	Burt	Ohio	Married	46	Republican.
Smith, Theo.	Farmer, Stockman, etc.	Tecumseh	Johnson	Pennsylvania	Married	45	Independent.
Smith, O. F.	Farmer	Ewing	Holt	New York	Married	55	Independent.
Smith, Julius	Farmer	Salem	Richardson	Germany	Married	42	Independent.
Soderman, F.	Farmer.s	Bertrand	Phelps	Sweden	Married	31	Republican.
Speecer, E. R.	Banker	Firth	Lancaster	New York	Married	53	Independent.
Stevens, John	Farmer	Edison	Furnas	West Virginia	Married	42	Independent.
Suter, Lewis H	Farmer & Stock Raiser	Neligh	Antelope	Pennsylvania	Married	28	Republican.
Sutton, A. L.	Lawyer	South Omaha	Douglas	Wisconsin	Single	47	Republican.
VanOulyn, John N	Examiner of Titles	Wilbur	Saline	Ohio	Married	48	Democrat.
VanHousen, John C	Farmer	Schuyler	Colfax	New York	Married	55	Republican.
Wardlaw, John M	Farmer	Pickrell	Gage	Kentucky	Married	42	Republican.
Watson, J. C.	Lawyer	Nebraska City	Otoe	Missouri	Married	42	Republican.
Wilson, John	Liveryman	Kearney	Buffalo	Pennsylvania	Married	47	Republican.
Withnell, G. H.	Contractor	Omaha	Douglas	England	Married	24	Democrat.
Woods, J. D.	Farmer	Hay Springs	Sheridan	Indiana	Married	43	Independent.

OFFICERS OF THE SENATE—TWENTY-FOURTH SESSION—1895.

Hon. Robert E. Moore, Lieutenant Governor, President.

NAME	OCCUPATION	POSTOFFICE	COUNTY	NATIVITY	MARRIED OR SINGLE	AGE	POLITICS
John C. Watson, President pro tem	Attorney	Nebraska City	Otoe	Missouri	Married	44	Republican.
Tim Sedgwick, Secretary	Editor	York	York	Illinois	Married	42	Republican.
P. W. Barber, 1st Assistant Secretary	Attorney	Grand Island	Hall	Canada	Married	39	Republican.
A. R. Keim, 2d Assistant Secretary	Attorney	Falls City	Richardson	Pennsylvania	Single	36	Republican.
R. Q. Stewart, Sergeant-at-arms	Farmer	Campbell	Franklin	Ohio	Single	49	Republican.
T. Williams, 1st Ass't Sergeant-at-arms	Painter	Geneva	Fillmore	Michigan	Single	44	Republican.
...... 2d Ass't Sergeant-at-arms							
J. Gannon, Doorkeeper	Farmer	Bancroft	Cuming	Illinois	Married	35	Republican.
C. S. Brindlare, Ass't Doorkeeper	Painter	Tecumseh	Johnson	New Jersey	Single	28	Republican.
J. E. Rule, Enrolling Clerk	Attorney	Western	Saline	Wisconsin	Married	33	Republican.
W. H. Pool, Engrossing Clerk							
...... 1st Ass't Enrolling Clerk	Farmer	Wabash	Cass	Ohio	Married	42	Republican.
...... 1st Ass't Engrossing Clerk							
H. S. MacAyeal, Chaplain	Minister	Cambridge	Furnas	Iowa	Married	34	Republican.

MEMBERS OF THE SENATE—Legislature 1895.

NAME	OCCUPATION	POST OFFICE	COUNTY	NATIVITY	MARRIED OR SINGLE	AGE	POLITICS
Harry C. Lindsay	Attorney	Pawnee City	Pawnee	Wisconsin	Married	33	Republican.
J. H. Hitchcock	Attorney	Tecumseh	Johnson	Ohio	Married	34	Republican.
John C. Watson	Attorney	Nebraska City	Otoe	Missouri	Married	41	Republican.
Orlando Tefft	Banker and Farmer	Avoca	Cass	Illinois	Married	51	Republican.
William J. Lehr	Farmer	Mead	Saunders	Illinois	Married	28	Republican.
Thomas D. Crane	Attorney	Omaha	Douglas	Massachusetts	Single	38	Republican.
William Stuefer	Banker	West Point	Cuming	Wisconsin	Married	47	Republican.
Sherman Saunders	Banker	Bloomfield	Knox	Nebraska	Single	29	Republican.
E. W. Jeffres	Farmer	Horace	Greeley	Ohio	Married	43	Populist.
W. D. Holbrook	Farmer	Everett	Dodge	Missouri	Married	44	Republican.
John T. Bressler	Real Estate and Loans	Wayne	Wayne	Pennsylvania	Married	45	Republican.
John C. Sprecher	Editor	Schuyler	Colfax	Ohio	Married	30	Populist.
John Crawford	Farmer	Atkinson	Holt	Scotland	Married	63	Populist.
H. G. Stewart	Farmer and Stockraiser	Crawford	Dawes	Wisconsin	Married	40	Populist.
W. M. Gray	Farmer and Stockraiser	North Loup	Valley	Pennsylvania	Married	48	Populist.
Joseph Black	Farmer and Stockraiser	Kearney	Buffalo	West Virginia	Married	60	Republican.
George H. Caldwell	Attorney	Grand Island	Hall	Ohio	Married	50	Republican.
J. N. Campbell	Farmer and Stockraiser	Fullerton	Nance	Missouri	Married	29	Populist.
Wm. E. Bauer	Attorney	David City	Butler	Ohio	Married	34	Populist.
John B. Wright	Grain Dealer	Lincoln	Lancaster	New York	Married	48	Republican.
Alex. Graham	Real Estate	Beatrice	Gage	Ohio	Married	49	Republican.
J. D. Pope	Attorney	Friend	Saline	Illinois	Married	38	Republican.
George Cross	Editor	Fairbury	Jefferson	Wisconsin	Married	53	Republican.
Chas. H. Sloan	Attorney	Geneva	Fillmore	Iowa	Married	31	Republican.
Edwin E. Mighell	Farmer	Aurora	Hamilton	Illinois	Married	44	Republican.
G. E. McKeeby	Physician	Red Cloud	Webster	Ohio	Married	30	Republican.
L. Hahn	Carpenter	Hastings	Adams	Germany	Married	47	Republican.
Walter F. Dale	Farmer	Atlanta	Harlan	Wisconsin	Married	38	Populist.
F. M. Rathbun	Farmer and Stockraiser	Cambridge	Furnas	Illinois	Married	45	Republican.
Wm. R. Akers	Farmer	Collins	Scotts Bluff	Ohio	Married	65	Republican.
Richard Smith	Contractor	Omaha	Douglas	Canada	Single	47	Republican.
Isaac Noyes	Farmer	Waterloo	Douglas	New York	Married	66	Republican.
J. C. F. McKesson	Stock Farmer	Emerald	Lancaster	Illinois	Married	37	Republican.

OFFICERS OF THE HOUSE—TWENTY-FOURTH SESSION—1895.

NAME	OCCUPATION	POST OFFICE	COUNTY	NATIVITY	MARRIED OR SINGLE	AGE	POLITICS
C. L. Richards, Speaker	Attorney	Hebron	Thayer	Illinois	Married	39	Republican.
W. M. Geddes, Chief Clerk	Mayor	Grand Island	Hall	Ohio	Married	58	Republican.
P. A. Harrison, 1st Assistant Clerk	Attorney	Pawnee City	Pawnee	Illinois	Married	30	Republican.
J. F. Zediker, 2d Assistant Clerk	Editor	Lincoln	Lancaster	Pennsylvania	Married	52	Republican.
H. Glasgow, 3d Assistant Clerk	Insurance Agent	Odell	Gage	Pennsylvania	Married	47	Republican.
H. Akin, 4th Assistant Clerk	Book-keeper	Omaha	Douglas	Kansas	Single	22	Republican.
W. W. Shoenberger, Sergeant-at-Arms	Real Estate and Col	Aurora	Hamilton	Pennsylvania	Married	49	Republican.
A. G. Tyler, 1st Asst. Sergeant-at-Arms	Real Estate	Ogalalla	Keith	Mississippi	Married	48	Republican.
J. L. Cook, 2d Asst. Sergeant-at-Arms	Painter	Fontanelle	Washington	Pennsylvania	Married	44	Republican.
P. Turr, Assistant Doorkeeper	Real Estate	Havelock	Lancaster	Wisconsin	Married	26	Republican.
W. J. Pemberton, Enrolling Clerk	Real Estate	Fairbury	Jefferson	Virginia	Married	43	Republican.
1st Asst. Enrolling Clerk							Republican.
F. L. Sargent, Engrossing Clerk	Farmer	Cedar Rapids	Boone	New Hamp	Married	49	Republican.
1st Asst. Engrossing Clerk							Republican.
M. S. Maze, Chaplain	Minister	Callaway	Custer	Indiana	Married	38	Republican.

MEMBERS OF THE HOUSE—LEGISLATURE 1895

Hon. C. L. Richards, Speaker.

NAME	OCCUPATION	POST OFFICE	COUNTY	NATIVITY	MARRIED OR SINGLE	AGE	POLITICS
David Guthrie	Miller	Superior	Nuckolls	Canada	Married	48	Democrat
T. G. Wilder	Farmer	Cowles	Webster	New York	Married	55	Republican
Peter Griffith	Farmer	Juniata	Adams	New York	Married	58	Republican
Randolph McNitt	Attorney	Red Cloud	Webster	Ohio	Single	24	Republican
W. H. Harrison	Lumber Dealer	Grand Island	Hall	Illinois	Married	34	Republican
G. L. Rouse	Farmer	Alda	Hall	Ohio	Married	48	Republican
H. Schickedantz	Implement Dealer	St. Paul	Howard	Germany	Married	34	Republican
P. H. Barry	Farmer	Greeley	Greeley	Ireland	Married	50	Populist
J. A. Robertson	Farmer	Joy	Holt	Indiana	Married	27	Populist
G. F. Smith	Farmer	Ewing	Holt	New York	Married	47	Populist
E. I. Myers	Lumber Dealer	Newport	Rock	Pennsylvania	Married	31	Republican
F. Rothleiter	Farmer and Merchant	Kilgore	Cherry	Austria	Married	36	Populist
Wm. Dempsey	Farmer	Alliance	Box Butte	Wisconsin	Single	33	Populist
R. D. Harris	Physician	Ogalalla	Keith	Ohio	Married	46	Republican
H. F. Rhodes	Farmer	Yale	Valley	New York	Married	38	Populist
W. P. Higgins	Farmer	Wescott	Custer	Missouri	Married	30	Populist
Isaac N. Goar	Farmer	Callaway	Custer	Indiana	Married	43	Populist
James W. Zink	Farmer and Stockraiser	Loup City	Sherman	Indiana	Married	48	Populist
John Brady	Farmer	Kearney	Buffalo	Wisconsin	Single	43	Republican
A. J. Scott	Farmer	Kearney	Buffalo	West Virginia	Married	45	Populist
Frank Bacon	Farmer	Gothenburg	Dawson	Illinois	Married	41	Republican
Oscar Carlson	Farmer	Axtell	Kearney	Sweden	Married	44	Republican
Henry Moehrman	Farmer	Macon	Franklin	Germany	Single	31	Republican
O. Hull	Farmer	Alma	Harlan	Pennsylvania	Married	45	Populist
E. Soderman	Farmer	Bertrand	Phelps	Sweden	Married	44	Populist
E. R. Bee	Lumberman	Cambridge	Furnas	West Virginia	Married	40	Republican
J. J. Lamborn	Real Estate and Loans	Indianola	Red Willow	Ohio	Married	41	Republican
D. L. McBride	Farmer and Clergyman	Quick	Frontier	Pennsylvania	Married	44	Populist
J. W. Cole	Attorney	Culbertson	Hitchcock	Indiana	Married	46	Republican

Name	Occupation	Town	County	State		Age	Party
Charles H. Chase	Farmer and Live Stock	Stanton	Stanton	Ohio	Married	39	Republican
George Mattison	Farmer	Ponca	Dixon	Wisconsin	Married	43	Republican
Henry S. Beck	Banker	Pierce	Pierce	Ohio	Single	57	Republican
M. H. Wart	Farmer	Creighton	Knox	New York	Married	59	Populist
L. H. Suter	Farmer	Neligh	Antelope	Pennsylvania	Married	41	Populist
L. P. Judd	Druggist	Cedar Rapids	Boone	New York	Married	36	Republican
F. W. Richardson	Farmer	Battle Creek	Madison	Illinois	Married	50	Republican
Gus G. Becher	Real Estate, Loans, Ins.	Columbus	Platte	Bohemia	Married	50	Republican
E. B. Speckman	Tinner	Fullerton	Nance	Pennsylvania	Married	48	Populist
John C. Van Housen	Farmer	Schuyler	Colfax	New York	Married	50	Democrat
R. C. Brownell	Farmer	Morse Bluff	Saunders	Canada	Single	34	Republican
James Havlik	Farmer	Abie	Saunders	Illinois	Married	37	Populist
C. D. Casper	Printer and Publisher	David City	Butler	Delaware	Married	49	Pop. & Dem.
M. C. Delaney	Farmer	Brainard	Butler	New York	Married	51	Democrat
W. A. Brokaw	Farmer	Ruby	Seward	Illinois	Single	52	Populist
D. D. Remington	Farmer	Bee	Seward	Wisconsin	Married	45	Populist
Joseph Burns	Contractor	Lincoln	Lancaster	Ireland	Married	46	Republican
Henry Harkson	Merchant	Davey	Lancaster	Denmark	Married	50	Republican
T. C. Munger	Attorney	Lincoln	Lancaster	Ohio	Married	33	Republican
W. D. Robinson	Attorney	Lincoln	Lancaster	Nebraska	Married	23	Republican
E. R. Spencer	Banker	Firth	Lancaster	New York	Married	33	Republican
W. O. Chapman	Editor	Crete	Saline	Indiana	Married	31	Republican
Wm. Kaup	Real Estate	Western	Saline	Germany	Married	45	Republican
J. C. Burch	Banker	Wymore	Gage	New York	Married	42	Republican
H. J. Merrick	Farmer and Stockdeal'r	Adams	Gage	Pennsylvania	Married	48	Republican
E. B. Hinds	Real Estate	Odell	Gage	Vermont	Married	52	Republican
F. W. Miles	Banker	DeWitt	Saline	Pennsylvania	Married	36	Republican
J. O. Cramb	Farmer	Fairbury	Jefferson	Maine	Married	61	Republican
E. M. Jenkins	Druggist	Alexandria	Thayer	Illinois	Married	46	Republican
C. L. Richards	Attorney	Hebron	Thayer	Illinois	Married	39	Republican
J. M. Perkins	Farmer	Fairmont	Fillmore	Pennsylvania	Married	60	Republican
Henry Langhorst	Physician	Ohiowa	Fillmore	Germany	Single	49	Republican
John B. Conaway	Farmer	York	York	Ohio	Married	54	Republican
Wm. McFadden	Farmer and Teacher	McCool Junc.	York	Pennsylvania	Married	51	Republican
Geo. Horst	Farmer and Stockdeal'r	Osceola	Polk	Wisconsin	Single	40	Populist
Robt. W. Campbell	Farmer and Stockman	Grand Island	Merrick	Iowa	Single	34	Republican
John B. Cain	Merchant	Aurora	Hamilton	Ohio	Married	39	Republican
A. N. Thomas	Attorney	Aurora	Hamilton	Pennsylvania	Married	55	Republican
E. E. Hairgrove	Farmer	Sutton	Clay	Illinois	Married	33	Republican
Wm. Ashby	Farmer	Fairfield	Clay	Illinois	Single	27	Republican

MEMBERS OF THE HOUSE—LEGISLATURE 1895.

HON. C. L. RICHARDS, SPEAKER.

NAME	OCCUPATION	POST OFFICE	COUNTY	NATIVITY	MARRIED OR SINGLE	AGE	POLITICS
John M. Brockman	Farmer and Stockraiser	Stella	Richardson	Illinois	Married	53	Republican.
T. P. Jones	Retired Farmer	Falls City	Richardson	Pennsylvania	Married	66	Republican.
John H. Shook	Farmer	Barada	Richardson	Illinois	Married	68	Republican.
James J. Bernard	Farmer and Stockdeal'r	Lewiston	Pawnee	Prince Edw. I'd	Married	42	Republican.
Wm. Sutton	Dairyman	Table Rock	Pawnee	Illinois	Married	50	Republican.
James F. Ely	Farmer	Auburn	Nemaha	New York	Married	51	Republican.
B. J. Johnston	Preacher	Howe	Nemaha	Missouri	Married	65	Populist.
V. Zink	Farmer	Sterling	Johnson	Germany	Married	51	Republican.
John H. Pohlman	Farmer	Johnson	Nemaha	Germany	Married	55	Republican.
Addison Wait	Produce Dealer	Syracuse	Otoe	Ohio	Married	48	Republican.
Patrick Roddy	Farmer	Nebraska City	Otoe	Ireland	Married	52	Republican.
Alfred S. Cooley	Farmer	Eagle	Cass	Ohio	Married	48	Republican.
John A. Davies	Attorney	Plattsmouth	Cass	Iowa	Single	38	Democrat.
Stephen W. Orton	Druggist	Weeping Water	Cass	New York	Married	50	Republican.
Edgar Howard	Newspaper Man	Papillion	Sarpy	Iowa	Married	36	Republican.
James Allan	Laborer	Omaha	Douglas	Scotland	Married	40	Republican.
E. Benedict	Contractor	Omaha	Douglas	Illinois	Married	41	Republican.
A. C. Harte	Attorney	Omaha	Douglas	Indiana	Married	38	Republican.
Richard H. Jenness	Builder	Omaha	Douglas	Kentucky	Single	34	Republican.
John W. Johnston	Printer	Omaha	Douglas	Illinois	Married	37	Republican.
M. O. Ricketts	Physician	Omaha	Douglas	Ohio	Married	39	Republican.
A. L. Sutton	Attorney	South Omaha	Douglas	Kentucky	Married	36	Republican.
Herman Timme	Merchant	Omaha	Douglas	Wisconsin	Single	28	Republican.
W. D. Haller	Druggist	Bennington	Douglas	Germany	Married	46	Republican.
E. F. Sisson	Farmer	Blair	Washington	Wisconsin	Married	47	Republican.
L. C. Weber	Druggist	Arizona	Burt	Ohio	Married	43	Republican.
Edward C. Barns	Druggist	Arlington	Washington	Kentucky	Married	49	Republican.
W. J. McVicker	Real Estate	Scribner	Dodge	New York	Married	56	Republican.
David W. Burke	Retired Farmer	North Bend	Dodge	New York	Married	44	Democrat.
Nick Fritz	Retired Farmer	Bancroft	Cuming	Canada	Single	55	Republican.
	Co. Treas. and Farmer	Pender	Thurston	Germany	Married	47	Democrat.

Appointive Officers of the House, 1897.

Custodian Cloak-room, D. Cosgrove, Omaha.
Assistant Custodian Cloak-room, L. S. Bruno, Central City.
Custodian Chief Clerk's Room, John Vanderburg, Indianola.
Time-keeper, E. W. Crane, North Platte.
Mail Carrier, D. S. Burkhard, Rowland.
Doorkeeper, J. C. Hammang, Arlington.
Assistant Doorkeeper, Charles Biven, Tecumseh.
Speaker's Private Secretary, W. N. Silver, Wahoo.
Engrossing and Enrolling Clerk, Lena Bromer, West Point.
    "   "   " John L. Cleaver, Falls City.
    "   "   " Anna Clegg, Falls City.
    "   "   " Joy Hackler, Springview.
    "   "   " P. W. Murray, Grafton.
    "   "   " I. D. Marks, Grand Island.
    "   "   " Katie Neville, Plattsmouth.
    "   "   " Lizzie Stevens, Hastings.
    "   "   " C. G. Wallace, Lexington.
    "   "   " Charles Yost, Kearney.
    "   "   " Ed. Westering, Clay Center.
    "   "   " Jud. C. Wilson, St. Edward.
Stenographer, Virginia E. Phillips, Omaha.
    " Sarah E. Striker, Wahoo.
    " George C. Kidd. Nebraska City.
Bill Clerk, J. M. Whisnand, Gilead.
Assistant Bill Clerk, H. F. Wasmund, Rushville.
Proof-reader, Mary Fairbrother, Omaha.
Assistant Proof-reader, Arthur L. Anderson, Omaha.
Copy-holder, Arthur Frantz, Tobias.
    " Jesse Pflug, Exeter.
Clerk of Committee on Elections, C. H. Challis, Ulysses.
    "   " on Accounts and Expenditures, C. N. Miller, Alma.
Clerk of Committee on Claims, J. B. Anderson, Holdrege.
    "   " on Finance, Ways, and Means, J. C. Low, Stella.
    "   " on Judiciary, Miss H. L. Knapp, Omaha.
Clerk of Committee on Engrossed and Enrolled Bills, J. H. Graves, Palmyra.
Clerk of Committee on Cities and Towns, Edwin Norris, Omaha.
Watchman, C. Marshall, Riverton.
    " Henry Taylor, Spring Green.
Night Watchman, W. F. Maddox, Aurora.
Janitor, W. S. Leiter, Seward.
    " Thomas Harrington, Central City.
    " D. K. Chaney, Stella.
Custodian of Basement, M. McGee, Lincoln.
Fireman, H. B. Schneringer, Callaway.
Boot Black, G. H. Holly, Lincoln.
Carpenter, George F. Daggett, Lincoln.
Chief Clerk's Messenger, O. C. Teel, Red Cloud.
Page, Ted Schneringer, Bradshaw.
    " Roy Platte, Lincoln.
    " Willie Smith, Salem.
    " Fred Wiebe, Grand Island.
Speaker's Page, Simon Kelley, Lincoln.
Page, William Hensley, Columbus.
    " James Boyd, Stark.
    " William Cunningham, Palmyra.
    " L. C. Edwards, Humboldt.
    " Harvey Grosvenor, Central City.
    " Oscar Phelps, Stratton.

OFFICERS OF THE SENATE—TWENTY-FIFTH SESSION—1897.

NAME.	OCCUPATION.	P. O. ADDRESS	COUNTY.	NATIVITY.	MARRIED OR SINGLE.	AGE.	POLITICS.
Hon. F. T. Ransom, Pres. Pro Tem.	Lawyer	Omaha	Douglas	Missouri	Married		Silver Rep.
W. F. Schwind, Secretary	Lawyer	Lincoln	Lancaster	Missouri	Married	32	Democrat.
H. A. Edwards, 1st Asst. Secretary	Lawyer	Grand Island	Hall		Married		Peo. Ind.
H. G. Stewart, 2d Asst. Secretary	Farmer	Bancroft	Dawes	Wisconsin	Married	42	Peo. Ind.
John Corlinn, Sergeant-at-Arms		Central City	Cuming				
D. H. Burke, Asst. Sergeant-at-Arms	Farmer	Papillion	Sarpy				Peo. Ind.
Charles Nownes, Doorkeeper		Hastings	Adams				
W. G. Willoughby, Asst. Doorkp'r	Farmer	North Loup	Valley		Married		Peo. Ind.
G. M. Petty, Enrolling Clerk		Wilber	Dodge				
Miss J. H. Abbott, Engrossing Clerk	Minister	Butte	Saline	Iowa	Married	32	Peo. Ind.
Frank T. Chatburn, Chaplain	Clerk	Pawnee City	Boyd		Single		Democrat.
Laura Forbes, Postmistress		Nebraska City	Pawnee				
F. J. Butler, Assistant Postmaster	Lawyer	Omaha	Otoe	Illinois	Married	40	Democrat.
W. M. Clary, Clerk Com. of Whole		Plattsmouth	Douglas				
J. G. Seay, Bill Clerk			Cass	Illinois			
J. J. Swoboda, Mail Carrier		Lexington	Cass		Single	22	
Nathan R. Greenfield, Bookkeeper	Lawyer		Dawson	Illinois	Single		Peo. Ind.

MEMBERS OF THE SENATE—TWENTY-FIFTH SESSION—1897.

NAME.	OCCUPATION.	POSTOFFICE.	COUNTY.	NATIVITY.	MARRIED OR SINGLE.	AGE.	POLITICS.
C. W. Beal	Editor	Broken Bow	Custer	Missouri	Married	37	Peo. Ind.
Smith T. Caldwell	Farmer	Edgar	Clay	Illinois	Married	51	Republican.
J. S. Canaday	School Teacher	Minden	Kearney	Indiana	Married	35	Peo. Ind.
J. B. Conaway	Physician	York	York	Ohio	Married	56	Republican.
William H. Dearing	Physician	Plattsmouth	Cass	Illinois	Married	38	Democrat.
John H. Dundas	Editor	Auburn	Nemaha	Illinois	Married	51	Peo. Ind.
J. H. Evans	Manager Laundry	Omaha	Douglas	Wales		48	Republican.
Thomas F. Farrell	Farmer	Chapman	Merrick	Canada	Married	38	Peo. Ind.
F. Q. Fett	Ranchman	Ogalalla	Keith	Iowa	Married	44	Peo. Ind.
Nick Fritz	Farmer	Pender	Thurston	Germany	Married	50	Democrat.
John N. Goudring	Lawyer	Columbus	Platte	Illinois	Married	40	Democrat.
Loyal M. Graham	Lawyer	Stockville	Frontier	Pennsylvania	Married	37	Peo. Ind.
O. Grothan	Physician	St. Paul	Howard	Norway	Married	37	Democrat.
W. D. Haller	Druggist	Blair	Washington	Wisconsin	Married	50	Republican.
J. W. Heapy	Farmer	Litchfield	Sherman	Canada	Married	42	Peo. Ind.
Edward E. Howell	Coal Dealer	Omaha	Douglas	Canada	Married	37	Democrat.
John Jeffcoat	Contractor	Omaha	Douglas	Illinois	Married	61	Peo. Ind.
L. L. Johnson	Farmer	Inland	Clay	Ohio	Married	46	Peo. Ind.
J. D. Lee	Minister	Lynch	Boyd	Virginia	Married	31	Peo. Ind.
Michael W. McGann	Lawyer	Albion	Boone	Illinois	Married	33	Peo. Ind.
William Miller	Farmer	Oakland	Burt	Alsace Lorraine	Married	45	Peo. Ind.
Charles T. Muffly	Farmer	Mead'w Grove	Madison	Pennsylvania	Married	68	Peo. Ind.
George A. Murphy	Lawyer	Beatrice	Gage	Indiana	Married	38	Republican.
Otto Mutz	Farmer	Springview	Keya Paha	Iowa	Married	41	Peo. Ind.
John M. Osborn	Farmer	Pawnee City	Pawnee	Indiana	Married	53	Peo. Ind.
Frank T. Ransom	Lawyer	Omaha	Douglas	Missouri	Married		Silver Rep.
William E. Ritchie	Farmer	Ulysses	Butler	Illinois	Married	49	Democrat.
William D. Schaal	Farmer	Springfield	Sarpy	Missouri	Married	37	Peo. Ind.
E. H. Spencer	Banker	Firth	Lancaster	New York	Married	35	Republican.
Calvin F. Steele	Merchant	Fairbury	Jefferson	Illinois	Married	53	Republican.
Tracy P. Sykes	Farmer	Hastings	Adams	New York	Married	33	Peo. Ind.
A. R. Talbot	Lawyer	Lincoln	Lancaster	Illinois	Married	57	Republican.
Edward G. Watson	Physician	Friend	Saline	Wisconsin	Married	38	Silver Rep.
Amos A. Weller	Merchant	Syracuse	Otoe	New York	Married	55	Democrat.

OFFICERS OF THE HOUSE—TWENTY-FIFTH SESSION—1897.

NAME.	OCCUPATION.	POSTOFFICE.	COUNTY.	NATIVITY.	MARRIED OR SINGLE.	AGE.	POLITICS.
J. N. Gaffin, Speaker	Farm. & Stock Dealer	Colon	Saunders	Illinois	Married	44	Peo. Ind.
Frank D. Eager, Chief Clerk	Publisher	Lincoln	Lancaster	Nebraska	Single	24	Peo. Ind.
U. E. Foster, 1st Assistant Clerk	Editor	Plainview	Pierce	Wisconsin	Married	30	Peo. Ind.
J. W. Barnhart, 2d Assistant Clerk	Editor	Auburn	Nemaha	Pennsylvania	Married	40	Democrat.
A. J. Webb, 3d Assistant Clerk	Accountant	Omaha	Douglas	California	Married	35	Democrat.
Rev. James Mailley, Chaplain	Minister	David City	Butler	Scotland	Married	56	Silver Rep.
L. A. Beltzer, Sergeant-at-Arms	Publisher	Osceola	Polk	Maryland	Married	54	Peo. Ind.
J. M. Nov. Ass't Sergt-at-Arms	Carpenter	Fremont	Dodge	Kentucky	Married	27	Democrat.
J. C. Hannang, Doorkeeper	Farmer	Arlington	Washington	Nebraska	Single	24	Peo. Ind.
Charles Bivens, Ass't Doorkeeper	Cigar Maker	Tecumseh	Johnson	Nebraska	Single	28	Silver Rep.
C. G. Wallace, Enrolling Clerk	Clk. in Lumb'r Yard	Lexington	Dawson	Illinois	Married	55	Peo. Ind.
John L. Cleaver, Engrossing Clerk	Insurance Agent	Falls City	Richardson	New Jersey	Married	28	Democrat.
C. A. Berry, Custodian	Real Estate & Ins	Wayne	Wayne	Switzerland	Single	60	Peo. Ind.
W. F. Wright, Bookkeeper	Farmer	Bethany	Lancaster	Michigan	Married	69	Peo. Ind.
Ralph D. Parsons, Postmaster	Farmer	Anselm	Holt	Indiana	Widower	70	Peo. Ind.
Miss Lura Lucas, Ass't Postmaster	Clerk	Lincoln	Lancaster	Illinois	Married	34	Democrat.

MEMBERS OF THE HOUSE—TWENTY-FIFTH SESSION—1897

NAME.	OCCUPATION.	POSTOFFICE.	COUNTY.	NATIVITY.	MARRIED OR SINGLE.	AGE.	POLITICS.
Frank B. Alderman	Marble Cutter	West Point	Cuming	Indiana	Married	44	Republican.
H. T. Ankeny	Farmer	Laurel	Cedar	Illinois	Widower	50	Peo. Ind.
C. W. Baldwin	Physician	Elkhorn	Douglas	Michigan	Married	31	Democrat.
James J. Bernard	Farmer	Pawnee City	Pawnee	P. Ed. Island	Married	45	Republican.
G. F. Billings	Farmer	Norden	Keya Paha	Iowa	Married	43	Peo. Ind.
Palmer Blake	Farm. & Stock Raiser	Tecumseh	Johnson	Vermont	Married	62	Republican.
Samuel Bower	Farm. & Stock Raiser	St. Paul	Howard	Pennsylvania	Married	59	Peo. Ind.
Frank Burman	Insurance	Omaha	Douglas	Sweden	Married	40	Republican.
E. J. Burkett	Lawyer	Lincoln	Lancaster	Iowa	Married	29	Republican.
John H. Butler	Builder	Omaha	Douglas	Indiana	Married	55	Republican.
H. D. Byran	Farm. & Stock Raiser	Decatur	Burt	Iowa	Married	42	Republican.
B. W. Campbell	Farmer	Clay Center	Clay	Illinois	Married	58	Peo. Ind.
James H. Casebeer	Editor	Blue Springs	Gage	Ohio	Married	57	Republican.
W. E. Chittenden	Farmer	Cortland	Gage	Illinois	Married	43	Republican.
Paul F. Clark	Lawyer	Lincoln	Lancaster	Wisconsin	Married	35	Republican.
Ralph A. Clark	Real Estate Dealer	Stella	Richardson	Kentucky	Married	29	Democrat.
William Cole	Farmer	Upland	Douglas	Illinois	Married	48	Peo. Ind.
Levi Cox	Live Stock Com.	South Omaha	Douglas	Ohio	Married	48	Republican.
J. H. Cronk	Farmer	Ord	Valley	New York	Married	35	Peo. Ind.
Joseph Crow	Lawyer	Omaha	Douglas	Indiana	Married	40	Republican.
C. E. Curtis	Merchant	South Omaha	Douglas	Indiana	Married	32	Peo. Ind.
Richard Dobson	Farmer	Grafton	Fillmore	England	Married	58	Peo. Ind.
DeWitt Eager	Merchant	BeaverCross'g	Seward	New York	Married	47	Peo. Ind.
W. G. Eastman	Farmer	Kingston	Custer	Illinois	Married	29	Peo. Ind.
P. H. Elghmy	Minister	Long Pine	Brown	New York	Married	58	Republican.
F. W. Endorf	Farmer	Tobias	Saline	Germany	Married	51	Democrat.
W. S. Felker	Lawyer	Omaha	Dongna	Maine	Married	60	Democrat.
Martin Fersow	Farmer	Roseland	Adams	Iowa	Married	29	Peo. Ind.
G. R. Fouke	Merchant	Liberty	Gage	Maryland	Married	43	Republican.
Fred Gaylord	Farm. & Stock Dealer	Colon	Saunders	Illinois	Married	44	Peo. Ind.
J. N. Gaffin	Mgr. Gas Works	Kearney	Buffalo	Iowa	Single	36	Peo. Ind.
Henry Gerdes	Farmer	Barada	Richardson	Illinois	Married	41	Democrat.
Felix Givens	Farmer	West Point	Cuming	Illinois	Married	52	Democrat.
J. S. Gosborn	Farmer	Chester	Thayer	Pennsylvania	Widower	67	Republican.

MEMBERS OF THE HOUSE—LEGISLATURE 1897—Continued.

NAME.	OCCUPATION.	POSTOFFICE.	COUNTY.	NATIVITY.	MARRIED OR SINGLE.	AGE.	POLITICS.
Joseph L. Graudstaff	Farm. & Stock Raiser	Bladen	Webster	Ohio	Married	49	Peo. Ind.
Claus Grell	Farmer	Chalco	Sarpy	Germany	Married	47	Democrat.
M. C. Grimes	Farmer	Chambers	Holt	Illinois	Single	33	Peo. Ind.
J. H. Grosvenor	School Teacher	Stark	Hamilton	Nebraska	Single	23	Peo. Ind.
D. W. Hamilton	Farmer	Rising City	Butler	Pennsylvania	Married	38	Peo. Ind.
Robert Henderson	Farmer	Henderson	York	Wisconsin	Single	45	Republican.
L. L. Hile	Farmer	St. Michael	Buffalo	Pennsylvania	Married	20	Peo. Ind.
R. H. Hill	Farmer	Edgar	Clay	Illinois	Married	64	Democrat.
W. D. Holbrook	Farmer	Everett	Dodge	Missouri	Married	47	Republican.
L. J. Holland	Farm. & Stock Raiser	Indianola	Red Willow	Tennessee	Married	66	Peo. Ind.
William Horner	Farmer	Lexington	Dawson	Wisconsin	Married	59	Peo. Ind.
O. Hull	Farmer	Alma	Harlan	Pennsylvania	Married	48	Peo. Ind.
N. Secor Hyatt	Farmer	President	Platte	New York	Married	54	Peo. Ind.
George E. Jenkins	Merchant	Fairbury	Jefferson	Pennsylvania	Married	50	Republican.
George U. Jones	Farmer	Wymore	Gage	Wales	Married	54	Republican.
D. N. Jones	Farmer	Brock	Nemaha	Ohio	Married	57	Peo. Ind.
D. A. Jones	Stock Feeder	Wayne	Wayne	Ohio	Married	39	Democrat.
Geo. F. Kapp	Lawyer	Butte	Boyd	Pennsylvania	Married	33	Peo. Ind.
H. C. Keister	Farmer	St. Edwards	Boone	Pennsylvania	Married	48	Peo. Ind.
C. M. Lemar	Farmer	Wahoo	Saunders	Indiana	Married	50	Peo. Ind.
John Liddell	Iron Moulder	Omaha	Douglas	Scotland	Married	35	Democrat.
F. F. Loomis	Farmer	Edholm	Butler	Ohio	Married	49	Silver Rep.
R. S. McCarthy	Farmer	Spaulding	Greeley	Ohio	Married	43	Peo. Ind.
D. McCracken	Farmer	Macon	Franklin	Indiana	Married	34	Peo. Ind.
Geo. H. McGee	Mechanic	Clearwater	Antelope	Iowa	Married	48	Republican.
Donald McLeod	Miller	Schuyler	Colfax	P. Eds. Island	Married	42	Republican.
W. H. Mann	Nurseryman	Wilber	Saline	New York	Married	64	Republican.
C. C. Marshall	Farmer	Arlington	Washington	Ohio	Married	34	Peo. Ind.
M. H. Mills	Stock Feeder	Waverly	Lancaster	Indiana	Married	59	Republican.
J. B. Mitchell	Pharmacist	Milford	Seward	Ohio	Married	70	Democrat.
O. S. Moran	Farmer	Creston	Platte	West Virginia	Married	43	Peo. Ind.
J. R. Morrison	Farm. & Stock Raiser	Chester	Thayer	Ireland	Married	34	Republican.
J. F. Nesbit	Merchant	Tekamah	Burt	Pennsylvania	Married	39	Peo. Ind.
C. W. Phelps	Farmer	Stratton	Dundy		Married	48	Peo. Ind.

Name	Occupation	Post Office	County	Nativity		Age	Politics
E. M. Pollard	Farm. & Fruit Raiser	Nehawka	Cass	Nebraska	Married	28	Republican
F. P. Prince	Hotel Keeper	Madison	Madison	Massachusetts	Married	42	Republican
Edson Rich	Lawyer	Omaha	Douglas	Illinois	Single	37	Democrat
John Fitz Roberts	LiveStck.Coun.Deal'r	South Omaha	Douglas	Illinois	Married	40	Democrat
John A. Robertson	Farmer	Joy	Holt	Indiana	Married	30	Peo. Ind.
Patrick Roddy	Farmer	Nebraska City	Otoe	Ireland	Married	64	Republican
G. L. Rouse	Farmer	Alda	Hall	Ohio	Married	59	Republican
*C. W. Schram	Farmer	Newcastle	Dixon	New York	Married	43	Peo. Ind.
O. A. Severe	Farmer	Palmyra	Otoe	Ohio	Married	43	Peo. Ind.
A. E. Sheldon	Editor	Chadron	Dawes	Minnesota	Married	25	Peo. Ind.
J. C. Shull	Farmer	Auburn	Nemaha	Missouri	Married	36	Peo. Ind.
Dudley Smith	School Teacher	Omaha	Douglas	Missouri	Married	40	Democrat
Jules Smith	Wholesale Grocer	Salem	Richardson	Germany	Married	69	Peo. Ind.
D. C. Snyder	Farm. & Stock Raiser	Elk Creek	Johnson	Pennsylvania	Married	48	Peo. Ind.
J. M. Snyder	Minister	Verdurette	Sherman	West Virginia	Married	72	Peo. Ind.
E. Soderman	Farmer	Bertrand	Phelps	Sweden	Married	47	Peo. Ind.
Luden Stebbins	Farmer	North Platte	Lincoln	Massachusetts	Married	64	Peo. Ind.
Vincent Straub	Farm. & Stock Raiser	Berlin	Otoe	Nebraska	Single	20	Democrat
William Sutton	Farmer	Table Rock	Pawnee	Illinois	Married	55	Republican
John H. Taylor	Farmer	Waterloo	Douglas	England	Married	57	Peo. Ind.
William H. Taylor	Merchant	Exeter	Fillmore	Ireland	Married	50	Democrat
Peter Uerling	Merchant	Ayr	Adams	Wisconsin	Married	38	Democrat
S. S. Van Horn	Farmer	Hooper	Dodge	New Jersey	Married	44	Democrat
Charles E. Waite	Real Estate Dealer	Lincoln	Lancaster	Ohio	Single	32	Peo. Ind.
E. M. Webb	Editor	Callaway	Custer	Wisconsin	Married	37	Peo. Ind.
William Welch	Farmer	Osceola	Polk	Ohio	Married	66	Peo. Ind.
C. F. Wheeler	Farmer	Precept	Furnas	Minnesota	Married	37	Peo. Ind.
C. E. Wiebe	Merchant	Grand Island	Hall	Iowa	Married	38	Democrat
T. M. Wimberly	Banker	Univ. Place	Lancaster	Illinois	Married	88	Republican
Wilson Winslow	Farmer	Bertrand	Gosper	Indiana	Married	40	Peo. Ind.
D. S. Woodard	Phys. and Surgeon	Hampton	Hamilton	Virginia	Married	48	Democrat
Charles Wooster	Farmer	Silver Creek	Merrick	Michigan	Married	53	Silver (rep).
J. H. Wright	Farmer	Ruskin	Nuckols	Illinois	Married	44	Peo. Ind.
John O. Yeiser	Lawyer	Omaha	Douglas	Kentucky	Married	39	Republican
Thomas T. Young	Farmer	Ashland	Cass	Ohio	Married	52	Peo. Ind.
D. S. Zimmerman	Stock Feeder	York	York	Ohio	Married	43	Peo. Ind.

*Died March 14, 1897.

STATE GOVERNMENT.

Governor.
Hon. Silas A. Holcomb, Broken Bow, Custer County.

Lieutenant Governor.
Hon. James E. Harris, Talmage, Nemaha county.

Secretary of State.
Hon. Wm. F. Porter, Clarks, Merrick county.

Treasurer.
Hon. J. B. Meserve, McCook, Red Willow county.

Auditor of Public Accounts.
Hon. John F. Cornell, Verdon, Richardson county.

Commissioner of Public Lands and Buildings.
Hon. Jacob V. Wolfe, Lincoln, Lancaster county.

Attorney General.
Hon. C. J. Smyth, Omaha, Douglas county.

Superintendent of Public Instruction.
Hon. W. R. Jackson, O'Nell, Holt county.

EXECUTIVE DEPARTMENT.

Governor, Hon. Silas A. Holcomb.
Private Secretary, Hon. Benton Maret.
Stenographer, Henry Blum.
Chief Clerk, Frank L. Mary.
Stenographer, Charles Q. De France.

Secretary of State.

Secretary, Wm. F. Porter.
Deputy, O. E. Weesner.
Book Keeper, Theodore Mahn.
Record Clerk, S. E. Starret.
Clerk, Miss Nellie Purcell.
Stenographer, L. W. Shrader.

State Treasurer.

Treasurer, Hon. J. B. Meserve.
Deputy, Samuel Patterson.
Book Keeper, W. H. Bradbury.
Stenographer and Book Keeper, C. J. West.

Auditor of Public Accounts.

Auditor, Hon. John F. Cornell, Verdon.
Deputy, C. C. Pool, Verdon.
Insurance Deputy, Samuel Lichty, Falls City.
Book Keeper, J. A. Simpson, Auburn.
Bond Clerk, June Abbott, Lincoln.
Recorder, J. M. Whitaker, Falls City.
Insurance Clerk, W. B. Price, Lincoln.
Stenographer, Miss Mamie Muldoon.

Commissioner of Public Lands and Buildings.

COMMISSIONER, Hon. **Jacob V.** Wolfe, **Lincoln.**
DEPUTY, Elon W. Nelson, Richland.
CHIEF CLERK, J. S. Hyatt, Lincoln.
DRAFTSMAN, Alex. Schlegel, University Place.
BOOK KEEPER, D. D. Lynch, Platte Center.
SALE CONTRACT CLERK, **Myrtle Shreve, Fremont.**
BOOK KEEPER, Albert Sjoberg, **Omaha.**
LEASE CONTRACT CLERK, J. H. **Graves.**
ASSIGNMENT CLERK, Rhoda H. Stewart, Lincoln.
ASSIGNMENT CLERK, Cora B. King, Schuyler.
DELINQUENT CLERK, Miss Clara Leese, **Lincoln.**

Attorney General.

ATTORNEY GENERAL, Hon. **C. J. Smyth,** Omaha.
DEPUTY, Ed. P. Smith, Omaha.
STENOGRAPHER, George F. Corcoran, York.

State Superintendent of Public Instruction.

SUPERINTENDENT, HON. W. R. **Jackson,** O'Neil.
DEPUTY, C. F. Beck, Lyons.
STENOGRAPHER, Bernice M. Jackson, **Lincoln.**
CUSTODIAN OF SUPPLIES, Alex Bentley.

SUPREME COURT.

CHIEF JUSTICE, Hon. **A. M. Post,** Columbus.
SUPREME JUDGE, Hon. **T. O. C. Harrison,** Grand Island.
SUPREME JUDGE, Hon. **T. L. Norval.** Seward.
COMMISSIONERS { HON. ROBERT RYAN, Lincoln.
HON. JOHN M. RAGAN, Hastings.
HON. FRANK IRVINE, Omaha.
CLERK **AND** REPORTER, **D. A.** Campbell, Lincoln.
DEPUTY CLERK, W. B. Rose, **Lincoln.**
ASSISTANT **CLERK, E. J. Streight, Lincoln.**
STENOGRAPHER, **Miss** Cora Outcalt, **Lincoln.**
STENOGRAPHER, E. C. Brunson.
LIBRARY CLERK, B. **M.** Howell, Lincoln.
ASSISTANT **REPORTER,** M. E. Collins, Lincoln.
BALIFF, **J. H.** Naden, Lincoln.
BALIFF, **O. D. Harris, Lincoln.**

STATE BOARDS AND ASSISTANTS.

Banking Department.

PRESIDENT, John F. Cornell, State Auditor.
MEMBER, J. B. Meserve, State Treasurer.
MEMBER, C. J. Smyth, Attorney General.
SECRETARY, P. L. Hall, Mead.
CLERK, H. Mathelsen, Omaha.

State Bank Examiners.

Reuben Lipp, Pawnee City.
John F. Coad, Jr., Omaha.
Frank A. Reynolds, Gothenburg.
Victor E. Wilson, Omaha.

State Board of Educational Lands and Funds.

Silas A. Holcomb, Governor, President.
W. F. Porter, Secretary of State.
J. B. Meserve, State Treasurer.
C. J. Smyth, Attorney General.
J. V. Wolfe, Commissioner Public Lands and Buildings, Secretary.

State Board Public Lands and Buildings.

J. V. Wolfe, Commissioner Public Lands and Buildings, President.
W. F. Porter, Secretary of State, Secretary.
J. B. Meserve, Treasurer.
C. J. Smyth, Attorney General.

State Board of Purchases and Supplies.

S. A. Holcomb, Governor, President.
W. F. Porter, Secretary of State.
J. B. Meserve, State Treasurer.
C. J. Smyth, Attorney General.
J. V. Wolfe, Commissioner of Public Lands and Buildings, Secretary.

State Board of Equalization.

S. A. Holcomb, Governor.
J. F. Cornell, Auditor Public Accounts.
J. B. Meserve, State Treasurer.

State Board of Printing.

J. F. Cornell, Auditor of Public Accounts.
J. B. Meserve, State Treasurer.
W. F. Porter, Secretary of State.

State Board of Escheats.

S. A. Holcomb, Governor.
W. R. Jackson, State Superintendent of Public Instruction.

State Board of Health.

S. A. Holcomb, Governor, President.
C. J. Smyth, Attorney General.
W. R. Jackson, Superintendent of Public Instruction, Secretary.

Secretaries.

F. D. Holdeman, M. D., Ord.
C. F. Stewart, M. D., Auburn.
B. F. Baily, M. D., Lincoln.
B. F. Crummer, M. D., Omaha.

State Board of Pharmacy.

C. J. Smyth, Attorney General, President.
W. F. Porter, Secretary of State, Secretary.
J. B. Meserve, State Treasurer.
J. F. Cornell, State Auditor.

Examiners.

C. M. Clark, Friend.
A. W. Buchelt, Grand Island.
H. R. Gering, Plattsmouth.
H. H. Barth, Lincoln.
Griff. J. Evans, Hastings.

State Board of Transportation.

John F. Cornell, State Auditor, President.
J. V. Wolfe, **Commissioner** Public Lands and Buildings, Secretary.
J. B. Meserve, State Treasurer.
C. J. Smyth, Attorney General.
W. F. Porter, Secretary of State.

SECRETARIES { J. W. Edgerton.
J. C. Dahlman.
G. L. Laws.

Miss Nellie Holland, Stenographer.

Nebraska Fish Commission.

PRESIDENT, W. L. May, Fremont.
VICE-PRESIDENT, J. S. Kirkpatrick, Lincoln.
SECRETARY, R. S. Oberfelder, Sidney.
SUPERINTENDENT, W. T. O'Brien, South Bend.

State Oil Inspectors.

CHIEF INSPECTOR, J. H. Edminsten, **Eddyville.**
DEPUTY, Wm. Dalley, Peru.
DEPUTY, F. B. Hibbard, Irvington.
DEPUTY, Warwick Saunders, Columbus.
DEPUTY, **Ed. F. Lyons,** Fairbury.
DEPUTY, **Nels O. Alberts,** Saronville.

Labor Commissioner.

DEPUTY LABOR COMMISSIONER, Sidney J. Kent.
CLERK, J. A. Edgerton.

NEBRASKA NATIONAL GUARDS.

Roster 1897-98.

Department Staff.

Adjutant General, Brig. Gen. Patrick H. Harry, Greeley.
Quartermaster and Commissary General, Col. William G Swan, Tecumseh.
Surgeon General, Col. R. Emmett Giffen, Lincoln.
Inspector General, Col. Nels P. Lundeen, York.
Judge Advocate General, Col. Edwin W. Hale, David City.
Chief Clerk, Adjt. Genl's. office, Ira J. Ayers, Lincoln.

Personal Staff.

Special Aid, Major Edmund G. Fechet, 6th Cav., U. S. A.
Aid-de-Camp, Col. James H. Peabody, Omaha.
Aid-de-Camp, Col. Fred A. Miller, Lincoln.
Aid-de-Camp Col. Lewis F. Walker, Benkleman.
Aid-de-Camp, Col. Herko Koster, Niobrara.
Aid-de-Camp, Col. Wm. F. Cody, North Platte.
Aid-de-Camp, Col. Emil Hansen, Archer.
Aid-de-Camp, Col. W. H. Barnes, Fairbury.
Aid-de-Camp, Col. J. M. Burress, Auburn.
Aid-de-Camp, Col. John G. Maher, Chadron.
Aid-de-Camp, Col. Walter Moise, Omaha.

STATE INSTITUTIONS.

Board of Education.

W. R. Jackson, State Superintendent of Public Instruction.
J. B. Meserve, State Treasurer.
B. E. B. Kennedy, Omaha.
J. S. West, Benkleman.
J. E. Lamaster, Tecumseh.
J. T. Spencer, Dakota City.
D. D. Martindale, Niobrara.

Insane Hospital, Lincoln.

SUPERINTENDENT, Dr. L. J. Abbott.
FIRST ASSISTANT PHYSICIAN, Dr. C. E. Coffin.
SECOND ASSISTANT PHYSICIAN, Dr. Minerva M. Newbecker.
MATRON, Mrs. Mary Thomas.
STEWARD, E. C. Rewick.

Insane Asylum, Norfolk.

SUPERINTENDENT, Dr. G. F. Keiper.
PHYSICIAN, Dr. W. H. Barber.
STEWARD, C. D. Jenkins.
MATRON, Mrs. L. Bowser.

Hospital for Incurable Insane, Hastings.

SUPERINTENDENT, Robert Damerell.
PHYSICIAN, Dr. J. T. Steele.
STEWARD, A. J. Scott.
MATRON, Miss Jennie E. Larsen.

State Penitentiary.

WARDEN, Geo. W. Leidigh.
DEPUTY WARDEN, Thos. Welch.
PHYSICIAN, Dr. H. C. Demaree.
CHAPLAIN, Rev. P. W. Howe.

Boys' Industrial School, Kearney.

SUPERINTENDENT, C. W. Hoxie.
ASSISTANT SUPERINTENDENT, James Holland.
MATRON, —— ——— ———.
PHYSICIAN, Dr. J. L. Bennett.
CHAPLAIN, Rev. E. Forrell.
BOOK KEEPER AND CLERK, John Brandt.

Soldiers' and Sailors' Home, Grand Island.

COMMANDANT, John W. Wilson.
SURGEON, Dr. S. Sadler.
ADJUTANT, J. H. Powers.
MATRON, Hannah Zimmer.

Institute for the Blind, Nebraska City.

PRINCIPAL, W. A. Jones.
PHYSICIAN, Dr. M. A. Carreker.
MATRON, Caroline E. Jones.
STEWARD AND BOOK KEEPER, B. S. Littlefield.

Home for the Friendless, Lincoln.

SUPERINTENDENT, Mrs. F. M. Williams.
ASSISTANT SUPERINTENDENT, Miss Lizzie Baldwin.
MATRON, Mrs. Mattie E. Wood.
PHYSICIAN, Dr. W. M. Knapp.

Girl's Industrial School, Geneva.

SUPERINTENDENT, Hon. B. R. B. Weber.
MATRON, Mrs. E. L. Philbrook.
PHYSICIAN, Dr. T. C. Canine.
BOOK KEEPER AND STEWARD, J. C. Brennan.

State Normal School at Peru.

OFFICERS.

B. E. B. Kennedy, Omaha, President.
W. R. Jackson, Superintendent of Public Instruction, Secretary.
J. B. Meserve, State Treasurer, Treasurer.

Deaf and Dumb Institute, Omaha.

PRINCIPAL, J. A. Gillespie, A. M.
PHYSICIAN, Dr. J. C. Denise.
CLERK, D. Clem Deaver.
MATRON, Helen J. Gillespie.

Institute for Feeble Minded, Beatrice.

SUPERINTENDENT, C. P. Fall.
STEWARD AND BOOK KEEPER, C. W. Phelps.
MATRON, Miss Maggie Wood.

Woman's Industrial Home, Milford.

SUPERINTENDENT, Mrs. Clara S. Carscadden.
PHYSICIAN, Julia E. Teele.
MATRON, Mrs. Elizabeth Kent.
BOOK KEEPER, Pearl Carscadden.

Soldiers' and Sailors' Home, Milford.

COMMANDANT, J. M. Fowler.
SURGEON, Dr. S. P. Tracy.
MATRON, Mrs. Elizabeth Ferguson.

STATE ASSOCIATIONS.

STATE AGRICULTURAL SOCIETY.

Officers for 1897.

PRESIDENT, Milton Doolittle, North Platte.
FIRST VICE PRESIDENT, J. N. Van Duyn, Wilber.
SECOND VICE PRESIDENT, J. B. McDowell, Fairbury.
TREASURER, Edmund McIntyre, Seward.
SECRETARY, Robert W. Furnas, Brownville.

Board of Managers.

J. B. Dinsmore, Chairman, Sutton.
S. C. Bassett, Gibbon.
W. A. Poynter, Albion.
E. L. Vance, Pawnee City.
E. A. Barnes, Grand Island.

STATE HORTICULTURAL SOCIETY.

Officers for 1897.

PRESIDENT, G. A. Marshall, Arlington.
VICE PRESIDENT, C. A. Hodkinson, Lincoln.
SECOND VICE PRESIDENT, J. W. Hesser, Plattsmouth.
SECRETARY, C. A. Barnard, Table Rock.
TREASURER, Peter Younger Jr., Geneva.
DIRECTOR, E. F. Stephenson, Crete.
DIRECTOR, J. W. Stephens, North Bend.
DIRECTOR, J. P. Dunlap, Dwight.
ANNUAL MEETINGS, January each year and Mid-Summer meeting.

NEBRASKA DAIRYMEN'S ASSOCIATION.

PRESIDENT, F. H. Vaughn, Fremont.
VICE PRESIDENT, J. W. Bush, Battle Creek.
SECRETARY, S. C. Bassett, Gibbon.

NEBRASKA SWINE BREEDERS' ASSOCIATION.

PRESIDENT, Z. S. Bronson, Waverly.
VICE PRESIDENT, L. E. Mahan, Malcomb.
VICE PRESIDENT, E. E. Day, Weeping Water.
VICE PRESIDENT, George E. Fenley, Geneva.
SECRETARY, Charles Dawson, Endicott.
TREASURER, J. L. Barton, Greenwood.
  Annual meeting held at state fair each year.

STATE BEEKEEPER'S ASSOCIATION.

PRESIDENT, E. Whitcomb, Friend.
SECRETARY, L. D. Stilson, York.

STATE POULTRY ASSOCIATION.

PRESIDENT, W. H. Haven, Fremont.
VICE PRESIDENT, Dr. A. Gaisen, Tecumseh.
SECRETARY, I. L. Lyman, Lincoln.
TREASURER, E. E. Greer, Beatrice.

Board of Managers.

Charles Ross, Omaha.
O. E. Gaines, Elk City.
C. A. Cook, Salem.
E. O. Spencer, Lincoln.
L. L. Fisher, Geneva.
E. A. Pegler, Superintendent, Lincoln.

STATE TEACHERS' ASSOCIATION.

PRESIDENT, J. W. Crabtree, Beatrice.
SECRETARY, L. U. Stoner, Valentine.
TREASURER, C. R. Atkinson, Fairbury.

UNIVERSITY OF NEBRASKA. LINCOLN.

Board of Regents.

Charles H. Morrill, President, Lincoln.
E. A. Hadley, Scotia.
C. W. Kaley, Red Cloud.
Charles Weston, Hay Springs.
Thomas Rawlings, Wakefield.
H. L. Goold, Ogalalla.
J. Stuart Dales, Secretary, Lincoln.

FACULTY BY DEPARTMENTS.

Agriculture.

George E. MacLean, Ph.D., LL.D.
T. Lyttleton, Lyon, Assistant Professor of Agriculture.

American History.

H. W. Caldwell, Professor.
J. A. Barrett, Instructor.
Frank Brown, Division Assistant.

Art.

Cora Parker, Instructor.
Henrietta M. Brock, Instructor.

Botany.

C. E. Bessey, Professor.
F. E. Clements, Laboratory Assistant.
F. A. Rydberg, Laboratory Assistant.
C. L. Shear, Laboratory Assistant.
Edna L. Hyatt, Botanical Artist.

Chemistry.

H. H. Nicholson, Professor.
John White, Instructor.
S. Avery, Instructor.
Rosa Bouton, Instructor.
Herman A. Senter, Instructor.
Robert S. Hiltner, Laboratory Assistant.
E. E. Nicholson, Laboratory Assistant.
Ward Hildreth, Storekeeper.

Civil Engineering.

O. V. P. Stout, Adjunct Professor.
W. R. Browne, Jr., Instructor.
G. R. Chatburn, Instructor.

216 UNIVERSITY OF NEBRASKA.

Electrical Engineering.

R. B. Owens, Associate Professor.
W. R. Browne, Jr., Instructor.
E. Podlesak, Electrician.
C. A. Skinner, Laboratory Assistant.
E. N. Corbin, Laboratory Assistant.

Elocution.

Mary D. Manning, Instructor.

English.

J. W. Adams, Professor.
E. A. Thurber, Instructor.
Prosser H. Frey, Instructor.
W. O. Jones, Journalism.
Frank Brown, Division Assistant.
Louise Pound, Theme Reader.
Ray E. Manley, Division Assistant.

English Literature.

L. A. Sherman, Professor.
H. C. Peterson, Instructor.
Louise Pound, Division Assistant.

Entomology.

Lawrence Bruner, Professor.
W. D. Hunter, Assistant.

European History.

F. M. Fling, Professor.
C. A. E. Holmes, Division Assistant.
Jessie Law, Division Assistant.

Geology.

E. H. Barbour, Professor.
J. P. Rowe, Laboratory Assistant.

German Languages.

Laurence Fossler, Professor.
P. B. Burnet, Instructor.
Amanda H. Heppner, Division Assistant.

Greek.

J. T. Lees, Professor.
W. F. Dann, Adjunct Professor.
Josephine Tremain, Instructor.

Horticulture.

F. W. Card, Associate Professor.

Latin.

G. E. Barber, **Professor.**
F. M. Johnson, **Adjunct Professor.**
Josephine Tremain, Instructor.
J. T. House, **Instructor.**
Alice C. Hunter, Assistant.
W. L. Westermann, Division Assistant.

Law.

M. B. Reese, Dean.
C. A. Robbins, Instructor.
H. H. Wilson, Lecturer, Secretary of Faculty.
Samuel Maxwell, Fremont, Lecturer.
W. W. Giffen, Pawnee City, Lecturer.
W. H. Munger, Fremont, Lecturer.
Frank Irvine, Omaha, Lecturer.
Joseph R. Webster, Lecturer.
W. S. Summers, Lecturer.
B. F. **Good,** Lecturer.
J. C. **Watson,** Lecturer.
J. C. **Watson,** Nebraska City, **Lecturer.**
Jacob **Fawcett,** Omaha, Lecturer.

Library.

Mary L. **Jones, Assistant Librarian.**
Mary E. **Robbins, Cataloguer.**
Florence S. Smith, **Assistant Cataloguer.**
May Hopper, **Assistant.**
Nellie J. Compton, Assistant.
Annie Fossler, Assistant.

Manual Training.

C. R. Richards, Adjunct Professor.
Cora Parker, Instructor.
W. B. Hampsen, Instructor.

Mathematics.

E. W. Davis, Professor.
H. E. Hitchcock, Emeritus Professor.
T. M. Hodgeman, Associate Professor.
A. L. Candy, Instructor.
G. R. Chatburn, Instructor.
J. J. Pershing, Instructor.
Juergen **Albers, Division Assistant.**
L. C. Walker, **Division** Assistant.
W. E. Brook, Division Assistant.
T. W. Howie, **Division Assistant.**

Military Science.

Capt. **J. F.** Gullfoyle, Commandant.
D. F. Easterday, Band Master.

Museum.

E. H. Barbour, Curator.
Carrie A. Barbour, Assistant.

Music.

Willard Kimball, Conservatory Director; Instructor Pipe Organ.
Martinus Sieveking, Instructor Piano.
Susie Schofield, Instructor Piano.
Emily M. Perkins, Instructor Piano.
John Randolph, Instructor Voice.
August Hagenow, Instructor Stringed Instruments, and Leader of University Orchestra.
Emma Hagenow, Instructor Stringed Instruments.
D. F. Easterday Instructor Wind Instruments, and Leader of University Cadet Band.
Mrs. P. V. M. Raymond, Instructor University Choruses.
F. M. Planque, Instructor Guitar and Mandolin.
E. L. Mouk, Piano Tuning.
Clara Spencer, Librarian.

Philosophy.

Professor.
E. L. Hinman, Instructor.
R. C. Bentley, Laboratory Assistant.

Physical Training.

R. A. Clark, Adjunct Professor, Director of Gymnasium.
Kate Wilder, Instructor.
Anne L. Barr, Instructor.

Physics.

DeWitt B. Brace, Professor.
Burton E. Moore, Instructor.
J. E. Almy, Laboratory Assistant.
W. E. Brook, Laboratory Assistant.
Rachael Corr, Laboratory Assistant.
M. E. Hiltner, Laboratory Assistant.
F. S. Philbrick, Laboratory Assistant.
H. E. Reagan, Laboratory Assistant.
D. T. Moore, Demonstrator.
J. Chowins, Mechanic.
Bert Spencer, Storekeeper.

Political Science.

W. G. L. Taylor, Adjunct Professor.

Romance Languages.

A. H. Edgren, Professor.
Clara Conklin, Adjunct Professor.

Sanskrit and Philology.

A. H. Edgren, Instructor.

Zoology.

H. B. Ward, Associate Professor
R. A. Clark, Instructor.
R. H. Wolcott, Instructor.
W. C. Hall, Laboratory Assistant.

United States Experiment Station.

T. L. Lyons, Director.
A. T. Peters, Investigator of Animal Diseases.
G. D. Swezey, Meteorologist.
G. A. Loveland, Weather Observer.
And six members of the University Faculty as Working Staff.

GRADUATES OF THE STATE UNIVERSITY.

	FOUR-YEAR COURSE	MEDICAL COURSE	MASTER'S DEGREE		FOUR-YEAR COURSE	MEDICAL COURSE	COLLEGE OF LAW	MASTER'S DEGREE
1873	2			1884	12	7		
1874	0			1885	6	13		
1875	3			1886	11	11		1
1876	5			1887	15	5		
1877	4			1888	21			1
1878	7			1889	24			1
1879	5			1890	30			10
1880	8			1891	24			3
1881	12			1892	35		13	5
1882	7			1893	42		28	2
1883	13			1894	44		21	7

It is estimated that more than 5,000 young people have received instruction in this University during the twenty years since its formal opening.

The Buildings and Grounds of the State University.

UNIVERSITY HALL, erected in 1869-70, at a cost of about $140,000, defrayed out of the proceeds of the sale of lots belonging to the site of the city of Lincoln.

CHEMICAL LABORATORY, erected in 1885-86, at a cost of about $35,000, of which sum $25,000 were defrayed out of University funds and $10,000 out of State funds.

GRANT MEMORIAL HALL, erected in 1888, at a cost of $20,000, of which $5,000 were defrayed out of University funds and $15,000 out of State funds.

NEBRASKA HALL, erected in 1888-9, at a cost of $50,000, all defrayed from University funds.

THE BOILER HOUSE, erected in 1889, at a cost of $12,000, out of University funds.

ELECTRICAL POWER HOUSE, erected in 1891, at a cost of $5,500, out of University funds.

LIBRARY BUILDING, the north wing erected in 1892, at a cost of $37,000 out of University funds. When complete will cost $100,000.

THE CAMPUS, of twelve acres, was reserved from State lands for University purposes when the city was laid out. It is now valued at $250,000.

THE COLLEGE FARM (including the Experiment Station farm), was secured by the exchange of State land and the payment of about $20,000 out of State funds. This property is now valued at about $250,000.

Value of University Property.

University campus, $250,000; buildings thereon (present value), $268,000. Libraries, apparatus, equipment, etc., $150,500. Steam heating plant, $25,000. College farm, with buildings, apparatus, stock, etc., $275,000. Total valuation, $978,500.

State University Tax.

On a valuation of $500 the tax is but 18¾ cents. On a valuation of $1,000 the tax is but 37½ cents. On a valuation of $10,000 the tax is but $3.75.

Advertisement.

THE LEGISLATIVE HAND BOOK AND MANUAL OF 1893.

RECOMMENDATIONS FROM MEMBERS OF THE TWENTY-THIRD SESSION.

The chapter on statutory provisions, and decisions of Speakers of House of Representatives on points of order are alone worth the price of the book.   G. C. LINGENFELTER.

I find it very much superior to our former blue book.
P. B. OLSON.

It is far better than the old in all respects; is is better arranged to find what you want; it also contains a great deal more valuable information
CHAS. S. ROBINSON.

Your Legislative Manual has been ably edited and admirably arranged.
JOHN A. DAVIS.

It is the best compiled work of its kind I ever saw.
L. H. SUTER.

It is just THE thing. There is method in its make up, and in fact it is just the thing.
G. F. SMITH.

The rules have been compiled in a perfect manner with the other valuable matter it contains, and all can be found without any trouble.
W. D. HALLER.

I think this blue book superior to any I have seen.
J. B. CAIN.

Your blue book is superior to any I have had the opportunity to examine, both in arrangement and typography.
GEO. R. COLTON.

You have added to the value of the work very largely by the introduction of new features.   R. H. OAKLEY.

I like the appearance and the method of classifying the different subjects.
R. C. RHEA.

It is out of sight.
JOHN C. VAN HOUSEN.

I think it a fine piece of work.
THEO. SMITH.

COMPARATIVE STATEMENT

OF THE

NUMBER OF OFFICERS AND EMPLOYES,

AND THE

SALARY AND WAGES PAID

DURING THE

20th, 21st, 22nd and 23rd Sessions

OF THE

NEBRASKA LEGISLATURE,

Compiled From The Auditor's Bi-Annual Report.

SENATE.

TITLE OF OFFICERS OR EMPLOYES.	NO. OF EMPLOYES				SALARY AND WAGES PAID.			
	1887	1889	1891	1893	1887	1889	1891	1893
Lieutenant Governor	1	2	1	1	$ 609 60	$ 680 40	$ 628 80	$ 628 00
Secretary to Lieut Gov			1				500	
President of Senate	1	1			180	231		
Secretary	1	1	1	1	600	600	600	568 00
Secretary Pro tem				1				44
Assistant Secretaries	3	4	3	4	1145	1620	1424	1790
Bookkeepers & typewriters	3	3	2	1	612	789	452	500
Stenographers		1	1	1			261	381
Sergeant-at-Arms	2	2	3	3	546	534	855	867
Chaplain	1	1	1	1	270	265	306 60	264
PostMaster and Assist'nts	2	2	2	3	546	513	564	567
Door-keepers	3	3	2	2	819	648	573	432
Eng. & Enrolling Clerks	26	13	23	9	6240	2913	5404 50	2004
Committee Clerks	27	1	17	13	4020	234	3623	2538
Senator's Clerks		32				6635 50		
Clerk to Auditor		1				231		
Clerk to Secretary of State				2			705	
Copy Clerks	1		2		81		331 50	
Bill Clerks	4	2	2	1	819	498	714	411
Janitors	17	9	11	3	3162	1985	2266	890 31
Custodians	2	5	5	7	546	1053	1266	1683
Messengers	7	5	7	1	1551	1104	1954 50	351
Pages	10	17	11	10	1228 50	1740 50	1510 50	1207 50
Mail Carriers	3	1	1	1	385 50	261	270	264
Proof Readers	1	2	2	1	306	678	564	354 75
Copy Holders	2	2	2	1	378	678	576	336 75
Watchmen	3	2	3	2	522	468	795	400 50
Firemen	2	1	1	1	399	222	270	432
Laborer		1				174		
Expert Accountant							230	
Special Sergeant-at-A ms		10					60	
Total	122	114	117	68	$24965 60	$24966 40	$26764 40	$16913 81

COMPARATIVE STATEMENT

OF THE

NUMBER OF OFFICERS AND EMPLOYES

AND **THE**

SALARY AND WAGES PAID.

DURING THE

20th, 21st, 22nd and 23rd Sessions.

OF THE

NEBRASKA LEGISLATURE,

Compiled From The Auditor's Bi-Annual Report.

HOUSE.

TITLE OF OFFICERS OR EMPLOYES.	NO. OF EMPLOYES.				SALARY OR WAGES PAID.			
	1887	1889	1891	1893	1887	1889	1891	1893
Speaker	1	1	1	1	$ 180	$ 231	$ 216	$ 180
Chief Clerk	1	1	1	1	600	600	600	600
Assistant Clerks	4	5	4	4	1881	2173	2356	2300
Sergeant-at-Arms	2	2	3	3	630	540	690	710 62
Chaplain	1	1	1	1	258	231	213	204
Postmaster and Assistant	2	2	2	2	615	552	480	514 50
Door-keepers	3	3	2	2	945	756	441	453 38
Engr'ng and Enr'l'g Cl'ks	26	34	20	11	5484	7561 50	3648	2467 16
Committee Clerks	19	25	12	6	4285	5178	2049	571 50
Bill Clerks	3	3	3	2	484	828	642	638 99
Clerk to Sec'y of State	1	1			249	300		
Clerk to Speaker		1	1	1		258	243	171 75
Messengers	1	3	2	1	480	748	504	204
Janitors	8	18	12	9	2229	4446	2553	1828 12
Custodians	2	14	4	3	474	3192	681	729 93
Pages	13	30	14	15	1377	3018 50	1316	1569 15
Proof Reader, Copy Holder	2	4	2	4	753	1218	633	760 50
Mail Carriers	2	2	3	1	549	510	423	282 00
Engineer and Fireman	2	3	1	2	476	827 75	273	457 50
Watchmen and Guards	1	3	4	3	261	729	561	827 00
Book-keeper		1				186		
Stenographers		1	3			60	354	
Time-keeper		1	1	1		192	216	331 30
Clerk Auditor's Office		1				201		
Supt. of Engrossing Room	1					258		
Elevator Boys		3				442 50		
Special Sergeant-at-Arms			11				204	
Carpenter				1				189
Clerk to recount ballots				1				33
Typewriters	1	1	3	3	243	273	729	590 62
Totals	95	165	110	76	$22453	$35510 25	$20025	$16624 02

www.ingramcontent.com/pod-product-compliance
Lightning Source LLC
Chambersburg PA
CBHW030316270326
41926CB00010B/1388